The Curse Of The Al Dulaimi Hotel
and other half-truths
from Baghdad

To Kathy
All the best

Colin.
x

The Curse Of The
Al Dulaimi Hotel
and other half-truths
from Baghdad

Colin Freeman

Monday Books

A CIP catalogue record for this title is available
from the British Library

2008 ISBN : 978-1-906308-02-5

Printed and bound by CPD Wales
Typeset by Andrew Searle
Cover Design by Paul Hill at Kin Creative

www.mondaybooks.com
info@mondaybooks.com

Contents

To my mum and dad

Foreword

I FIRST SET FOOT in Iraq on May 1st 2003 – the day George W Bush officially declared that major hostilities were over. Timing was never my strong point: being the last reporter to make it to Baghdad while the war was just about still on is not much to boast about. But then, for every big shot correspondent who writes the world-exclusive *I-was-there-first* pieces, there are legions of us who stream in afterwards and scratch about trying to make some sort of sense of what's left. This book is an attempt to give them – or, let's face it, me – a share of the limelight for once.

Bigger, better and brighter names have passed through Iraq, but this is not an account of the country as seen by some omniscient grandee of war reporting, for whom dodging bullets and bombs is second nature: it's an account by, effectively, an ordinary punter... someone who is often slightly scared and confused, frequently disorganised and incompetent, and, yes, who bottles it from time to time.

There are gaps and holes in this book – characters who might have benefited from a little more description, and sub-plots which hit sudden dead ends. That's because I was there earning a crust, day-to-day and hand-to-mouth, as a freelance reporter. The pressures of daily deadlines – and the dangers – mean that you get to spend very little time in one place, with one person; often, it's just minutes. As a result, your experience is patchy. There's no great, over-arching theme, either, but in a way that's the whole point: post-war Iraq is an unpredictable and chaotic country and it's often hard to make proper sense of anything. There is little reliable information, lots of gossip and hearsay. Officialdom often propagandises and exaggerates, while the opposition would often rather behead you than give you an interview to 'put their side across'.

I'd like to thank the following people, without whose help and encouragement this book would never have been written: *Evening Standard* photographer Cavan Pawson, who put the whole idea of going to Iraq into my mind in the first place; former *Standard* reporter Hugh Muir, who persuaded me it might actually not be a complete fool's errand; freelance reporter Jacqui Goddard and photographers Chris Hackett and Marcus Bleasdale, for their practical advice; and, of course, my friend Dominic Casciani from the BBC for his invaluable 'hostile environment' course on the mean streets of Streatham. Thanks to the newsdesks of the *Scotsman*, *Sunday Telegraph* and *San Francisco Chronicle* for keeping me in work while I was out there, and of course the Evening Standard – for all my whinging about them, they were great people. Thanks also to my friend Neil Chandler, Mirror reporter Chris Hughes and the staff of Monday Books for persuading me that the book was worth writing. And, finally, thanks to the iraqis, whose civility and friendliness made my time out there a lot more pleasant than it might have been.

Milkbottles On A Doorstep

THE PATH TO IRAQ – for me, anyway – began on Christmas Eve 2002, on a sunny pavement outside Cheryl Barrymore's house.

Cheryl lived in a block of maisonettes in a posh street in Swiss Cottage, a part of London that boasts – as we journalists like to say – more celebrities in a few square miles than the rest of Britain put together. Like many who have spent time in the lower echelons of British journalism, I've visited a lot of them – generally getting about as far as the doorstep, where I'd pitch camp for as long as my editor wanted me to.

'Doorstepping', as the practice is known, is no more than legalised stalking. The idea is that if you hang around outside somebody's house long enough, they will eventually talk to you just to get you to go away. Or hit you, which always makes a good picture.

The trouble is that this seldom actually works. These days, even the thickest, most publicity-addicted *Big Brother* has-been is media-savvy enough to say 'No comment' or 'Call my PR' if he doesn't want to talk. In all my years hanging around outside celebrity addresses – and it probably does add up to years – all I've ever got out of it is a skin as thick as a rhino's and a collection of extremely banal celebrity anecdotes. Liam Gallagher from Oasis told me to fuck off. The late George Best said something similar, I think (it was unintelligible). Various nonentities have called me a 'ghoul', a 'vulture' and a 'sad, sleazy little twat'. A few minor royals have called the police.

Cheryl, of course, was the ex-wife of Michael, the TV 'entertainer' whose life has resembled a sort of slow motion car wreck in recent times. Yet another unflattering tale about her ex-husband had appeared on the front page of the *Sun* that day, and my newspaper, the *London Evening Standard*, wanted her reaction to it.

I'd got to the office at five o'clock that morning – despite having the word *'Evening'* in its title, the *Standard*'s first edition actually comes out at around 11am. I'd had a heavy night at a Christmas party and was still badly hungover as I was briefed by Mike Leese, the paper's feared deputy news editor. Mike was an early-morning operator par excellence, with a bizarre ability to function on vast amounts of alcohol and very little sleep, but he also doubled as the unofficial newsroom enforcer. Most newspapers employ at least one hard nut like him to keep the reporters on their toes, and they give the place a permanent frisson of danger. I read an interview once with a former warden at Broadmoor psychiatric hospital: he said most of the time everything was fine, but the moment you dropped your guard someone would try to stab your eyes out with a Biro. It's a bit like that in newspapers.

Mike had stood over my desk under the harsh office lights, puffing on a strange plastic cigarette he used during his periodic attempts to quit smoking; judging from the ferocity of his drags, he had some way to go. 'Get down to Cheryl's, see if you can get some reaction,' he had muttered, brandishing the front page of the *Sun*. 'Take a photographer with you.'

Then he was gone. News editors rarely hand out detailed briefs, preferring you to use your alleged skill and judgment as a reporter to work the finer points out yourself. Then, if it doesn't work out how they want, they can blame you. So there I was. Sat outside an eight-storey mansion block set back from the road behind a high brick wall. December 24th. Early morning. No sign of Cheryl.

It looked like a long wait.

The concierge refused to tell us which flat she lived in, whether she was in, or even if we had the right address, which we weren't sure of. Newspapers' information on celebrities' whereabouts isn't as accurate as you might think. It's not unknown to spend several days on a doorstep only to find that your intended victim has been coming and going all week from a house round the corner, or has just been photographed at a movie premiere in Los Angeles.

The photographer, Cavan Pawson, and I sprawled in his car for a while, drinking coffee, moaning, and getting bored, like we were stuck in a stake-out scene from a bad episode of *Starsky and Hutch*.

By about 9.30am, we had weighed up the options. There were at least three possible entry and exit points to Cheryl's block. Which meant that if she left the building and we didn't spot her, we could hardly be blamed. Not much, anyway.

'Starbucks?' asked Cav with a yawn, starting the engine. I nodded. Out of sight and out of mind, with any luck we could spend the rest of the day doing nothing and then knock off early for Christmas.

Unlike mine, Cav's star was in the ascendancy at the *Standard*. For a while he'd been a journeyman like me but on September 11, 2001, he'd been in America covering New York Fashion Week when the news broke that two aircraft had just been hurled into the World Trade Center. With only around half an hour until the *Standard*'s final deadline, he jumped in a taxi and got close enough to reel off several brilliant shots of the towers before they collapsed. The photo on the *Standard*'s front page won him the British Photographer of the Year award, and Cav's fortunes had been transformed. He'd gone to New York to photograph skirts and dresses, but came back as someone who could handle himself in a Major World News Story. As a result, Cav was now off to war.

Nobody knew exactly when the much-talked of US invasion of Iraq was going to take place, but by December 2002 there was little doubt it would happen. All the whispers from government to the *Standard*'s political and defence correspondents suggested it was cut and dried. After all, Britain and America were already sending 250,000 soldiers out to the region, something they wouldn't do if they thought it'd be resolved diplomatically. What was even more certain was that I wouldn't be there to report on it. The *Standard* was planning to send a whole team of journalists to cover the war, but it would be the usual coterie of their most favoured news and feature writers. Of which, it was fair to say, I was not one.

To my intense frustration, and despite working as hard as I realistically could, I'd never quite made it to the top rung at the *Standard*. The only assignment I'd ever been hand-picked for was to cover London's roadworks. With its large commuter readership, roadworks were a subject the paper was obsessed with, but reporting on them every day was less exciting than filling them. I'd made the mistake of doing a good job at it, assuming I'd get rewarded with something more interesting after a few months. Instead, they'd mistaken my eagerness to please for genuine enthusiasm, and now refused to let me palm the job off on anyone else. So while Cav would be out covering the biggest story of his life, I would be revealing that the A23 through Streatham had been dug up because of a gas leak.

'When are you off then?' I asked, half-hoping he'd say, hadn't I heard, I was going, too. The roads were going to be bombed to shite in Iraq, after all.

'Sometime in January,' he said. 'We fly out to Kuwait, then follow the Brits in when the invasion starts. But that might not be till February or March.'

'Scared?'

'A bit. I've never done a war before, I suppose. But I might not get another chance.'

'You lucky bastard.'

There was a silence, while we slurped our coffees.

'Didn't you put your name down for the war team?' he said.

'Nah.'

'Why not?'

'Already been decided, hasn't it? The team's picked already, plus all the reserves. I'm not even on the subs' bench.'

'Have you asked?'

'No point, is there? Not flavour of the month, me.'

Cav looked at me. 'If they won't send you, why don't you just go yourself?' he said. 'As a freelance?'

'*Freelance?* To a *war?*'

'Why not? You don't even have to go to Iraq itself. Once it starts, it could spill into all the neighbouring countries. Turkey, Syria, Jordan. The *Standard* will want their own people there as well in case anything happens. And you could work for other papers too.'

I mulled it over, briefly. I wouldn't even know where to start. I could see myself turning up wherever nothing was happening and getting precisely nowhere.

'What have you got to lose?' he said.

What had I got to lose? Well, my job. My savings. And my life.

Cav gestured back up the road towards Cheryl's house. 'You might be still on that doorstep in 10 years' time, wishing you'd done it,' he said.

Jesus Christ. Saddam Hussein or Cheryl Barrymore.

Two hours later, we wandered back up Cheryl's flat. Still no sign of life. We rang the office and got permission to knock off for Christmas. A few days later I heard she'd been in Spain the whole time.

* * * * *

Cav's words echoed round my head later that afternoon as I sat in the pub with Max, my ex-girlfriend. We'd gone out together for 18 months before splitting up in the summer. It wasn't that we didn't get on well – just that when the question of getting married and having children came up, I couldn't get enthusiastic. Unfortunately, with no problems in our relationship other than its lack of long-term prospects, we'd continued to spend nearly all our time together. Until two weeks ago, that was, when Max had given me an ultimatum. Either we started going out properly again, or, with New Year beckoning, we made a resolution to stop seeing each other.

'How was your day?' she asked, draining a glass of Pinot Grigio.

I debated whether or not to tell her what Cavan had said about Iraq. In all practical terms, his suggestion of going to Iraq as a freelance seemed about as feasible as going there as a mercenary. I had a full-time, salaried staff job on a proper newspaper in London, even if it was a bit crap. Wasn't it a bit silly to give all that up? Yet I couldn't deny the spark of hope inside me, the thought that, somehow, my stagnating career might find direction again. I was planning to keep quiet about it until I'd checked it out properly, but was so excited I blabbed to Max straight away.

Best to keep quiet though, until I'd actually checked out whether it was possible or not.

'Max, I'm thinking of going to go to the war as a freelance.'

'Which war?'

'*The* war. How many are there? The one in Iraq. The one that's going to start in the spring.'

'Yes, yes, I know. But isn't a bit difficult to get into Iraq?'

'I thought I might base myself in one of the neighbouring countries. Saddam might invade them or something. Or, er, fire chemical weapons at them. Then I'll be right on the spot.'

A less understanding woman might have stressed the potential drawbacks of this but Max was both a fellow journalist and at the end of her tether: she'd heard me whinging about my stalled career so often that she was like a probation officer stuck with a persistent re-offender. Any new resolve, in no matter what direction, represented potential progress.

'So which countries might you go to?' she said, an encouraging expression on her face.

'Er... dunno. Jordan, maybe, or Syria.'

Max knew even less about the Middle East's geography than I did.

'Are they next door to Iraq?'

'Er… Jordan is. And Syria is, too, I think. To the left, and down a bit.'

'Will they let you in?'

'Dunno.'

'Would you get any work?'

'Dunno.'

'What sort of stories would you do?'

'Dunno.'

'Where did you suddenly get this idea from?'

'Dunno. Well, Cav suggested it outside Cheryl's today. I… I need to look into it a bit more, obviously.'

Max had met the crackpot barstool explorer in me before. Last January, in a fit of despair at work, I'd suggested we both resign and backpack across Africa for six months. She sensibly dithered, while I actually got as far as handing in my notice. Then, forced to think about it properly for the first time, I realised I'd get fed up within about a fortnight. There were only so many epic bus rides, vibrant markets and historic temples that I could handle before I'd get crashingly bored. Humiliatingly, I'd asked for my job back, and returned to work.

I tried to make my case. 'This wouldn't be like Africa, though? I'd be working, so I wouldn't get fed up. And if it didn't work out, it'd just be like backpacking with a difference. But yeah, I doubt it's possible. It's probably a daft idea.'

'No, it's not,' she said. 'It's exactly what you need.'

She also knew what else it meant. Unlike Mission Africa, this particular birdbrained scheme would potentially mark a final parting of our ways.

'So we won't be getting back together, will we?' she said.

I stared at her, pouring white wine into my mouth where profound or soothing words should have come out.

'No.'

She smiled. 'I don't mind, you know. I just want you to be honest.'

We headed off to spend Christmas with our respective families.

Six hours before, the Iraq war had been something to discuss while killing time outside Cheryl Barrymore's. Now it was shaping up as my future.

George W Bush had better not cancel it.

* * * * *

I rapidly realised that one big drawback to my new plan was that I knew nothing about war reporting whatsoever. I'd seen it done on TV, by people like Martin Bell, the BBC man with the 'lucky white suit' who got shot in the Balkans. You'd see them crouched down in a trench somewhere, explosions and gunfire going off around them. Occasionally their colleagues – Spanish cameramen or Japanese sound guys – would get killed. They came across as earnest, serious individuals, who enjoyed great respect for the bravery and integrity of their reporting. They were the polar opposite of anything I did. Interestingly, even the big names complained that the reports they risked their lives to get were being chopped to make room for more 'news' about celebrities – the kind of stuff I was trying to leave behind, in fact.

If I knew little about war reporting, I knew even less about the Middle East. The *Standard* covered international news, but we rarely sent staff on anything but the biggest of foreign stories. Most of the rest of the time we relied on the Reuters and Associated Press wire services, rewriting their copy in the office and running it under the byline 'By our foreign staff'. I was an unchallengeable expert on the New Roads and Streetworks Act 1991, and my *Mastermind* specialist subject might have been The Love Life of Anthea Turner, but virtually all I knew about Iraq was from watching a bit of TV coverage of the first Gulf War in 1991, when I'd still been at university. We'd had a party the night Operation Desert Storm began, beers in hand as if it was a football match. After a couple of hours of watching green explosions, we'd got bored and switched channels.

The only way to find out how to freelance out there was to ask around, but that would be tricky in itself. For a start, people with war zone experience weren't exactly thick on the ground in Kensington. I'd also have to be careful that nobody at the *Standard* found out I was making inquiries. I was already a marked man for having resigned and then un-resigned the year before. Any further evidence, rumour or otherwise, that I was thinking of quitting again would be seen as a further sign of disloyalty.

Over the first few weeks of New Year I asked around. I vaguely remembered that Allan Ramsay, a New Zealander who'd left the Standard recently, had tried freelancing during the Balkans wars in the early 1990s. I rang him up and arranged to go out for a beer.

Allan's tale of war started brilliantly.

'Another Kiwi hack just rang up one day and said, "There's a bunch of us driving down to the war in Bosnia, do you wanna come?"' he said. 'I figured I could work for the Standard and freelance for some of the Kiwi papers, so off we went.'

'Excellent. How did it go?'

'When we first got there we stayed in some tower block in the middle of a small town. Then during the night, a huge firefight broke out, with one half of the town firing at the other. It was bloody terrifying, actually. You could hear injured people screaming.'

'Blimey,' I said. 'The Standard must have loved it.'

'To be honest, mate, I was so frightened I couldn't write a thing. And they weren't interested anyway. That sort of thing was happening all over the place. Just because I'd seen it myself didn't make it a story. In the end, I decided it wasn't for me, and went back home again.'

'But at least you tried, though. Must've raised your standing at the paper?'

'Not really. When I got back, the news editor just asked me if I'd enjoyed my little bit of war tourism.'

At least Allan had been able to get to where the action was. The more I asked around, the more it seemed that going to Iraq itself was completely out of the question.

'Not really a place for freelancers, mate,' said a Daily Telegraph photographer I knew, who'd just come back from Baghdad. Iraqi government officials had made it impossible for anyone other than staff correspondents to work there, he said, because of their desire to screw as much money from everyone as possible. Not only did they charge you astronomical rates for a bugged hotel room, you coughed up hundreds of dollars a day for Ministry of Information 'minders' to watch you, hundreds in visa 'renewal fees' every week or so, and hundreds to 'rent' a telephone line. All for the privilege of being there when America flattened the place.

'You want to try Kurdistan,' he said. 'That's the Holy Grail for freelancers. Great access, but very difficult to get in.'

'Yes, good idea,' I said, having no idea where Kurdistan was or whose side they were on.

A session in the *Standard*'s cuttings library revealed all. Kurdistan was a small, mountainous enclave in northern Iraq which had broken away from Baghdad's control after the first Gulf War. The Kurds loathed Saddam for massacring 5,000 people in a gas attack on the Kurdish Iraqi town of Halabja in 1988. Now they were hoping to get revenge by helping the Coalition stage a northern assault on Saddam's frontlines. The assault would be spearheaded by the Kurdish *peshmerga* militias, whose name translated as 'those who willingly face death'. It was potentially even more perilous than being in Baghdad: because of his long and nasty history with the Kurds, it was widely predicted that Saddam would unleash the bulk of his feared chemical weapons arsenal against them. Maybe it was a Holy Grail for the combat-hardened, but it looked a bit vertical, learning curve-wise, for a novice.

Still, I looked into it. As Kurdistan was a NATO protectorate, rather than a proper country, it didn't really exist, diplomatically-speaking. The only way in or out was via its other neighbours, Iran, Turkey and Syria. Because they had restive Kurdish populations of their own, they were reluctant to recognise Kurdistan officially, and therefore rarely gave permission to foreigners – especially journalists – to cross the border. A few freelancers had somehow managed it, either by smuggling or bribing themselves in. But when I emailed them asking for tips, I got no response whatsoever. It gradually dawned on me that I was, potentially, their competition. The only people who could really help me, in other words, had a direct interest in not doing so.

Eventually someone put me in touch with a guy who'd been to Kurdistan before and was planning to go again for the coming war. Marcus Bleasdale was exactly how I'd imagine a war zone photographer: wiry and serious, with a heavy growth of stubble on his face. I'd never met this kind of photographer before, which wasn't surprising since he seemed to spend most of his time in places like the

Congo or Afghanistan as opposed to drinking coffee outside Cheryl's. He generously agreed to meet up for a beer to answer any questions that I might have. Like, how to get to Kurdistan, where I did I stay, how did I find stories, and how did I avoid getting killed.

To his credit, he didn't snort contemptuously when I grilled him. It could be done, he reckoned, even by someone without experience. You could get into Kurdistan via Iran, as long as the Iranian Embassy in London would grant you a transit visa. Then, once the war started, you just stuck with other hacks at first and didn't take too many risks. But it would still be seriously expensive. Translators and drivers were at least £30 a day each, as was a hotel for the night. For communications with the outside world, I would need a satellite phone, which cost around £1,000 and a dollar-a-minute for calls. Plus a laptop, flak jacket, helmet, gas mask and chemical protection suit, coming in at a further £3,000 minimum. And that was just for starters. Once the fighting got under way, war zone economics would kick in. Translators and drivers would demand danger money, doubling or trebling their charges. Hoteliers, shopkeepers and purveyors of virtually every other commodity would do likewise.

I did the maths.

Even if I was lucky enough to be able to share drivers and translators with some other freelancers, as Marcus suggested, my bills could easily be £200 a day – £6,000 a month. The flak jacket, satphone, laptop, flights and so on would push it to around £10,000. Worst of all, because Kurdistan had no functioning banking system, your entire money supply for the trip had to be taken with you, in $100 bills. I'm the kind of bloke who gets nervous withdrawing £50 from the cash machine in case I'm mugged. Taking half my entire life savings and wandering around with them in a war zone didn't seem like a good idea.

'What happens if you get robbed?'

'Make sure you don't.'

'But if every journalist is carrying that kind of cash around, won't all the locals realise that you're a target?'

'Yes.'

'Is there anything you can do about that?'

'No.'

I thanked Marcus for his time and said I'd buy him another beer if I ever saw him in Kurdistan. He smiled in a friendly sort of way, but I suspected he'd lie low the moment he heard I was in town.

A couple of weeks later, I headed down to my favourite beach in Devon for a surfing break. The weather was beautiful, spring sunshine lighting up the mist off the waves as it streamed over the sand dunes. I savoured every moment. Never in my entire life had my future seemed more up in the air. It was now late February, and some time in the next month or two the war was expected to start. I'd applied to the Iranian embassy for a transit visa, but so far I'd heard nothing back from them. And the closer the invasion got, the more likely they were to seal the border altogether. Overall, the odds on getting out there seemed about as promising as those on Saddam winning the war. Sooner or later, though, the call would have to be made. Either give up the job, lash out vast amounts of money, and leave my old life behind, or stick it out at home.

When I got back that weekend my mind was made up. Come what may, I'd give it a try. First I told my parents. To my surprise, they didn't seem horrified at all. If anything, they were a little too encouraging.

'You've been so down in the dumps recently, dear,' said my mum, breezily. 'If it cheers you up, I think you should do it.' It was as if I had announced I was joining a local church group.

The *Standard*, when I told them, seemed equally blasé. All they asked for was a week or two's notice. Anyone would have thought they were happy to get rid of me.

Streatham: A Hostile Environment

BY MARCH, THE *Standard* was gearing up into full war mode. Every reporter who was being dispatched to the region was being sent on week-long 'hostile environment' training courses run by firms of ex-SAS men. The courses were done at country house hotels in Wales, and covered everything from how to recognise incoming mortar fire, through to how to seal a bullet-punctured lung with a credit card. At the end, there'd be a fake 'crisis' scenario, complete with actors dressed up as terrorists and crazed militiamen. It was all very different from the old days, when reporters in war zones had simply learned on the job. But, increasingly, newspapers' insurers were beginning to demand that staff attended the courses: the more a paper could show it had tried to prepare reporters for the risks, the less chance that anyone who came unstuck – or his surviving relatives – could sue.

At £3,000 a pop, though, I couldn't afford to pay out of my own pocket. Luckily, my friend Dominic, who worked for the BBC's internet news service, had been on almost every course on offer. He wasn't actually going to the war, because his wife, Tracey, was pregnant. Yet with its virtually limitless resources, the Beeb had still trained him up anyway. He was now schooled in how to survive World War III in virtually any conflict zone in the world. In the upstairs cupboard of his flat in Streatham, he even had a full chemical and biological survival suit, ready for him to clamber into within the requisite four minutes of an air raid warning. So far, the only practical use he'd had for it was cleaning out his chimney, where the gas mask came in handy against the soot.

Dominic agreed to teach me what he could remember, and one Saturday afternoon I went round to his house for a crash course. He'd prepared a detailed programme, with suburban Streatham recast as a hazard-strewn, post-apocalyptic wasteland. His back garden would serve as the theatre for a simulated chemical and biological weapons attack. Sessions in battlefield first aid would be held in his front lounge. And landmine awareness training would take place in his local playpark.

Sat at his breakfast table, Dominic bit into an apple and started talking. He sounded like a cross between an SAS sergeant and a management consultant. 'Right, first of all you've got to identify both your destination and your mission once you get out there.'

'Uh?'

'Your destination and mission. Where are you going, and what will you do when you get there? The whole idea is to think systematically about these things. So that you know exactly what threats you're going to face.'

'Er, my idea is to go to Iraq, if I can get in. And then report.'

'And what will be your greatest fear once you get out there?'

I thought hard. It sounded suspiciously like one of those trick questions they fire at you in interviews.

'Saddam Hussein?'

'No.'

'Chemical weapons?'

'No.'

'Nuclear weapons?'

'No.'

'Getting killed?'

'No.'

'How can getting killed not be my greatest fear?'

'Think about it.'

'Fear? My greatest fear is fear itself?'

'Wrong again.'

'Failure?'

'No. Your greatest fear,' Dominic announced triumphantly, 'is ignorance. And that's what we're going to be talking about today. Right, let's hit the kids' park.'

The Streatham Hill Children's Play Area does not closely resemble the killing fields of the Balkans or Cambodia. A small patch of sloping, litter-strewn grassland, the only people it is potentially hazardous to are the under-fives, who are advised not to attempt the climbing frames without an appropriate guardian present. We sat on a scuffed park bench, near a smelly pooper-scooper bin. Dominic pointed out across the grass.

'Now, imagine that the pooper scooper rules had never been introduced, and that this park was like the old days, with dog crap everywhere.'

'Right.'

'Back then, would you have wandered through here without looking where you were going?'

'No.'

'Absolutely. So if you're travelling in an area that might be landmined, think about it in the same way. They could be anywhere. And remember, where there's one mine, there's probably more. So if the car in front of you hits one, don't go rushing in to help straight away. You might run into another yourself.'

'But what if the person in front is bleeding to death?'

'Well, just tread very carefully. There's no point in adding to the casualties. You're in a war zone. You could be hundreds of miles from a hospital.'

Parts of Kurdistan, I'd read, were heavily mined. I imagined myself stuck there in some mine-hit convoy, a companion missing half a leg, going crazy with pain and me completely unable to help. A few days later, at great risk to themselves, a rescue team would turn up, by which time my colleague would have died. At a subsequent press conference, the rescue team commander would denounce the 'naive and inexperienced' journalists who'd entered a mined area without any proper training. There was no mere doom-mongering, either; it could really happen.

Dominic pointed to another park bench, where a man sat, minding his own business and swigging from a can of Kestrel Super. 'Right, imagine that's you. Your colleague has been blown up by a mine, totally vaporised. Nothing left except a few bits splattered all over you. No point worrying about him, but now you've got to get out. You can hear enemy forces coming. You need to hide. What are you going to do?'

'Give up and have a drink, like your man over there.'

'Be serious.'

'Sorry. I guess I'd walk very carefully, checking for mines, and head out that gate over there.'

'Why that way?'

'It's the nearest exit.'

'Boom! Dead again.'

'Huh?'

'Second rule of laying mines. You anticipate human behaviour, which is always to take the easiest possible route. If there's a gate, or a gap in a fence, people will use it, so it's the obvious place to plant a mine.'

'Hmm. Fair enough. But it seems like you're stuffed, whatever you do.'

'Well, yes. But that's all hostile environment training does. It makes you aware of the risks.'

Class moved on to the dangers posed by weapons and gunfire. Dominic pointed to the climbing frame at the far end of the park, where a group of unaccompanied nine-year-olds were playing what appeared to be a game of Yardie crack dealers. At least we weren't the only ones in the realm of fantasy.

'An important thing with gunfire is to be a good judge of distance,' Dominic said. 'Walk to that climbing frame, counting your paces. One pace equals about one metre. Then pace it back again the same way, to check.'

I set off, half expecting to hear that I'd been blown up by another bloody landmine. It was 46 paces there, and 50 on the way back.

'Right, so take the average, which is 48. Round it up to 50 for convenience. Now fix that distance in your memory. You're not going to be able to get out a tape measure if you get in a firefight. But you do know that the distance from the bench to the climbing frame in the swingpark at Streatham is 50 metres. Now imagine those kids are hostile militiamen. If they've got assault rifles, their guns probably won't be accurate beyond about 25 metres, especially if they're not properly trained. And if they've got pistols, the accurate distance is reduced to only 15 metres. So on that basis, you can make a judgment about whether you're really within range or not. If not, perhaps you can take a chance and make a run for it.'

I nodded, half-impressed. Here, at least, was some solid fieldcraft. Dominic was less clear on what to do if you couldn't see who was firing at you. On the one hand, it was wise to stay absolutely stock still, as sudden movement attracted attention. On the other hand, it was also a good idea to run like crazy, as moving targets were harder to hit.

'So how do you decide?'

'It's all down to your experience and judgment.'

'But I haven't got any.'

He conceded my point. 'But everybody's a beginner at some point, aren't they? The best thing is to stick with someone who's been in these kinds of situations before. Preferably someone who's married with kids. The instructor on our course said they tend to be a lot less gung-ho, because they've got their nearest and dearest depending on them back home.'

'But if they've got kids, won't they just be sensible and not go in the first place? Like you?'

'Probably.'

Having survived the dog mess minefield and the nine-year-old gunmen, we turned to coping with being taken hostage. Dominic was something of an expert on this, having been 'kidnapped' during his hostile environment courses by various actors posing as IRA men, Serb paramilitaries and Arab mujahideen. So we pretended to be on a pretend kidnap course.

'You've been abducted at a roadblock by a group of mujahideen,' he said. 'They want to kill you right now. You've got to give them a reason not to. What you are going to say?'

'Best to say silent?'

'Wrong. Remember, these people may not like you or your country, but they're still human beings. Try and establish a rapport. The more they see you as a person, the harder it is just to kill you in cold blood.'

'So how do I do that?'

'Ask for food or medicine. Or to go to the toilet. The moment your captors have to look after you, you're striking up a relationship with them. Or try praying. Even though they might be Muslims or whatever, you're better off pretending you're not some godless heathen. Another good idea is to show them a picture of your child from your wallet. Let them realise there's a wife and family who will miss you.'

'But I haven't got a wife or a family.'

'Doesn't matter. Just take a photograph of some kid with you.'

'But what happens then if they kill me anyway? And then the photo's found on my body? Everybody is going to remember me as some weirdo paedophile for carrying around some picture of a kid I've never met.'

'Everybody thinks you're a weirdo anyway. Anyway, I'm the mujahideen leader, I've just put my revolver to your head. Death to the infidel, the dirty nonce, whatever. Come on, think quick, or you're dead. Five seconds.'

'I offer to play him at Russian roulette, like Robert de Niro in *The Deerhunter*. Then I load the gun with three bullets and shoot him when it's my turn.'

'No way. He says he's seen the stupid Yankee film *The Deerhunter*, and you're a stupid infidel pig for thinking he's the kind of simple peasant who would fall for that. He's angry now. Shit, he's cocked the hammer of the gun, he's about to pull the trigger.'

'Tell him that I'm a big star on TV back home. If he kills me, Tony Blair will personally ensure that his home village is razed.'

'Actually, somebody came up with a story like that on my kidnap course. The instructor said it was so outrageous, it might actually work. But no, what you need to be doing now is trying to win their confidence as a journalist. Tell them you've come to get their side of the story.'

'Bollocks, I try that line on doorsteps every day. People never buy it.'

'Ah, that's here. Remember, in some parts of the world, journalists are still respected.'

I doubted that. Like most other hacks, war zone journalists had been using the 'let's get your side of the story' excuse for decades in order to wangle interviews with dictators and warlords. And every time, they still stitched them up. Surely the baddies had cottoned on to that by now.

'Did that line work with your kidnap gang on the course?' I asked.

'Yes. I told them I worked for the BBC, and that through me they could tell their story to the rest of the world.'

'And they believed you? They can't have been very good terrorists. Did you escape?'

'Not quite. The moment after they let me go I trod on a pretend landmine.'

'Oh dear. Shall we go for a pint?'

'Good idea. You've just been executed, though.'

We adjourned to the pub around the corner from Dominic's house, a shabby, flat-roofed shambles of a boozer that had somehow avoided the rest of Streatham's gentrification. Dominic had never been there before, and as we wandered in I could see why. Its tattoo-per-patron quotient was at prison levels. I edged nervously past several beer-bellied men in shellsuits and baseball caps, bought two Stellas and took them to a table in the furthest corner of the room.

'Right dump, this.' I whispered.

'It's the next stage of your hostile environment training. Remember, if you find this bad, you're going to struggle once you get to any kind of war zone.'

I pictured the slobs at the bar as a Balkan militia, the People's Beerbellied Liberation Front. Kalashnikovs in one hand, pints in the other. After all, in the anarchy of a war zone, where civil society gave way to the law of the jungle, it would be lowlifes like these who ran the show, not the local vicar. What would happen if I fell into the hands of people like these? They'd call me a soft ponce, beat me up, have a few more Stellas, and then execute me in the function room upstairs.

Dominic sipped his lager, one eye monitoring the rest of the bar. 'So was anything of what I said any use?'

'Sort of,' I said. 'It's just that I think if I ever got in any kind of shoot-out or whatever, I'd just forget it all and end up in a total blind panic.'

'That's only natural. The idea is just to make you think a bit, so that if the worst happens, you at least know what you should try and do. If nothing else, that keeps your mind busy and stops you panicking.'

'Do you think I'm mad even *thinking* about doing this?'

'Not for me to say. But if anyone asks, don't say the only safety training you had was from your mate in the local park.'

* * * * *

A few days later, Dominic and I went war zone shopping. With him acting as technical adviser, we toured the budget electrical goods stores on London's Tottenham Court Road and bought a laptop, a satellite phone and a tangle of connecting cables. I also bought a mini DVD camcorder, on the off chance that I might film a world exclusive of Saddam Hussein entertaining Osama bin Laden in a café in downtown Baghdad. Failing that, I was going to use it to make a video diary. The whole thing felt like such a giant leap into the unknown that I'd decided to record it day by day. If I got to Iraq but didn't manage to get anything into print, which seemed quite likely, I could at least bore all my friends silly with a special home video night when I got back. We also visited a place called the 'Spymaster' shop in Mayfair, which sold security equipment to rich and paranoid businessmen. They had everything from bulletproof cars through to spy cameras hidden in fake Coke cans. For £400, I picked up an Israeli Army-issue gas mask and chemical and biological survival suit. Or that was what they said it was, anyway. The suit was in a sealed packet that wasn't supposed to be opened except in emergencies; it could have been a beekeepers' outfit for all I knew.

By the time we'd finished, I'd blown nearly £4,000 on new equipment. Few journalists are particularly techno-literate – on my first local paper, I remember someone holding up a computer mouse and complaining that the 'footpedal' was very unresponsive – and I was no exception. Back at home, I couldn't even figure out how to switch the laptop on. I poked and prodded curiously at it like some curious Neanderthal, then gave up. Max, who'd come round for a drink, finally mustered an intelligent observation.

'Have you got all this stuff insured?' she asked.

'Well, I'll get travel insurance.'

'Can you get it if you're going to a war zone?'

'I hadn't thought of that. Does that mean I wouldn't get cover for accidents either?'

'Well, it's not like going to Ibiza.'

The next day I investigated. I'd assumed that getting cover wouldn't be a problem, given how much insurance companies seemed to have adapted themselves to the adventure holiday market. You could, after all, buy blanket round-the-world insurance policies that covered places like Colombia, where violent robbery was almost part of the tourist experience. But Iraq was in a different league, and the only cover I could find was something called a brokered policy, tailor-made for your specific plans – the sort of thing that stuntmen and people marching solo across the South Pole use. I tracked down a broker who specialised in dealing with journalists.

'Can you tell me how much you charge for Kurdistan, please? It's in northern Iraq.'

'Kurdistan? Just a second.' At least he had heard of the place. Other insurance firms had denied it existed. 'Kurdistan policies start at about £3,000. That's for £100,000 worth of cover.'

'£3,000 a year?' I said, half to myself. 'That's a lot.'

'Er… that's per *month*.'

'Per month?'

'Yes. It's very high because everyone's expecting the war to start.'

I put the phone down. The only saving grace was that, at £3,000 a month, there was no agonising about it. If I was going, I'd be as uninsured as my laptop and satellite phone were. And that big stash of $10,000 that I was going to have to carry in my underpants. It was a sobering thought. Adventure was one thing, foolhardiness another. If I got crippled and wasn't insured, I could end up a burden not just to myself but to my family. My parents might end up re-mortgaging their house, just so I could remain paralysed on a life-support machine in their front room.

On the other hand, wasn't that what real adventures were all about? Real risk? Christopher Columbus would never have crossed the Atlantic if the insurers and actuaries had been around: too much risk of dropping off the edge of the earth, or getting eaten by sea monsters.

And then there'd have been no America.

And nobody to invade Iraq.

Put That Statue Back Up

ON THE NIGHT OF Thursday March 19, 2003, the war started. Acting on a CIA tip, President Bush signed an order raining bombs down on a bunker in Baghdad where it was thought Saddam and his sons were hiding. The next day, the invasion proper got under way, with British and American troops streaming across the Kuwaiti border. I watched with mixed feelings. On the one hand, I was profoundly relieved the whole thing hadn't been called off at the last minute. On the other, the opening of hostilities meant any chances of getting into Kurdistan via Iran were gone. I changed my plan, booking a flight ticket to Amman in Jordan for mid-April. Lots of other journalists were already there, hoping to go into Iraq whenever the war ended. My plan was to sit it out there, glean as much info off the grapevine as possible, and then head into Baghdad if it ever looked safe enough.

April Fool's Day was my final day at the paper, an omen if ever there was one. Leaving was almost a relief. Already, I was fed up with people asking me why I was still in the office when the war had already started. Mike Leese, the deputy news editor, wandered over to wish me luck.

'Just be careful,' he said. 'Really careful.'

'I will.'

'I mean it. Remember, these war reporter guys get a hard-on from what they do.'

'You what?

'A hard-on. You know.' His eyes gestured downward. 'They get a sexual turn on from the fighting. They're a certain kind of people, it gives them that kind of buzz. I'm not knocking what you're doing, just remember that you might find it's not for you. Don't do anything crazy just because other people do.'

'Sure, I won't.'

We shook hands and I walked out the *Evening Standard* offices for the last time, wondering what to make of what Mike had said. It had to go down as one of his most bizarre pieces of advice ever, which was saying something.

A week later I was a nervous wreck. Problems that I'd previously been too busy to deal with now loomed large. Getting the laptop to work with the satellite phone, so that I could send stories from Iraq, was beyond me. Given that the only people who generally used satellite phones were Colombian drug barons and international terrorists like Osama bin Laden, virtually nobody in Britain knew how to work the damned things. So far, despite paying £100 to a computer expert, all I'd been able to do was text message Dominic the GPS co-ordinates of my flat in Camberwell.

Meanwhile, the Coalition invasion was making alarmingly smooth progress. On April 9th, I turned on the TV to see an American tank pulling down a statue of Saddam Hussein in central Baghdad, as a cheering crowd of Iraqis looked on. From the way the TV reporters on the ground were burbling excitedly, it was clear that this would become the defining image of the fall of Saddam's regime. As history was made that day, I was one of a tiny number of people who watched in dismay, along perhaps with Saddam himself and a few other remaining despots. 'Put that statue back up,' I felt like shouting. 'The war's not allowed to finish until I get there.'

The night before I left for Jordan, Max threw a small party around at her flat. The atmosphere was convivial, but also had something of the feel of a wake held in advance. I filmed bits of it for my new video diary, feeling like some death row inmate making a documentary about his last few days on earth. By 11pm I was half-drunk, as I'd been for most nights in the last few weeks. It was the only way I could relax and become vaguely optimistic about my plans.

At 6am the next day, I headed for Heathrow, accompanied by Dominic and Max. I hugged them both and said goodbye, wondering whether I'd ever see them again. In the duty-free bar, I ordered a large Scotch, opened my new copy of the *Lonely Planet Middle East*, and tried to not to feel scared. If all else failed, I'd already got a plan B: head for a beach resort on Jordan's Red Sea coast, chill out for a month or two, and then quietly come home when no-one was looking.

*****

Flight 4041 to Amman was finally called. It was the last fixed bit of itinerary I had. Once I got to Amman, I'd have no real idea where I was going, or what I was going to do, other than try to get into Iraq. It wasn't even clear yet if the border was open. And if I did get in, I'd know nobody, have no work lined up and no real idea of what to do. The newspapers I'd read on the plane brought little cheer. Since the toppling of Saddam's statue the week before, law and order had completely broken down. Looting was rampant, and reporters were getting robbed at gunpoint left, right and centre. It was the worst possible environment for an uninsured freelance. I reminded myself of my Christopher Columbus theory: that a genuine adventure, by definition, carried a high risk of going disastrously wrong. It was, therefore, reasonable to be utterly paranoid.

Sat a couple of rows back on the plane was a Dutch bloke who I'd seen earlier on loading TV camera gear into the overhead lockers. He had the look of many of the reporters I'd seen on TV in Baghdad – suntanned but also haggard, like a junkie who'd been on holiday. He didn't seem particularly keen to talk, but I couldn't afford to be polite anymore. If I wanted to find out what to do next, I was going to have to get used to asking complete strangers dumb questions. Like: 'Er, excuse me, have you been in the war in Iraq?'

'Yah, I have. But I left just before the bombing started. Now I'm going back in.'

'Can you get into Baghdad from Jordan yet?'

'Yah, I think so. There are no longer any Iraqis guarding their side of the border, so you don't need the visa anymore. But it's dangerous, man. People are getting robbed everywhere on the road in. The only way to do it is with a convoy of cars, with lots of other people for safety. But it costs a lot of danger money. Last I heard, it was $2,000 one-way.'

I went back to my seat. There was no way I was forking out $2,000 for the journey into Baghdad. But at least the Jordanian border was open, unlike the Syrian, Turkish and Iranian ones. If nothing else, I was heading to the right country.

At around 1am, the plane finally touched down in Amman. I checked into a £12-a-night hotel down an alleyway in the old part of the city, cracked open a beer from the mini-bar and watched the latest news from Iraq on CNN. It wasn't good. Gangs of 'Ali Baba' looters were everywhere, ransacking government buildings, shops and private homes. Like the tail-end of the January sales, it seemed that most of the best bargains had gone: one looter had found a speedboat but not its tow-trailer, so his pick-up truck was just dragging it down the road on its hull at about 30 mph. Otherwise, the only thing left to steal seemed to be a large amount of Ba'ath Party office furniture, particularly grey swivel chairs, which were being wheeled away in huge fleets down the street.

The Palestine Hotel, the *de facto* headquarters of the press corps, was becoming the unofficial meeting point between Iraq and the outside world. Crowds of newly-liberated Iraqis flocked outside, some waving banners, some begging interviews with foreign journalists, others begging for jobs as translators. To prevent the place being over-run, the US military had thrown a protective security cordon around it. As night fell, the soldiers began blasting away at some unseen enemy in the pitch-dark streets beyond, streams of tracer fire lighting up the blackness. Some reports said it showed the city was still awash with resistance fighters. Others said the soldiers had just fired off a few rounds to help the TV crews fill their bulletins that night.

Overall, the place looked scary, but manageable. If the looting ended, the danger money that drivers were charging from Amman would drop. Then all I'd need to do was find a dirt-cheap hotel, a translator willing to work for bugger all, and someone who wanted me to write stories for them. It was still a bit of a long shot, a complex, five-horse accumulator kind of gamble, but somehow the odds looked better when seen close up. In a fit of optimism, I cracked another beer, channel surfed in a fruitless quest for some porn, and fell asleep.

The next morning I went up to the Intercontinental Hotel, the main *rendezvous* for journalists going to and from Baghdad. On a notice board in the lobby, various reporters had posted hand-written notices looking for people to share convoy costs. *'Car going to Baghdad tomorrow. One extra place. Contact Fabrice from Le Monde or Miguel from El Pais.'* I got vaguely excited until I saw the going rate, which was still hovering around the $2,000 per person.

Over the next few days, I loitered around the hotel lobby, quizzing every other journalist who went past. Those who'd just come back from Baghdad often sometimes looked slightly askance, as if I was some weird war zone groupie. But those on their way in were often just as keen to pool knowledge. Nobody, though, seemed willing to hang around in the hope that the price of a place in a convoy might eventually drop. Once that happened, they reckoned, there wouldn't be a story worth reporting on anymore.

When not at the Intercontinental I spent time in internet cafés, surfing the net on super-slow computers and emailing the foreign desks of all the national newspapers to ask if they needed a spare Baghdad correspondent. Several sounded positive, saying they'd be pulling their own staff reporters out soon. But none were willing to stump up the $2,000 for the journey in. I could understand why. If I was subsequently killed, whichever hapless foreign editor had stumped for the trip would face a sanctimonious inquest from every other newspaper. 'Did he have any experience?' No. 'Was he insured?' No. 'Had you ever met him?' No. It wouldn't look good.

After a fortnight in Amman I finally took the plunge. The looting in Baghdad had finally subsided – probably because there was little left to steal – and the price of the journey in was dropping. I answered an ad on the wall in the hotel lobby. *'Car leaving for Baghdad tomorrow,'* it read. *'With Tokyo TV. Extra people needed. If interested, meet in Intercontinental lobby 6pm tonight.'*

The leader of the Tokyo TV trip turned out not to be Japanese but a British-Iraqi guy about my own age called Omar Hadi. His family had left Baghdad in the 1970s, as Saddam Hussein's rule became increasingly authoritarian. He was still fluent in Arabic but had been educated at a British public school and spoke English better than I did. He wore white linen trousers, an expensive-looking shirt and sports jacket, and a trilby. Yet he still looked a lot more dashing than me, in my new war reporters' utility vest, a waistcoat thing with lots of pockets for notebooks and cameras. I'd bought it hoping I would look like James Woods in the film *Salvador*, but instead I took on the appearance of a posh farmer.

Omar was going back to Iraq for the first time since the age of five, to track down relatives he hadn't seen for more than 20 years. Tokyo TV, consisting of two Japanese photographers he'd met in Amman, were going to follow him around for a documentary. The other passengers would be Omar's elderly Iraqi aunt, who'd left Baghdad for the duration of the war, and a clean-cut looking American guy about my own age called John Dawkins, who didn't say much. I had him down as some kind of volunteer aid worker.

The deal seemed like as good as it was going to get. Omar had hired a GMC, an enormous American-made sports utility vehicle that was the standard form of transport for the run to Baghdad. The price, including an Iraqi driver, was only $150 each. The plan was to leave the next night at 2am. That got you to the Iraqi border by dawn, leaving as many daylight hours as possible to negotiate the dicey 300-mile stretch to Baghdad.

That evening I went for a quick beer in a bar down the road and recorded what would be my final pre-Iraq video diary entry. In the past few weeks it had become like my personal therapist, a repository for endless worries, whinges and fears. I had the uncomfortable feeling, as I filmed myself, that this might turn out a bit like *The Blair Witch Project*: 'In May 2003, a young journalist with a video camera disappeared while travelling into Iraq. A year later, his footage was found. Unfortunately, it was rubbish, so it could never form the basis for a major motion picture.'

The Road To Baghdad

'I, COLIN FREEMAN, pledge to leave the Jordanian territories to Iraq on my personal account and accept that the government will not be responsible for guaranteeing my safety or anything else that might arise from my departure to the Iraqi territories.'

The blurb on my Jordanian press card reminded me of the disclaimer I'd once signed while doing a bungee jump. Without it, the Jordanians would not allow you through the border, so we all had one, a piece of cheap, laminated blue card with English on one side and Arabic on the other. The six of us stood with our bags outside the Intercontinental, casting envious glances at the people gassing away in the restaurant and bar. Shortly after midnight, the GMC arrived, a tatty-looking thing with a windscreen sporting numerous frosty bruises from stones kicked up on desert roads. My mind flashed back to one of Dominic's hostile environment course maxims: 'If going through dangerous terrain, always check that your vehicle is completely roadworthy'.

'Don't worry, it's better to have an older-looking car,' said Omar, sensing the collective unease. 'Less chance of getting robbed.'

We piled in, Omar's auntie up front with the driver. That wasn't just so that she could have more space. If any robbers saw the car approaching, they'd see an elderly Iraqi woman rather than a bunch of Westerners loaded with dollars and expensive electronic equipment. That would hopefully trigger their chivalrous instincts, if they had any. The word was that often they just killed their victims anyway.

We set off, passing through the endless suburbs of Amman before reaching the highway to the border. As the rest of the car gradually fell asleep, I sat awake, staring into the darkness. It was April 30, four months and one week since the morning outside Cheryl Barrymore's house. After all that hassle, worry and indecision, this was finally it. I pulled out my notebook, ready to jot down a few profound thoughts to tell the video diary the next morning, but none came. All I could think about was the broken springs in the seat, already digging painfully into my legs.

Eventually, I dozed off. Three or four hours later, I opened my eyes again. As I massaged the circulation back into my thighs, dawn began breaking, a pinkish strip along the horizon sandwiched between the inky blacknesses of the desert floor and the night sky. An hour later, the Iraqi border loomed, marked by two large yellow arches stretching either side of the dual carriageway that made Iraq look like a giant drive-in McDonald's. As we sat waiting for the car to be searched, I got everybody to speak to the video camera, recording their reasons for the trip and what they hoped to achieve.

Omar Hadi and John Dawkins, it turned out, were business associates. They'd met in Kazakhstan, the former Soviet republic in Central Asia, where Omar had been involved in the oil and gas trade and John had worked in IT. Dawkins seemed something of a specialist in frontier countries: prior to Kazakhstan, he'd done business in Afghanistan and Russia.

Now, with Omar as his guide, he was hoping to tap into post-Saddam Iraq, cut off from the outside world since 1991 and one of the world's last virgin commercial territories. His first plan was to tout his services to US Army bases. Nobody doubted that the Americans would be here for some time to come, and soon they'd want equipping with internet access, telephones and all manner of civilian comforts for bored, war-weary troops. Whoever could supply them out here could virtually name their price. To stake a claim, though, he had to get in ahead of the big American multi-national contractors like Kellogg Brown and Root and Halliburton, the company once run by US vice-president Dick Cheney. TV Tokyo was just a cover story to get the press card that allowed him into the country straightaway.

We handed over our passports in a dirty, half-empty visa processing hall and waited for exit stamps. A passport official, bleary and unshaven, handed them back once they were stamped, calling out the names like a bored school teacher taking a register. Western names like mine jolted out amongst the endless rollcall of Hassans, Mohammeds and the odd Saddam. We rolled on to the US checkpoint, where several tanned, grinning faces in helmets and sunglasses appeared at the windows. 'Welcome to Eye-raq!' said the troops, and we were in, and driving past a statue of Saddam that lay broken on the ground.

Iraq was like a massive beige billiard table, utterly featureless, like the surface of some distant planet. Other journalists had spoken of the road being littered with dead bodies just a couple of weeks before, but now there seemed to be nothing other than the odd burned-out car by the roadside. On that score, it wasn't much different from Camberwell.

'Not much to it, is there?' said Omar. The trickle of traffic from the border post thinned out rapidly, and within a few miles, we were completely on our own. The emptiness of the landscape was rather unsettling. I scanned the road ahead and behind for hazards. Robbers, I'd been told, often used scout vehicles, following at a discreet distance before racing on ahead and setting up an ambush. Sometimes they'd also get shepherds to block the road with their flocks. The standard technique used by most convoys was just to drive non-stop the whole way at about 100mph, so I looked up when our driver began going slower rather than faster. When eventually he dropped to about 30mph, Omar leaned over and asked what was wrong.

'Er… something the matter with the gears,' Omar reported back.

Minutes later we were sat on the hard-shoulder, the driver's legs protruding from beneath the GMC as he inspected its innards. He'd parked underneath a motorway flyover. Whether that was to protect us from the sun or to hide our presence, I couldn't tell. What was it Dominic had said about breaking down in hostile environments?

Rule one: Don't get out of the car in case you make yourself a target.

Rule two: Don't wander off the road in case of landmines.

Too late. John Dawkins was already sat by the hard shoulder, while one member of Tokyo TV was busy taking pictures from on top of the flyover, visible to any robber for miles around. A light wind whistled eerily through the ramparts of the bridge. It was very easy to imagine that someone out there was watching us.

Omar called us all back to the GMC. 'The driver needs to go into a town near here to get the car repaired,' he said.

'Is it safe?' I asked.

Omar didn't reply. I had a feeling he was engaged in a spot of news management. We crawled on down the road for another few miles, before turning off along a slip road. 'What's this place called?' I asked. Omar muttered something unpronounceable beginning with

R. I didn't repeat the question. From the terseness in his voice, he was obviously concentrating very hard on getting us in and out quick.

'R' was unbelievably run-down. No buildings seemed to be more than one storey high, and even then they struggled to stand upright. The main drag was made of jerry-built shacks, leaning lopsidedly against each other for mutual support. Piles of garbage lay in varying states of decay, some still recognisable as household debris, some left so long it had congealed into a kind of black, urban compost. Mechanical and agricultural detritus littered the streets, amid pools of oil, leaked sewage and other smears and stains of indefinable origin.

A few Iraqis hung about, huddled around barrels of petrol that they'd turned into makeshift filling stations. Most wore dirty white dishdashas or cheap-looking black leather jackets. They looked like the Jordanians in the scruffier parts of Amman, only rougher, more unshaven, and, unless it was just paranoia, bigger. The driver headed for a street lined with gloomy workshops, surrounded by piles of tyres, spare doors and other car giblets. He shouted to a garage owner, who waved us into his premises.

'Stay inside the car,' warned Omar. 'The driver says people here aren't that friendly.'

As two mechanics worked on the GMC, I could see the other garage hands stealing occasional glances at us. They didn't smile, but they didn't look hostile either. Or not as hostile as I would be to foreigners whose armies had just invaded my country. Here we were in their town, after all, Western, wealthy and totally defenceless. Yet rather than robbing us, they were helping us on our way. No wonder Iraq was in a mess. Its ordinary people clearly lacked any sense of natural justice or opportunity.

Ten minutes later the driver came over and spoke to Omar, waving his hands apologetically. 'He's going to have to stay at least a day here to get the gears repaired, possibly longer,' Omar said. 'He doesn't think it's safe for us to stay here, so he's suggesting we take two taxis from here to Baghdad. He'll pay them the money we were going to pay him.'

We had no choice. Minutes later, we were transferring our gear into two elderly-looking Nissan saloons. The one I was in had a dashboard decorated in strips of maroon and gold carpet, and a windscreen with so many pebble marks it looked like it had been raked with machinegun fire. We left via the east side of 'R', where we saw our first bomb site, a grey brick building that looked like it might have served some official function. Inside, you could see exactly where the munition had plunged through the roof, creating a tunnel of struts, cables and fibres in its wake. Rather than blowing outward, as you would expect, the whole place appeared to have collapsed in on itself, as if the explosive had acted like a giant vacuum. Further down the road, a flyover that straddled a greasy-looking creek had been flattened like a giant had stepped on it.

The next five hours on the motorway were like the first, the road stretching through endless desert like a film on a repeat loop. All that changed was that it got even emptier and emptier. Often we'd go half an hour without seeing another vehicle. When any other car did approach, I watched for the passenger windows opening slightly and Kalashnikov barrels poking out. This was apparently a standard signal in the Iraqi highwayman's code. The rough translation being: *'A carful of armed men is behind you. Pull over to the nearest convenient point on the roadside and hand over your valuables. And please forget that Dick Turpin bullshit about not being harmed as long you co-operate.'*

The afternoon sun was beating down fiercely, creating a mirage that turned the central reservation ahead into blurred quicksilver. In the distance mini-tornadoes spiralled in the thick layer of heat on the desert floor. Every extra mile felt good, as if we were escaping some unseen foe, although the real danger lay on the approach to Baghdad. The roads around the city of Ramadi, west of the capital, had been a robbers' haven even in Saddam's time. As the last proper city before the great empty expanse between Baghdad and Jordan, it was easy for bandits to lurk a few miles outside town, do a couple of hold-ups, and then nip back home along the backroads with their loot.

The motorway started to show more scars of battle. Bits of the central reservation had been squashed and torn aside, presumably by tanks or armoured vehicles. Here and there the road had been peppered by strafing runs from US warplanes, each round throwing up a mound of brown earth like a giant molehill. Nearing Ramadi, we saw an armoured US troop transporter, similar to the one that had been used to tear down Saddam's statue. A huge, squat metal box with no windows or turrets, it was tearing down the road at about 40mph, its tracks leaving stress marks on the concrete. It was, I realised, the first US Army presence we had seen since the border.

The sun was lowering by the time we finally reached the outskirts of Baghdad. The place looked like trouble even from a distance. Rising above the skyline were huge palls of dirty smoke, while the lay-bys on the approach road were littered with burnt-out Iraqi tanks and artillery pieces, roasted to a rusty bronze. Previously we'd gawped at every burnt-out vehicle we'd seen. Now there were too many even to count. Bridges and buildings bore scorch marks and craters, lampposts lay flattened and twisted, and many of the palm trees that lined the streets had been reduced to charred stumps, as if the US Army had used them as target practice. On an overhead gantry, punctured with bullet holes like the sign for a Wild West town, read the words we'd both longed for and dreaded: *Welcome to Baghdad*.

Even if the Americans hadn't dropped thousands of tonnes of ordnance in the last three weeks, I got the impression that Baghdad would still have looked pretty grim. The *Lonely Planet Middle East* had given due warning. In its brief three-paragraph résumé on Baghdad, it said that most of the traditional architecture that once made it a beautiful city had been destroyed. Not so much by the cruise missiles of the 1991 Gulf War, but by Saddam's equally ruthless urban modernisation programme a decade before. In had come a drab hybrid of Arab and Soviet architecture, endless sprawling blocks of arches and domes coated in a vomit-brown harling. Thanks to the economic sanctions of the last decade, most places hadn't had a lick of paint in years. Even the poorest Third World cities usually have a few freshly-painted houses or newly-done-up shops to brighten things up a bit. Here, there was nothing. Kerbsides had crumbled, paintwork had cracked, and even the ubiquitous brown breezeblock had developed ugly ulcers. The whole place had a starved, malnourished feel, made all the sadder given that, only 20 years ago, it had been one of the most developed cities in the Middle East. There was also a pungent smell which hung everywhere, a potent reminder that the city hadn't washed properly, had its rubbish collected or taken a civilised crap for nearly two months.

Ten minutes later we were heading into a downtown area of high-rise buildings. On our left was the bombed-out remains of a modern supermarket, a low, flat-roofed building like the Safeways near my Camberwell flat. As we passed, two scruffy-looking children crawled out from beneath the hulking debris like ants. Seconds later we were on a bridge heading over the Tigris, its sewage-brown waters stretching in a long, dirty streak through what was left of the city centre. This was where Operation Shock and Awe had been at its show-off worst. The Baghdad Telephone Exchange, a 15-storey tower overlooking the river that bristled with antenna and receiver dishes, had several huge holes punched in its walls by missiles.

Across the bridge we disappeared into a jungle of vast, hulking office blocks fashioned from a uniform grey concrete. One or two had been bombed, black soot smothering their upper tiers like giant cakes with icing dripped over them. The few people who were wandering around, I noticed, all looked either scary, scared, drugged or plain mad. I remembered reading that just before the war Saddam had released all the country's prisoners – not just the nice political ones, but all the ordinary murderers, cut-throats and crazies, too. I wondered how crazy you'd have to be to commit crime in a police state like Iraq. Downtown looked like where they all hung out. At a roundabout, a potbellied man in a red checked shirt was arguing with a fellow street loiterer. As we drove past, Potbelly stripped his shirt off and began poking his companion in the chest, as if preparing for a bout of bare-knuckle boxing. Just visible at the top of his jeans waistband was the black handle of a pistol, its barrel wedged into his ample backside. Our taxi turned the corner before I could see what happened next, not that I really wanted to know. The whole thing felt like something out of *Grand Theft Auto*.

Then, long before we'd put anything like a comfortable distance between us and Potbelly, the Palestine Hotel finally loomed. It was a huge, 18-storey block, its balconies studded with hundreds of TV satellite dishes. With the rest of Baghdad in near-anarchy, it had become the lone oasis of safety and order in the whole city. American troops had parked tanks around it and were manning a barbed wire cordon round its perimeter. Omar consulted with an Iraqi at the car park entrance. 'Rooms are $80 a night,' he said. 'What do we want to do?'

'Let's just book in here before it gets dark,' I said. '$80 a night's OK for me.'

It wasn't really, but after what I'd just seen down the road I didn't care. All I wanted was somewhere safe. If Baghdad was as scary as it looked, I wouldn't be staying long anyway. John Dawkins, though, wanted to check out a hotel that Shamil, one of the Japanese photographers, knew of a mile away. Shamil had stayed there while posing as a human shield during the war, and said it was very cheap, and before I could protest we'd driven off again. Ten minutes later we found the place down a filthy sidestreet. It was called the Al Andalous Palace, a brown eight-storey splodge within retching distance of several overflowing skips of stinking rubbish. A palace it wasn't. Inside the gloomy lobby, the odour wasn't much better. There was an overpowering smell of rotten fungi, as if the place had once been badly flooded and they'd never quite dried the carpets out properly. The decor was unbelievably drab, like stepping into a Soviet Intourist hotel from the early 1980s.

An elderly receptionist led us to the first floor and opened up a suite. The two single beds inside were unmade, and lying on the floor were several empty vodka bottles. It looked and smelt like a couple of tramps had been on honeymoon in there. If this was the 'showroom', Christ only knew what the rest were like. We made our excuses and checked out another hotel next door called the Al Majalis. It looked, unbelievably, even tattier, despite boasting a 'Four Star' sign above the front door, but the rooms looked cleanish and it didn't smell of rotting mushrooms. Before I could suggest going back to the Palestine, everybody started unloading their gear. Cursing under my breath, I followed suit. Even if I could remember where the Palestine was, there was no way I was travelling anywhere on my own. I took a room next to John and Omar on the third floor, muttered that I'd look them up a bit later and flopped on the bed. It was about as comfortable as a snooker table.

Staring up at the broken ceiling fan, I tried to calm myself down. The street fight scene down the road had rattled me. I tried to remind myself that anywhere remotely nasty always feels a lot worse on the first visit. As a student in Manchester University, my friends and I had rented a house in the slum district of Moss Side, notorious for riots, drug dealing and gangland killings. The first time I went there was like travelling into a different world. Drug dealers seemed to hang on every corner, nearly half the houses were burnt-out or boarded up, and packs of wild dogs roamed everywhere. It was terrifying, and the only reason I agreed to move in was because I didn't want to look like a coward in front of my friends. Yet as soon the area became familiar, it became much less threatening. The less was left to the imagination, the more things assumed their true proportions. There were in fact only two or three groups of drug dealers, not dozens, only around one in ten houses was derelict, not half, and the dogs were friendly. Baghdad, I reasoned, might be the same. Once you got to know your bearings, things would assume a bit of perspective. And staying in the Al Majalis would probably be better than staying in the fortified Palestine, where it would be easy to develop a siege mentality.

An hour or two later John, Omar and I assembled in the hotel lobby again. We'd decided to walk down to the Palestine – it was reasonably safe as long as you were careful and observed the 11pm curfew. *En route* we passed a strip of restaurants. Only one, down a sidestreet, was open, so we dropped in for a bite to eat. It had been popular with foreigners before the war and most of the staff spoke English. Canaries and budgerigars chirped from cages hung up around the windows and a waiter thrust a three-page menu in front of us.

'Everything is off except chicken and lamb kebabs,' he said.

Ten minutes later, they arrived, served on rice with a side salad of aubergines and onions. The chicken kebabs seemed to be mainly bits of leg, while the lamb kebabs had a strong, gritty mince that tasted like it might have been dogfood. Even though I'd no idea where my next meal was coming from, I couldn't do more than pick at them.

When we got inside the Palestine complex, Omar and John explored downstairs while I went to see a *Daily Mail* reporter, Richard Pendlebury, who was staying there. The *Mail*'s foreign desk had rung me in Amman and asked me to deliver him $5,000 in cash. Being a courier wasn't exactly what I'd had in mind as my first foreign desk assignment, but they'd offered me a fairly generous fee to do it. Richard counted the money, gave me a cold beer, and we chatted for half an hour or so. By the time I got downstairs again, Omar and John had gone. So much for sticking together. I looked for a taxi. There'd been lots outside the hotel earlier on. But now the street was completely deserted. After ten minutes of increasingly anxious waiting, I wandered over to the soldier manning the checkpoint and asked him where they'd all gone.

'Curfew time, sir,' he said. 'No vehicles or people allowed out.'

'Curfew isn't until 11pm, is it?' I said, looking at my watch. 'It's just gone 10.'

'Your watch is an hour slow, sir.'

Shit. I'd had no idea that Baghdad was an hour ahead of Jordan. If I didn't get back to the hotel, John and Omar would be worried sick about me. I went back to the soldier. 'Excuse me, my hotel is just about a mile down the road,' I said. 'Do you think it'd be OK if I walked?'

He whistled. 'Can't really answer that one, sir.'

'Well, you're not going to shoot me or anything, are you?'

'Not me, no. But it's at your own risk, sir.'

I strode straight off, clutching a bottle of whisky that Richard had given me. I realised I'd made no accurate fix on where the hotel was, other than it being roughly straight down the road from the Palestine. Luckily, that was also one of the few roads that had working streetlamps; 10 minutes in a straight direction and I'd be back. As I walked, though, nervous sweat gathered in the small of my back. The street was completely silent, and my footsteps echoed loudly. It was eerily reminiscent of late nights wandering home through Moss Side, where the streets were similarly empty after dark. Suddenly, the street lights began cutting out. Within seconds, everywhere was pitch black. Unable to see more than three feet ahead, I tripped on a hole in the pavement and went sprawling, nearly breaking the bottle of whisky. I got up, nursing a sprained ankle and limped on, trying to control a rising tide of panic.

As a roundabout loomed, I realised I was lost. Hadn't the road gone to the right a bit? Or was I too far already? I couldn't remember a single landmark on the way from the hotel. Any passing American patrol would probably now shoot me on sight.

'A British journalist has been shot dead by US troops on his first night in Baghdad. The US military said that Colin Freeman, who was wandering round after curfew with a bottle of whisky, was mistaken for a looter.'

I ducked into a side alley and tried to calm down. Dominic's hostile environment training hadn't included getting lost in a pitch-dark city after curfew while armed with only some cheap and nasty spirits. I couldn't even find my way back to the Palestine now. What would Dominic have done now? I could hear him now, dispensing wisdom from the park bench in Streatham.

Well, frankly Col, I wouldn't be so stupid in the first place as to…

Never mind that! Just get me out of here!

Well, if I were you, I would make a careful note of my exact location, and then press on from there a little bit at a time. Then, if it didn't work out, I would come back to my starting point and keep trying in different directions. Then if that didn't work either, I would just stay where I was and spend the night outside. At least I wouldn't have strayed any further, and would hopefully be able to find my way back at first light.

Is that the best you can do?

I tiptoed for another hundred yards, scarcely daring to breathe. Then, to my immense relief, a sign saying BBC loomed on a house to the right. The former BBC studio – Shamil, the Japanese photographer, had pointed it out earlier – was right at the end of our street. Sure enough, the Al Majalis was just 50 yards away. I felt pathetically grateful. The hotel door was locked. Despair surged again. Then, inside the darkness of the lobby, an oil lamp detached itself from the reception desk and hovered its way over, revealing a grinning young Iraqi face behind it.

'Hello, I am Ali,' he said, in not bad English. 'Where you go? Everyone very worried when you don't come home.'

'Sorry, I got lost,' I said. I was touched to hear that the hotel staff had been worried about me. Given their standards of hospitality, the welfare of guests had not seemed likely to be a major concern.

'This way please. Sorry for no electricity. This Iraqi hotel. Now we are living in 18th century.'

He led me over to a corner of the lounge, where a group of men sat on settees eating pistachios. I told him what had happened and he laughed, translating for the others. His teeth, I noticed, were rotting.

'At night, Baghdad very dangerous!' said Ali. 'Many Ali Baba! So we have this!' He pulled up the cushion of the settee he was sitting on. Sticking out was the blue-black barrel of a Kalashnikov. 'No problem!'

A few pleasantries later, I went upstairs, sat at the balcony of my room and poured myself a generous slug of Richard's Scotch. It was 'Dimple', a brand I'd never heard of, despite its claim to being 'one of Scotland's most famous whiskies'. As a nerve-calmer, though, it did the job. Especially after half a pint. Somewhere in the night, shots crackled – possibly fighting, or possibly what the Americans called the 'celebratory gunfire' of newly-liberated Iraqis.

It had been a memorable day. I'd got into Iraq. Survived a day in Baghdad, both before and after curfew. Seen a machine-gun that wasn't in the hands of a soldier, policeman, or otherwise legitimate authority. And to cap it all, I'd heard someone say that George W Bush had officially declared the conflict to be over as of today, May 1st, 2003. But he hadn't said so until about midday my time. Which meant that technically, I'd been in a war zone, even if it was just for a few hours. True, being the very last journalist to get into Baghdad for the war was not the greatest claim to fame. But it was better than nothing. I toasted myself with more Dimple and then collapsed on the bed asleep.

Lost In Translation

I WAS WOKEN UP the next morning by a sudden deafening roar of machinery. It was just after 7am. I peered over the balcony to see an electricity generator the size of a large shed about 20 feet below. It had just started up, belching out grey-blue smoke as it choked on fuel impurities. Across the road, where two scruffy-looking goats were feeding on rubbish, another one was also sputtering into life. Generators had been used in Iraq for years now because of power shortages under Saddam. With electricity now down to just a few hours a day, they were now the default rather than the back-up power supply. Living in this room would be like living in a ship's engine chamber. It was probably one reason, though presumably not the only reason, why it was only $5 a night. I tried closing the windows, which were crisscrossed with black tape to prevent them shattering from bomb damage, only to find two panes were missing anyway.

I languished in bed, nursing a Dimple hangover and putting off getting up. Ever since leaving London, morning had been the hardest time, when my radical career change seemed at its most daunting. Any booze-inspired optimism worked up the night before had worn off, and the day ahead stretched out with all its challenges and uncertainties. A good few hours of effort, of hustling and cajoling, were obligatory before one could justifiably give up, crack open another beer, and hope for better luck tomorrow. Also, what exactly was I going to do anyway? Much as I whinged about it, as a staff correspondent on a newspaper you always had set tasks, no matter how ludicrous they were. Now, as a freelancer, it was entirely down to me what I did and when I did it. I felt like a paroled jailbird hankering for the familiar rules of prison.

Around 9am I got up and wandered out to look for John and Omar. The windowless corridor outside had no electricity and was almost pitch dark. To get to their room I had to feel my way down the wall, counting the doors until I reached theirs. There was no reply. So much for thinking they'd be worried about me. In the lobby, Ali, the friendly nightwatchman, was fast asleep on the settee, and reception was unmanned. No other guests were around. Clearly the Iraqis, like me, were not in the mood to jump up and greet the new day. I sat down for a few minutes and formulated an action plan. The best way to overcome the fear of the world outside, I figured, was to do it gradually. Start off with little trips of no more than a few blocks at a time. Then cover the whole neighbourhood, then the next neighbourhood, and so on. All the while memorising a safe bolt-route back.

My first journey would be back to the restaurant where we'd eaten, or half-eaten, the night before. I still had no appetite, but it was easy to get to. Out the door, past the Bombed Out Building and the Bricked-up Shops, and left again. First, though, there was the small question of what to do with my $10,000 cash. It had been a source of constant worry every since I'd picked it up. So far I'd followed the advice of the *Lonely Planet Middle East*, which was to carry it around in a moneybelt underneath your trousers. Unfortunately, the wad of $100 bills was as thick as a medium-length novel. The moneybelt bulged out like a giant codpiece, chafing uncomfortably against the groin area. I'd worn it in on the journey from Amman and it had carved vicious welts on my nether regions, as well as getting sweat-soaked. A few weeks more of that and the cash inside would go mouldy. Keeping a few hundred dollars aside to placate any muggers, I grabbed my dirty laundry bag and hid the rest of the cash in a stinking sock. Hopefully that would deter all but the most unsqueamish of hotel thieves. I left the hotel and strolled off down the road, Dominic's voice ringing in my ears once again.

'Always look like you know where you're going, even if you're lost. That way people will think you know the area and will be aware of the risks.'

I tried to look as casual as possible, as if going for a stroll through downtown Baghdad was an entirely normal thing for an unaccompanied Westerner to do. Passing motorists seemed to think differently. Nearly every car that drove past, taxi or otherwise, slowed down and honked their horns. 'Meesta, you need taxi?' It wasn't clear whether they were asking or telling. Up ahead loomed the day's first major test of nerve. A large group of villainous-looking Iraqi men were gathered round a car. They were looking at something laid out on the bonnet, but had now all turned to stare at me. I felt a twinge of the panic from the night before.

What should I do, Dom?

Evasive action should always be your first option. Can you switch to the other side of the road?

Nope, they'd see I was trying to avoid them.

How many of them are there?

God knows. About 30. Well, five or six.

What do you mean when you say they're villainous?

Well, they've got dark skin and moustaches for a start. Like that psycho fat guy yesterday with the pistol wedged down his backside. Like every bloody Iraqi. They all look scary, frankly. Even the kids. Even the dead ones on TV.

Cool it. Remember, they're not expecting to see you, so you've caught them unawares. Carrying out a street robbery requires planning and a little presence of mind. Just walk on past and say a quick 'Salaam al ay coom', the traditional Arab greeting. Remember what that means?

'Hello, and peace be upon you', or something. How d'you say it again?

'Salaam al ay coom'. I thought you said you were learning Arabic?

Saloon, ak al aam!

Six pairs of Iraqi eyes looked over, slightly nonplussed as I mangled their age-old greeting. The crowd around the car parted, as one man in a tatty tee-shirt wandered forward. To my astonishment, he proffered a can of beer. 'Hello meesta, you like beer, please?' He gestured to the car bonnet, effectively a mobile off-licence complete with bottles of spirits and beers of unknown provenance. From the way he and his companions were grinning, it looked like it doubled as a bar as well.

In front of me, I suddenly realised, was the new Iraq. During sanctions, Saddam had banned public consumption of alcohol, shutting down the bars and nightclubs that once made Baghdad the most fun city in the Middle East. He'd figured it would give Iraq a more pious, Islamic sort of image, which, in turn, would encourage other Muslim nations to protest if America invaded. It hadn't worked, not least because Saddam was known as a boozer himself. His favourite tipples, according to a book I'd read, were Johnnie Walker Black Label whisky and, bizarrely, Matheus Rose, a Portuguese wine that my parents served at dinner parties in the 1970s. Now Saddam was gone, the nation was back on the bevvy again, taking to *al fresco* drinking with all the enthusiasm of a Camberwell tramp.

Despite the conviviality, joining a group of street drinkers didn't seem like a good idea on my first full day in Baghdad. I smiled weakly, waved my hand and scurried onwards to the restaurant. Breakfast was the same as dinner: everything off except chicken and lamb kebabs. It wasn't really what I fancied at 9am, but I ordered a chicken kebab anyway, along with a pile of naan breads that instantly went rock hard. I squeezed a bottle labelled 'Brown Sause' over the kebab; the top came off and half a pint of pungent brown liquid splashed all over the plate. The waiter dashed over with a tissue, and swabbed the mess away with a practised hand. 'Very sorry. This Iraqi bottle.'

That, I was soon to learn, was a poignant universal disclaimer for anything that didn't work properly. *This Iraqi car. This Iraqi hotel. This Iraqi people.*

*****

'To be, or not to be, this is the question. Whether it is nobler in the mind to suffer slings and arrows of outrageous fortune, or to take arms against the sea of troubles, and by opposing er, um, end them.'

Haider, my newly-hired translator, broke off in mid-quote and looked at me through his half-moon spectacles for approval, as if taking the curtain call at the Globe Theatre. He'd told me that he was a retired linguistics professor from Baghdad University, and that Shakespeare was his favourite author. Elizabethan English, however, seemed to be about all he could manage. He had terrible trouble understanding me, even when I did my best to impersonate a BBC continuity announcer. Among the questions that had stumped him so far were 'How long were you a professor of linguistics?' and 'What is your favourite Shakespeare play?' Both times he'd simply replied: 'Yes.'

I'd picked Haider up in the car park of the Palestine Hotel, where every morning hundreds of Iraqis now gathered to tout their services as translators, fixers, drivers and pretty much anything else that people would pay them for. Middlemen worked the crowd, asking the foreigners what they needed and matching them to the limited talent on offer. People brandished photocopied degree certificates, CVs and yellowing letters of recommendation, boasting of everything from PhDs in chemical engineering through to references from long-departed diplomats. One man offering to be my driver told me his granddad had done the same job for the British Ambassador in 1920. I was quite impressed, until the next man said exactly the same.

Haider's sole recommendation was that he was cheapest. The middleman had hardly been able to hide his disgust when I'd told him what my top rate of pay was. '$5 a day? You are a journalist, no? The journalist always pays at least $50 a day.'

'I am freelance,' I said. 'Independent. No office in London to pay for me. Everything comes from here.' I patted my back pocket for emphasis. 'Very poor. Like human shield!'

His face dropped. 'OK, no problem, I try find. But maybe not good person working for this price.'

The middleman conferred with half a dozen different people, who in turn conferred with others. Eventually someone produced Haider. He stood out because he was far older than the rest. He was about 70, and wore cheap grey trousers and plastic shoes. A few strands of swept-back silver hair wisped across a nervous, freckled face. I felt like a trader at a slave auction, buying the weak and infirm lots that no-one else wanted. Even Haider wanted $30 a day to start off with, but with a bit of take-it-or-leave-it disinterestedness I got him down to $5 for just the morning, with the tempting offer of further labour that afternoon if he wanted it. This, we agreed, would be for both 'translating and fixing', although frankly Haider didn't look like he could fix anything. He was also somewhat short on ideas, as was I. It had dawned on me that although the collapse of Saddam Hussein's Iraq was the biggest story of the decade, I couldn't actually think of anything to report on. In the absence of any functioning government, economy or civil society, all the bread-and-butter events with which we filled newspapers at home were absent. There were no press conferences, no politicians to interview, no organisations pumping out surveys or press releases, no court cases to attend, and – thank God – no celebrities to doorstep. Nor was there any TV, radio or other newspapers to steal stories from. Instead, one would have to work entirely 'off-diary', ferreting out stories directly from the streets. That was what was known back home as 'real' journalism, the kind that elderly news executives used to say we youngsters knew nothing about. 'Real' journalism was also hard work. Particularly if you were a lone freelancer in a war zone, with only a geriatric Thespian for company.

'Shall we hire a taxi and drive round town for an hour?' I suggested. It wasn't likely to unearth any stories, but it would give me a chance to check Haider out a bit. We wandered to the hotel and got picked up by the first car that came along, an ancient brown Datsun Cherry like the one I learned to drive in back in 1988.

'Let me get the price,' said Haider, sticking his head through the window. After two minutes of animated discussions he turned around. 'Five dollars for the hour.'

'Five dollars for the hour?' Omar had said the going rate for an hour's ride was no more than about a dollar or so. Either Haider was planning to take commission, or his fixing skills were even worse than I thought. 'Tell him I can hire someone for the whole day for that,' I said.

Haider reconferred. 'He says three, lowest price.'

'OK.' It was still too much, but I didn't want to be seen dithering by the roadside for too long.

We clambered in. I'd thought the taxis that had taken us into Baghdad were clapped-out, but this was a whole other order of decrepitude. The dashboard, panelling and upholstery were all completely stripped away, leaving just the car seats and a bare carapace of exposed metal. The driver started the ignition by fiddling with wires in the steering column and, as we lurched off in a cloud of diesel, I could feel the chassis flexing and straining. Even so, other people still tried to flag us down. There seemed to be some rule by which only the cars most eminently unsuitable for public carriage touted for business on the streets. Somehow, I doubted that even the most comprehensive £3,000-a-week war zone insurance policy would have covered travelling in a deathtrap like this.

'From weech country, meesta?'

Our cabbie, a fat, stubbly chap in an off-white vest and shellsuit suddenly took an interest. Because his rear view mirror was missing, he turned right round to look at me, apparently unconcerned about the random traffic ahead.

'I am from Britain.'

'*Breetan*. Breetan good. Tony Blair. And Rothman cigarette. I have cousin live Breetan. In Heathrow, the capital of London.'

'Oh really? What does he do there?'

'Yes. Welcome to Iraq!'

It lacked the fluency of Haider's Hamlet soliloquy, but it was a nice gesture. In fact, it was surprising how agreeable people seemed. I'd never seen the point of hiding the fact I was British, but I'd assumed there'd be at least a few hostile looks. So far I'd had nothing but friendliness, if of a slightly bemused sort.

As we drove around I tried to quiz Haider about his life. Other journalists had told me that one of the great things about Iraq was that everybody you met had a story. You didn't need to seek out prominent dissidents or outspoken human rights activists – so insane and brutal was Saddam's regime that even your taxi driver, hotel bellhop or translator would have some newsworthy tale of being jailed, tortured or otherwise spectacularly mistreated. The only solid info I could get from Haider, however, was that he had fathered nine children and fought in one of Saddam's conscript armies during the Iran-Iraq war 20 years ago. Given his frailty, the idea of him doing either seemed pretty unlikely. We plunged down the wrong way onto a dual carriageway, the cab swerving in and out of the oncoming players like a rugby scrum-half heading for the tryline.

'Tell me Haider, why is it that people drive the wrong way down the road here?'

'These Iraqi drivers,' he said, as if no further explanation was necessary.

'Yes, but *why*? Isn't it dangerous, yes?' I pointed at the cars hurtling past us on either side and grimaced and whistled. Conversation with Haider, I realised, was going to be like playing charades. With a bit of gesturing, persistence and intelligent guesswork, the two of us could sometimes reach a breakthrough.

'Ah, we call this driving "wrong side". Same as in English. Is from Saddam time. The cars of all the big government people would drive down wrong side, making common people get out of the way. Now everybody is free, so they want to try this themselves.'

To my surprise, an overloaded red double decker bus suddenly drove past, with what seemed to be about 200 passengers hanging out the windows.

'Are the buses still running?' I asked.

'No, this Ali Baba bus. After the war, all the buses in Baghdad stolen. The thieves drive them around, pick up passengers, the same as before. But now they go wherever they like, take bus home to their house at night.'

I felt a flash of inspiration. The *Standard*, being a commuters' paper, was obsessed with stories about buses, even though they were almost as dull as stories about roadworks. This might just interest them. I could see the opening lines now.

'He has already stripped Baghdad's shops and banks bare, and saturated the market in stolen office furniture. But when the going gets tough, the enterprising "Ali Baba" does not get on his bike to look for work. Instead, he steals a double decker bus...'

OK, it needed a bit more work, but that could wait. Right now we had to secure an exclusive interview with the bus driver.

'Haider, tell the driver to turn around. Follow that bus!'

As he manoeuvred around, I tried to explain the story to Haider. He was as hard to convince as the *Standard* newsdesk after they'd been in the pub.

'But Mr Colin, why do you want to speak to the people driving the buses? They are Ali Babas, bad people.'

'Never mind. Just take it from me. My newspaper will be interested in this story.'

'Your newspaper is interested in stories about buses?'

'Er, yes.'

'Maybe we can go to the bus garage,' suggested Haider, showing unexpected initiative. 'Very near here.'

'Good idea. But hasn't it been looted?'

'Looted? What please is meaning of "looted"?' asked Haider. Shakespeare had clearly never used the word.

'To loot means the same as to steal.'

'Ah yes, the bus station is very looted. But some of drivers are there.'

'Why are they there if there are no buses to drive?'

'They are hoping the Americans will come to pay their wages.'

The bus garage was a couple of miles away. Through a rusting set of double gates, torn and twisted open by forces unknown, we stepped into a vast concrete compound half the size of a football pitch. Scattered around were numerous red buses, squatting on their innards after being gutted by looters. Even their destination boards were missing. As a stolen commodity, it was hard to see what resale value they would have.

Sheltering outside an office was a crowd of around twenty bus drivers. Chaos ensued as Haider tried to interview them. First two drivers would talk at him at once, then a third would join in, then a fourth. Eventually, the entire crowd was simultaneously jabbering and arguing, with Haider and with each other. Haider stood, bewildered, in the middle, trying courteously to listen to each person and failing miserably. After a couple of minutes I pulled him aside. Nobody seemed to notice.

'What are they saying, then?' I shouted.

'So far, nothing.'

'What do you mean, nothing? You've just had 20 people yelling at you non-stop for the last two minutes.'

'Ah, they were just talking about the general things. The bad life for the Iraqi people. No security, no electricity.'

'Did you ask them about the buses?'

'No.'

'Why not?'

'Please Mr Colin, we must do things slowly. These Iraqi people. It will take a little time.'

'Look, just pick one guy out of the crowd. Whoever sounds least crazy.'

We honed in on one of the quieter drivers and dragged him into a corner of the yard. I pulled out my notepad.

'What's his name?'

'Chiad.'

'How do you spell that?'

'Z-I-A-D.'

'You mean Ziad?'

'Yes. As I said. Z-E-A-D.'

I settled on 'Ziad'. Slowly we got him to talk. For some reason, even the simplest of questions elicited answers that were nothing to do with what I'd asked. I couldn't work out whether it was Haider mistranslating me, Haider mistranslating Ziad, or Ziad just choosing to ignore the questions.

Ziad reckoned that about 200 buses were now being driven around town by thieves. Most had no idea how to drive a bus properly, hardly ideal when there was no traffic laws and US tanks driving everywhere. One bunch of looting brothers, he said, had an entire row of buses parked outside their house, and were using them for taking their extended family on picnics.

'Why don't the drivers go and take the buses back?'

'The thieves will shoot them.'

After ten minutes I'd had enough. The sun was already hot and my notebook was soaked in sweat from trying to take down Haider's translation, which had a habit of starting in long, multi-claused sentences before stopping halfway through, like a Shakespearean actor who'd forgotten his lines. As we turned to go, Haider was once again collared by several fingerjabbing drivers.

'They are saying why don't you write a story about the bad security here, and the problems with the electricity. This they want the world to know.'

'Tell them that the problem with the buses is a story about bad security.'

'They say buses not important story.'

I felt my teeth gritting. There wouldn't be much point in telling them that back home, everyone had been writing about the electricity and security problems for weeks. As a freelance, I needed a new line.

'Tell them that when the Americans read about the stolen buses, maybe they will come and give them new ones. Anyway, let's go and see if we can find a stolen bus.'

We headed back towards the Palestine Hotel, and down towards the scary downtown area where I'd seen the man with the pistol wedged in his arse. Fortunately, in mid-morning the area didn't look too bad. A few streetcafés had re-opened, their customers glancing nervously over glasses of chai, as if they couldn't quite believe that such a normal, harmless activity was allowed again. A few shops were open, half-empty shelves touting a mix of elderly looking stereos and cameras like some Communist-era store in Eastern Europe. Parked up near a square full of fruit vendors was what looked like another Ali

Baba bus. As we wandered along, I suddenly felt Haider's hand slip around mine.

'Er, why are you holding my hand, Haider?'

'Mr Colin, this place called The Market of Thieves. Many Ali Baba. We do not want to be lootered. You must hold my hand for protection.'

What should I do, Dom? He's holding my hand!

First rule of security. Always use local knowledge. If your translator feels the area is dangerous, I'd do whatever he says. And remember, in Arab countries, it's not unusual for men who are friends to walk around hand in hand.

Squirming inwardly, I left my hand where it was, trying to touch Haider's as little as possible; it reminded me of going on dates as a teenager with girls you didn't really like. We wandered towards the fruit market, watched by what seemed like several hundred onlookers. I fretted about the TV crews we'd seen at the Palestine Hotel that morning, heading out for another day's filming on the streets. It would be just my luck to end up in some 'Life in Baghdad returns to normal' feature on the BBC.

The bus was loading up with passengers again. A skinny ruffian in an oily white t-shirt, oily shorts and equally oily mullet hairdo was behind the wheel, while a kid about 14 wandered up and down taking money. Haider chatted to the driver.

'He tells passengers "pay whatever you like". He has two friends with pistols sit among the passengers. If there is any trouble, bang.'

'Can we speak to the guys with the guns?'

'Please, Mr Colin, no. This dangerous.'

'Ask him, is this his bus?'

Haider said something to the driver. Whatever it was, it didn't sound like the question I'd asked. The driver just muttered and stared ahead.

'He says yes, it's his.'

'Where is his permit?'

'At home,' said Haider, without bothering to ask for an answer.

I gave up. We repaired to a nearby café at the end of a long sidestreet, made up of Italianate-style villas with elegant balconies and pillars. They would have been stunning at one time, but now they looked on the verge of collapse. Haider ordered chai, little schooner-shaped glasses of maroon tea that came with about six teaspoons of sugar heaped at the bottom. After yet another morning without breakfast, the sugar rush was quite energising. What could we do next? Aside from electricity and security, the other big story was the gun markets. Prior to the war, Saddam had distributed vast amounts of weapons among the civilian population, in the vain hope that they'd turn every Iraqi city into a re-run of Stalingrad. Instead most people had sat quietly at home and then flogged their weapons as soon as the war was over. Arms bazaars had now sprung up all over the city, flogging everything from Kalashnikovs to rocket launchers at ultra-cheap prices. Grenades could apparently be picked up for just $1. The story had already been done, with endless TV footage of gun traders obligingly test-firing their wares, but I still fancied visiting one just to see what it was like.

'Haider, do you think we could visit a gun market?'

He looked horrified. 'You need a gun, Mr Colin?'

'No, I just want see a gun market for a story.'

'We can't. They're full of bad people.'

I dropped the subject and we supped our tea. As Haider chatted to a man in a straw hat at another table, I reviewed his performance. He seemed trustworthy, and certainly cheap, but he clearly wasn't streetwise. If things kicked off anywhere – let alone at a weapons market – he'd be about as much use as my mum.

Haider tapped my arm. 'You want to see a gun market?' he asked, grinning at the man in the straw hat. 'There is one right here.'

'Eh? Where?'

'Right here.' As he spoke, he nodded to the man in the straw hat, who got up and disappeared round the corner. Minutes later he came back with a pistol and a Kalashnikov, making the chai glasses rattle as he placed them on the table. Nobody else paid the slightest bit of attention. Straw Hat demonstrated the pistol's loading and cocking mechanism, laughing along with Haider at my astonished face. He then thrust the pistol into my hand. It was surprisingly heavy.

'You see?' said Haider with a grin. 'This is Iraq. Guns everywhere. No need for gun market! Give me your camera – let me take a photo.'

Dom's voice piped up immediately.

For God's sake Col, you're not really going to pose for a picture holding a gun, are you? That is just pathetic war tourism of the worst kind.

Get away, you're just jealous. Remember, in Arab countries it's not unusual for grown men to wave guns about together in public.

I sat there, scared to hold the thing too tight in case it went off. My wrist bent under the gun's weight, making me look like a camp Dirty Harry. Haider snapped away. 'Smiling, please!'

*****

That evening, I felt my way down the corridor to Omar and John's room. Despite their indifference as to whether I'd been murdered or not on the first night, I was still keen to maintain some kind of contact. If something awful did happen, at least they'd be able to tell the Foreign Office when I'd last been seen alive. To my surprise, Omar welcomed me like an old friend.

'Colin! Come in, buddy. I was just about to have a drink. Got some Johnnie Walker that I brought in from Amman.'

'Yeah, OK.' I tried not to sound too eager, as if weighing Omar's company up against numerous other social options.

Dawkins was sat on his bed, working on a spreadsheet on his laptop. He'd seemed pretty taciturn until now, letting Omar do the talking. So far, all I'd gleaned out of him was that he was married, originally from California, currently living in Istanbul, and possibly about to be a father. Or already was one, I couldn't remember. He'd seemed so cagey when he'd talked that I'd stopped paying attention. Now, just as I was wondering whether it was even worth saying hello, he changed tack.

'Colin, how you doin' man? How's things? Sorry we've not been around much – been working totally flat out for the last few days.'

'No bother, mate. You going to join us for a drink?'

'Not tonight, no – too busy. Once I'm clear, though – you bet.'

Omar and I perched on two sweaty plastic seats on the balcony, swilling Johnnie Walker out of a couple of misted, cracked old glasses he'd found in the bathroom. The sun was disappearing behind an apartment block, silhouetting a couple of distant pyres of smoke. Not far away, a pall of flame burned from an oil refinery tower. Saddam had built it within a residential area to make it difficult for foreigners to bomb it without massive civilian casualties. We stared out, jumping occasionally as gunfire cracked, and compared notes so far.

51

Omar had a lot more to relate than I did. Since arriving, he and John had been touring various US Army bases around Baghdad. They'd also been to Saddam's old presidential palace complex in the city centre. It was now being used as the main administrative base for the Americans, who'd given them a guided tour round in a Humvee.

'They're using teams of ex-British Army Ghurkas as private security guards for the place,' said Omar, laughing. 'John thought they were Filipino houseservants. You should get yourself a tour of the palace. It's fascinating.'

'Yes, it's on my list of things to do,' I lied. I hadn't even been aware it existed. Since getting here I'd been completely incommunicado, knowing nothing other than what I saw with my own eyes. There was no TV, no internet, no newspapers and no other Westerners to chat to. Even the BBC World Service, supposedly a lifeline in the remotest corners of the world, emitted nothing more than a fuzzy crackle on the short-wave radio that Max had given me as a present before I left.

'So what've you been up to?' asked Omar.

'Not a lot, really. Just finding my feet. Experimenting with translators, driving around checking the place out. It's hard to know where to start, really, especially when you're on your own.'

He nodded. 'D'you have any work lined up? You work for the *Standard*, right?'

'Not any more. I quit them so I could come out here. I'm freelance now. Just looking to write for whoever I can.'

'Do you know Lyse Doucet?'

'Who?'

' Lyse Doucet. News presenter on the BBC World Service. Very good.'

'Never heard of her.'

'I met her at a book launch in London once.' He mentioned the names of a few other journalists he knew, all Middle East specialists, along with the various books they'd written. I hadn't met, heard of or read any of them.

'So you've never covered the Middle East before? What made you come out here?'

'Just got bored with my old job. Used to spend all the time writing shite about roadworks, plus sitting outside celebs' houses. Figured I'd try something different before I got too old.'

'If I hear any good stories I'll let you know.'

'So tell me a bit more about yourself,' I said. 'Why exactly did your family leave Baghdad?'

'A number of reasons, really. One was Saddam. My parents got worried when I was coming home from school aged five, reciting poetry that praised him. They thought I'd end up indoctrinated, so they decided I should go to school in England.'

'Let me guess. Eton, right?

'Close. They thought about Eton. In the end it was Bedales. A hippy school. One of those ones where you only have to attend class if you feel like it. No real rules.'

'A bit like here then.'

Omar grinned and poured more whisky. I was warming to him, even though I still didn't really feel like I'd worked him out. In my experience, most children from upmarket hippy schools went on to run self-expression workshops or become respectable drug addicts. They didn't become businessmen, certainly not ones trying to turn a profit in war zones.

'So tell us a bit more about what you plan to do here,' I said. 'Are you going to do oil and gas stuff?'

'Maybe eventually. Right now I'm not really working, just helping John out as a friend. He's in procurement.'

'Which is… ?'

'Supplying anybody who's out here with whatever it is they need. Say you're a commander at a US Army base. Soon the weather's going to be hot, really hot, and you desperately want shower units for your soldiers. It will boost morale. But who can you buy from out here? Everything's in chaos. That's where someone like John comes in. He turns up at their bases, meets the commander in charge, and offers to do it all for him. He organises a supplier from say, Turkey, fixes up the transport and arranges for workers to set them up. All the commander has to do is hand over the money.'

'You could be onto a good thing.'

'The profit margins can be pretty good, if you keep the overheads down. Some work you can sub-contract to Iraqis, but you are the Western face who actually strikes the deal, the people the commander feels he can trust.'

'How do you actually get the work? Do you just go to each Army base and introduce yourself?'

'Pretty much. They have contracting officers whose job is to deal with supply issues. And John has some people he knows. But often it's just cold-calling. John's good at breaking the ice. Asks the soldiers where they're from in the States, tells them the scores from whichever American football team they follow, to remind them of home. I think he actually memorises the scores deliberately. All good marketing.'

'So are you going to settle down here?'

'We'll see. I'd like to help rebuild this country if I can.'

'You excited to be here?'

'Of course. You?'

'Yeah. Still can't quite believe I'm here. All I need now is a decent translator.'

I told him about my day with Haider and his difficulties with the Ali Baba bus drivers. Omar nodded sympathetically. 'The problem is that people here constantly interrupt each other when you're talking to them. They say "No, don't tell him that!", or "What kind of fool are you? Tell him the truth!" Especially when they see a foreigner present. They want to give a certain impression.'

'I guess so. If you come across any decent translators, let me know. What's your plan for the next few weeks?'

'Keep looking for work, so we can start earning a living.'

'You and me both.'

*****

'This bit's from Tikrit. Went there on embed last week. Fuckin' crazy, man.'

Jim hit the rewind button on his camera and pointed to its playback screen. A US Army soldier could be seen leaning out of a Humvee, blasting away at some unseen gunman across a dusty track. A muffled crump then sounded as another Humvee hit the insurgent position with a rocket, accompanied by laughter and whoops. It was a lot more exciting than anything on my video diary.

Jim was the first other freelancer I'd met since arriving here a week ago. He, Haider and I were sat on an ornate, 20-foot long settee in a gym-sized drawing room in Saddam's presidential palace, waiting to apply for 'embeds' with the US Army's press centre. It had taken Haider and me two whole days to find it: Saddam's presidential palace turned out to be not just one building but an entire campus containing dozens of places that looked grand enough to qualify as a palace. Eventually we'd found it by spotting Jim with his camera and following him. He was decked out in what I now recognised as the war zone cameraman's standard get-up: knee-length utility shorts, t-shirt, hiking boots and a Celtic-design arm tattoo. He'd been in Iraq since mid-April and was working for one of the American networks. Already he'd toured the country. Already he was a font of information. Already he was starting to get on my tits.

'Embeds, that's the fuckin' way man,' he said, fast-forwarding to yet another one-sided bloodbath with US soldiers shooting up some Iraqi neighbourhood. 'Eat with the Army, travel with the Army. You been on one yet?'

'No. Trying to sort one out today.'

'Where else you been so far?'

'Nowhere. Just Baghdad.'

'You ain't been out of Baghdad yet? Man, you're wasting your time. You need to see Tikrit and Fallujah. Go on patrol. I tell you, no point in hanging around here. Too many other reporters. Nothing to yourself.'

'So what exactly was the story you were covering in Fallujah?'

'How the locals fuckin' hate the Americans. Totally different from here in Baghdad.'

'Yeah, the problem is that story's been done a lot already. Need something new on it really to sell it as a freelancer.'

'Hey, if you don't go out there, you'll never find it, will you?'

In a sense he was right. Baghdad did have too many reporters chasing every story. But his idea of freelancing was very different from mine. As a retained cameraman for a big TV network, all he had to do was go where he wanted, shoot footage of gunfights – known as 'bang-bang', apparently – and pass it on to his network. Given that they were still running vast Iraq packages every night, the chances were they'd use it sooner or later.

For me it was very different. The British newspapers that were still closely following the war – *The Times*, *The Financial Times*, *The Daily Telegraph*, *The Guardian* and *The Independent* – had sent their correspondents out to places like Fallujah several times already. They'd have no interest in me going there unless I could offer a completely different angle. I'd have liked nothing more than to charge around Tikrit in a tank like Jim, but the fact was that nobody back home needed me to. And unlike him, I didn't have teams of company-paid drivers, translators and producers on hand to ferry me around, look after me and generally organise my life.

The fact that I was wallowing in self-pity was also a sign that things weren't going particularly well. I'd been in Baghdad nine days now, and was still nowhere near selling a story. Being incommunicado all the time didn't help. The only people who actually knew what was going on were the staff correspondents, who themselves were briefed by their newsdesks back home. Each day there was normally a story they all covered, such as the re-forming of the Iraqi police or the arrest of another of Saddam's cronies, but I didn't usually hear about it until the morning afterwards. Even finding out *yesterday's* news wasn't easy. You had to go to the offices of one of the TV networks in the Palestine Hotel, bribe a producer or technician with a couple of beers, and ask if it was OK to surf the internet on their satellite link for half an hour.

My main hope was to become a 'stringer'. This is someone who provides a freelance service to any news organisation that doesn't maintain their own correspondent in a particular country. I'd hoped there'd be demand from the British tabloids, who'd pulled their staff correspondents out of Iraq pretty much as soon as the war had ended. Having done a few shifts on a tabloid before joining the *Standard*, I knew they generally weren't too fussy about whom they used as foreign stringers. Many of them were boozy, semi-retired expats who wrote appallingly, and whose only qualification was that they lived in the country concerned. The idea was that they would provide 'man-on-the-spot' reporting, adding in local knowledge and colour. But mostly they just nicked what was in their local paper, re-wrote it badly, and filed it back well after deadline. The newsdesk, though, didn't really care. All they wanted was to give readers the impression that the paper still had staff all round the world, even if Joe Bloggs in so-and-so was just some lush who never ventured further than the bar of his local taverna. But if that was how it worked, I was more than happy to profit from it. The problem was that now that the war was over, the tabloids would only be interested if something major happened, like Saddam getting caught, or British soldiers or citizens getting killed. And so far, nothing like that was happening. Just in case, though, I made a mental note to get a photo of Omar.

Otherwise, the only light on the horizon at the moment was *The Scotsman*, whose foreign editor, James Hall, had said he'd look at any story ideas I offered now that I was in Baghdad. *The Scotsman* wasn't in quite the same league as the *Times* or *Telegraph*, but it was still a serious broadsheet with big foreign pages to fill every day. Since they couldn't afford a staff correspondent out here, there was potentially the chance to become their full-time stringer. The only drawback was that, so far, I had no story ideas worth offering them. Not even the *Standard* had been interested in the Ali Baba bus drivers, and otherwise, my 'news list' was pretty uninspiring:

1. Interview Saddam's astrologer. Apparently Saddam was a big user of mystics, consulting them for his political and military strategy.

For: Could provide fascinating insights into the man who ruled Iraq. Maybe said medium will reveal that Saddam only defied America because his tea-leaves told him to.

Against: Fortune teller is already in hiding, pursued by every American TV network in Iraq. If they can't find him, nor will Haider and I.

2. Track down the man who was filmed hitting Saddam's statue with his slipper as it was pulled down. Apparently a Kuwaiti TV station has now offered him $250,000 for the slipper, but he has refused to sell it.

For: great follow-up tale of a participant in a key moment in Iraqi history.

Against: It came from Haider, who said he'd heard it from his cousin. Who'd heard it from his cousin. And so on.

3. Report on how Jews are buying up Baghdad's old government buildings while they're still going cheap.

For: exposing a Zionist conspiracy to corner the Iraqi property market and charge exorbitant rents.

Against: blatantly anti-Semitic rumourmongering, again sourced mainly from Haider's cousin.

It was a crap list. Much as I resented Jim the cameraman's simplistic analysis of what made a story, I hoped he was right about embeds. After we'd waited about an hour, a US Army press liaison officer appeared. He was tubby, balding and with round glasses. With a military uniform and a loaded pistol, he looked like an accountant on a paintballing expedition.

'Can I help you gentlemen?'

We explained our respective missions. While Jim inquired urgently about 'special forces embeds', I asked for just a day's patrol around Baghdad. The guy took my satellite phone number, and told me to expect a call within the next 24 hours.

That night, as Omar and I were tucking into his Johnnie Walker again on the hotel balcony, my satellite phone rang.

'Hi, this is Sergeant Craig Jason, US military. Is that Callum Freeman?'

The low, disembodied drawl sounded straight out of a Vietnam movie. If an M16 rifle could talk, this was how it would sound.

'Er, yes, I think you mean Colin Freeman. Yes, that's right, this is him.'

'Good. Callum, you wanna come on ridealong with us tomorrow?'

'I'm sorry?'

'A ridealong. With my patrol?'

'Oh I see, yes, to ride along! Er, yes please, that would be marvellous!' Against Sgt Jason's ultra-laid back, all-American drawl, it was impossible not to sound like Bertie Wooster. 'Er, where should I report, or whatever?'

'0800 hours tomorrow. You git there late, we go without you. Gotta pen? I'll give you the grid co-ordinates for the rendezvous.'

'Co-ordinates?'

'Shoot, you ain't on the military system, are you? Well, it's the west gate of the presidential palace. Just go the checkpoint and ask for my subordinate, Specialist Yoff.'

'Specialist who?'

'Yoff. Let me give you that phonetically. Yankee, Oscar, Foxtrot Foxtrot. Good to talk to you, Callum.'

'Thanks. By the way, it's Colin, not Callum.'

'It's what?'

'Colin.'

'Got a phonetic of that?'

'Er, C as in, er, cat. O as in, er otter, L as in, ah, Lucy, like the girl's name, that is. I as in ice cream. N as in, um, nobody.

'Uh, roger that. See you at 0800.'

At 7am the next day I headed off, with a cabbie that Ali the nightwatchman had fixed up the night before. He was a gnarled old fellow who looked like he'd be more at home driving a herd of goats, but Ali had vouched for his honesty. Unfortunately, the vast presidential palace complex turned out to have not one, but several gates. I had no idea which was the west one. Neither did the cabbie, despite having nodded knowledgeably when Ali had asked him. Half an hour of aimless driving later, we approached a roadblock manned by US soldiers on top of a tank. Perhaps they could give us directions.

Zing! Zing!

Two rifle shots pinged overhead, issuing tiny, high-pitched hums like supersonic wasps. We were still a good hundred yards from the checkpoint, but I could see a soldier waving his arm at us frantically. The cabbie ground to a halt. What had we done? I tried to remember Dominic's wisdom on checkpoint etiquette. We'd covered it, but only with reference to drunken Balkan militiamen who couldn't shoot straight. Not sober Americans armed with laser-sighted M16s.

I got out, hands held aloft, feeling both scared and stupid. 'I'm a British journalist!' I shouted. 'I'm here for an embed!'

Whoever answered certainly wasn't the laid-back Sgt Craig Jason.

'This here's no fuckin' entry! Read the fuckin' sign! Fuckin' turnaroun'! Turn the fuckin' vehicle roun'. Fuckin' *now*!'

I spun round, shoulders hunched in expectation of a bullet, and yelled at the cabbie to do the same. He began manoeuvring, only for the decrepit engine to conk out. For a few seconds he fiddled with the wires under the steering column, looking horribly like a suicide bomber experiencing technical difficulties. Then the engine sputtered back into life. We pulled away, each shooting the other looks that said *'I can't believe I'm in a vehicle with this idiot.'*

It was now 8.10am. I wrote off the embed. There was no way I was going near any checkpoint again. And besides, we were now completely lost. We cruised down a sliproad onto a deserted dual carriageway, where, in the distance, I saw a fleet of enormous US Army trucks coming towards us. They were huge amphibious things designed to drive through swamps, with tyres as big as those on tractors. Then, with horror, I realised they were on our side of the road. I wasn't sure which of us was driving 'wrong side', but there was no doubt who'd end up coming off worst if we collided. Rather than trying to get out of the way, the cab driver simply stopped in the middle of the road, like a rabbit caught in headlights. One by one, the lorries swerved to avoid us, blasting their horns furiously and missing the cab by no more than a couple of feet. Had any of them even clipped it with a wheel, it would have disintegrated. I felt like I was starring in one of those 'look-at-this-idiot-motorist' bits from *Police, Camera, Action.*

I got back to the hotel and holed up in my room for the rest of the day. Two brushes with death was enough for a single morning. If I also counted wandering home after curfew on the first night, that was three near-misses in ten days. Assuming I had nine lives, at this rate I was likely to be dead within the month.

The Colonel

'HEAR THE CRIES OF the martyrs. The tyrants must never think of staying in our land. Alexander the Great tried before you but failed. No to Turkish intervention.

'Our basil calls that it cannot grow with a tyrant. We will never allow them to hurt the already anguished mothers of the martyrs.'

(Badly-subtitled patriotic song on Kurdish satellite TV, Al Majalis hotel)

As the weeks went by, Omar, John and I became honoured guests at the Al Majalis. Perhaps they were impressed by the fact that we'd stuck it so long. I was given a new room at the front of the building, away from the noisy generator and with a commanding view of the rubbish skips outside.

With the help of Ali the nighwatchman, I got to know the rest of the staff, or as much as was possible given the language barrier. Ali's daytime counterpart on reception was Nasir (old, thin, cheerful). Then there was Narro (young, friendly, yellow golf jumper, brother once worked in Holland) and Mohammed (fat, grumpy, ripped me off on change once). As well as the regular staff, there was also an omnipresent delegation of semi-employees, who seemed to do nothing but sit in the front lounge and watch TV. Several further groups of dedicated loiterers frequented the street outside. There were the Men Who Hung Around Outside The Shop, The Men Who Hung Around Outside The Tea Stall, The Friends Of The Men Who Hung Around Outside The Tea Stall, and, finally, The Men Who Hung Around At The End Of The Street. All were unfailingly friendly. The short stroll to the main road could involve shaking hands with anything up to about 50 people, depending on how sociable you were feeling.

Mr Omar, the hotel's general manager, was a rotund, affable chap who spoke some English. He was Kurdish, as were most of his staff. This surprised me. I'd assumed that no Kurd would ever have dared set foot in Baghdad, given Saddam's fondness for gassing them and

61

their role in helping the Americans topple his government. In fact, Baghdad had always had a large Kurdish population, co-existing happily with their Arab neighbours and seldom letting the odd frenzy of state-sponsored genocide get between them.

Because the Al Majalis was Kurdish-run, word had got round in Kurdistan that it was a good place to stay. Many of the rooms were now occupied by gangs of Kurdish businessmen visiting Baghdad for the first time in years. By day they traded looted Iraqi government 4x4s in the hotel's front courtyard. By night they lounged around in grubby white longjohns, looking like Victorian pugilists relaxing after a boxing match. Some claimed to be Kurdish peshmerga fighters who'd helped the Americans in the military offensive from the north. They were now visiting Baghdad as tourists, checking out the territory they'd conquered. One wondered if they thought it had all been worth it.

What the Al Majalis made up for in conviviality, however, it took back in lack of comfort. Quite apart from the failing electricity and its lack of air-conditioning and hot water, decades of neglect had sown the place with endless booby-traps. The wooden furniture stabbed endless splinters into your hands. The ancient plugs and light fittings dished out shocks whenever the power was on. The static from the cheap nylon carpet was as bad – just walking down the corridor could give you as much charge as a car battery. One time, I grabbed the metal door of the elderly elevator and sparks shot from my fingertips like some low-powered wizard. The elevator was scary, too. Its concertina metal doors could snip your fingers off, and if the power cut out it would often get stuck halfway between floors. You then had to wriggle out, risking being cut in two if the power suddenly started again. Even more dangerous was a second, derelict lift shaft at the other end of the corridor, which had a gaping drop three floors down the basement. Feeling my way to my room in the dark one drunken night, I went too far and nearly fell right down it.

Mr Omar would occasionally invite me for cups of tea in the lobby, where he would tell his life story and lament the hotel's many woes. He was an engineer by trade, who'd worked in Yugoslavia and then returned to Iraq to work for a company that made ball-bearings. For some baffling reason, the company's owner then diversified into hotels, buying the Al Majalis and installing Mr Omar as a manager.

Several other hotels nearby had also been bought by ball-bearing people. It was hard to see where the investment synergy lay. Mr Omar constantly griped about the way the owners had let the place fall into such a decrepit state. While I simply accepted it as normal, his Kurdish guests expected better and gave him no end of grief.

Still, at only $5 a night, it was an ideal place in which to acclimatise. Because the West had helped out the Kurds in the war, we were looked after like family. Mr Omar even turned a blind eye to us drinking alcohol in our rooms, something he tried to forbid among Iraqi guests who, when pissed, would embark on drunken rampages worthy of The Who or Led Zeppelin. 'When Iraqi peoples drinking, sometimes they fire guns into the ceiling,' Mr Omar complained. 'Go to room 607, you will see the holes are still there.'

To stop such behaviour, his team of women cleaners reported any suspicious bottles or cans they found. It didn't make much difference. Every night, drunken yowls would emanate from one hotel balcony or another, as groups of guests partied away. As the drink flowed, they would turn to baiting Hassan, the local shoeshine man who had a stall on the street outside. Unfortunately, the same polish that Hassan put on peoples' shoes by day went up his nose at night, so later on he'd turn up outside the hotel, drugged out of his mind and shouting the odds, at which point guests would take great delight in chucking things at him from their balconies. Not just bits of food, but beer cans, bottles and even medium-sized lumps of masonry, which were in abundant supply in the Al Majalis's derelict eighth floor. Some of the missiles were big enough to kill him, yet nobody regarded it as anything other than good, clean fun. Luckily, conditions were normally too dark and drunken for proper aim.

*****

Back in my days at the *Standard*, one of the jobs on the 5am shift was to ring the Scotland Yard media voicetape. A recorded voice would deliver a round-up of the most newsworthy crimes in London overnight, followed by a touch-dial menu of murder, rape and pillage: *'Press one to hear more about the murder in Islington, two for the double shooting in the Hackney nightclub, three for the indecent assault in Bromley,'* and so on. The Dial-a-Story line, as the voicetape was known, made London sound like quite a scary place the first time you called it. By contrast, the Lincolnshire Police voicetape, which I'd rung as a trainee at the *Grimsby Evening Telegraph*, seldom had anything more than thefts of underwear from washing lines and warnings about pig rustlers. After a while, though, you realised that even London rarely had more than one or two murders a day. In a city of nearly eight million people, that gave you fairly good odds.

It was less easy to apply that calm statistical rationale to Baghdad, where the daily crime figures made the Scotland Yard tape sound frankly pathetic. Without a police force to speak of, nobody really had an accurate picture of just how bad things were, but every now and then the US Army would post snapshots of their progress in the press information centre in Saddam's palace. *'In the past 24 hours, 1st Armoured Division have detained 87 people for murder, looting, weapons violations and drug-dealing, and seized 130 AK47 rifles, 13 pistols, 6 grenades, 40 anti-aircraft missiles and 3 rocket propelled grenades.'*

These crimefighting results were not thanks to some major operation, either. Instead, they were just the routine, on-the-beat arrests, of criminals who hadn't been bright enough to hide when they heard a 50-tonne tank coming down their street. God only knew what the real villains were up to.

To improve law and order, the Americans re-formed the Iraqi police service. I spent a morning at the newly-opened police training college, where US military policemen were trying to teach the old Iraqi coppers the niceties of Western-style policing, such as the art of interrogating suspects without the aid of 240 volts. A female instructor asked one class: 'When you were in the old Iraqi police, was there a code of conduct?' Half the room half said 'no', the other half lied and said 'yes'. After just a few days of training, they were back on the streets, wearing makeshift uniforms of a blue shirt and slip-on armband embroidered with the words 'Iraqi Police'. They looked like a badly-underfunded Scout troop. Counterfeit armbands, along with matching police ID cards, were soon doing a thriving trade in the downtown markets. It quickly became clear that the only way to tell the fake cops from the real cops was that the fake ones generally had better weapons and looked more motivated.

One evening at the Al Majalis, Omar and I watched from the balcony as a police patrol pulled up alongside three Kurdish traders unloading their van. There was a brief discussion in low voices, which ended with the sound of one of the policemen cocking his Kalashnikov. Money changed hands, and the police car drove off into the night, sirens blaring. Afterwards, the traders came into the hotel, shaken up. The police had accused them of carrying stolen goods, and then demanded about $150 at gunpoint not to arrest them. I'd noted down the number on the police car, but Mr Omar, the hotel manager, didn't seem very keen on my idea of handing it to the Americans. It would have been too easy for the policemen to work out who'd complained.

Also hampering Mr Omar's desire for a quiet life was the re-opening of the café-brothel right opposite the Al Majalis. A small, neon-lit place, decked out in rattan furnishings, it was back in business for the first time since the war. It didn't tout its wares too obviously, but every now and then a middle-aged, kebab-meat-dressed-as-lamb Iraqi prostitute would wander out and clamber into a passing car. Like every other business on the street, the brothel had its own group of Men Who Hung Around Outside, led by a vicious-looking Sudanese in a straw hat. Occasionally he'd get in rows with the punters, usually over the quality of the wares. 'Always trouble there,' Mr Omar told me. 'They say to customers "here you shall find pretty womens". But often the womens are not so pretty. Then the customers make problems.'

Among the few Iraqis drawing inspiration from the violence, sleaze and chaos were Acrassicauda, Iraq's only heavy metal band and perhaps the only metallers in history whose songs about slaughter and mayhem weren't drawn purely from adolescent imaginations. I bumped into their lead singer, Walid Rabiaa, in the lobby of the Palestine Hotel one morning during yet another visit to look for a new translator. Although he had short hair, he was otherwise an absolutely typical metaller, with the true fan's obsession with the minutiae of the genre. 'Actually, we're not heavy metal as such really,' he said. 'More a cross between death metal and speed metal.'

Walid and four schoolfriends had formed Acrassicauda back in 2000, borrowing the Latin name for a particularly venomous scorpion found in the Iraqi desert. They'd honed their sound – and their English – through pirated CDs and videos of Western heavy metal bands like

Slayer and Megadeth. Walid could now speak, sing and issue guttural grunts in almost perfect English.

'Don't you do any songs in Arabic?' I asked.

'Not really, it doesn't work.'

'Why not?'

'Don't know – we tried, to start off with, but for some reason the syllables are too soft. Makes you sound like a girl or something. You need English to make the proper heavy metal sound – hard and angry. The only other one language that works is German.'

Whatever language they sang in, being a member of Acrassicauda in the old days had been a risky business. Saddam was more of a gypsy folk music man and distrusted anything that smacked of the West. Even the Iraqi Symphony Orchestra, who performed nothing more subversive than the odd Bach recital, had to make do with scratchy old instruments because he starved them of public funds. Another heavy metal band, Scarecrow, had been jailed for two months on sedition charges in 1999 and Acrassicauda had looked destined for a similar fate until their crafty music teacher came up with the idea of legitimising themselves by writing a pro-government song. Hence was penned probably the only heavy metal song ever written in praise of Saddam.

'Living in the dark, shining like a spark,' went *Youth of Iraq.* *'Living with the pride, so to fight we decide... Evil forces are the Jews, so we will never refuse.'*

Not exactly Led Zep, but it had gone down well with the local secret policeman, who was also the dean of the Baghdad art gallery where Acrassicauda then put on their first gig. Yet the song wasn't the cynical sell-out it seemed. Instead, like all the best heavy metal music, it contained subversive subliminal messages.

'The line about "living in the dark" is actually about not having enough electricity,' said Walid. 'Where we talk about fighting, we mean fighting against the regime. And when we talk about the Jews, we really meant Saddam. Because he did more to help the Zionists than anyone else, by taking us into stupid wars.'

Fearing that anti-Semitism might now dent their chances of getting picked up by a Western record company, Walid was now actively courting the Jewish death-metal/speed metal fanbase, a niche market if ever there was one. 'We'd really like to see some Jewish people at our gigs,' he said.

I, however, had other plans for his vocal skills. Walid was clearly the perfect candidate to be my next translator – friendly, polite, and in command of almost perfect English. As a former teenage metaller myself, we would also have plenty to talk about. Sadly, the fact that I could discourse knowledgeably about AC/DC, Motorhead and the early 1980s period of the Ian Gillan Band was not enough to tempt him into working for $10 a day. 'I'd work for you for free for a while just to help you out,' he told me. 'But I've already got a job lined up with the BBC.'

I felt a pang of despair. Over the last fortnight I'd canvassed at least half a dozen would-be candidates for the job, assessing their language aptitude, fixing skills, and personalities. The process had convinced me that translators were like girlfriends. Every single one had some fault or other. If I met one who spoke fluent English, he'd turn out to be vain or boorish or untrustworthy. If I met one who seemed like a nice guy, he'd barely be able to string a sentence together. Those who were both fluent and pleasant invariably wanted $100 a day or more, as indeed did many who were neither. Some had other shortcomings, like strong body odour or terrible facial warts. As the translator was my *de facto* speaking voice, I somehow felt that people would associate those defects with me. One eminently suitable candidate I rejected simply because he was fat. I sat in the Palestine's lobby, watching jealously as other reporters came and went, their Iraqi employees hanging attentively at their sides. Already I'd had to turn down a couple of jobs from newsdesks because I had no Iraqi translator to help me. What was the point of being here if I couldn't work?

A few days later I was stood by the road near the Al Majalis, trying to hail a taxi to an internet café that had recently opened. A rusting, green 1981 Nissan jerked to a halt. Inside was a man with a large moustache, big 1980s-style sunglasses and a shirt open at the neck revealing a hairy chest. I'd thumbed a lift from Burt Reynolds. As I clambered in and launched into my usual repertoire of pidgin taxi Arabic, he raised a hand. 'It's OK, you can speak English.'

'Great, do you know Zayuna district? I want to go a café there.'

'Of course. It is just three kilometres. You are a Britisher, yes?'

'How did you know?'

The moustache flattened into a grin. 'I listen to the BBC sometimes, where they are talking in this accent of yours. You want to hear the BBC?'

He fiddled with a radio dangling by its innards from what remained of the dashboard, and the BBC World Service came on, tinny but clear. I was impressed. So far, all I'd got from my short-wave radio was what sounded like Russian shipping forecasts.

As we drove I looked at him. He was tall and well-built, about early 40s, and spoke English in a slightly monotone voice, rather like a Dalek. He was fluent, though, if not quite Walid's standard. When he didn't know the right word or phrase, he improvised quickly.

'Where did you learn English?'

'First in the school, and then in the army,' he said. 'I am a colonel. A colonel staff.' He pronounced the first 'l' in colonel, and put particular emphasis on the word 'staff'.

'Oh really? What's a colonel staff?'

'This means, sir, that I have been selected for the military staff academy of Baghdad, and completed all the necessary examinations and procedures.' He spoke like he was testifying to a military promotion board.

'Right. And you were in the Iraqi army?'

'Since 1986. Tank commander in the armoured corps.' He pronounced the silent 'p' in 'corps', making it sound like 'corpse'. I wondered if he'd seen many.

'So what are you doing now?'

'Now the army is finished, so no job. I went to the Americans at the palace of the president, because I was hearing they wanted translators. But nothing yet.'

It might just be your lucky day, I thought. I asked him to detour down to the money changers near the Palestine Hotel, to buy me more time to size him up. He reminded me of a famous picture I'd seen of Saddam, in which the former leader was sporting a very similar set of sunshades. Only this guy was younger, leaner, and, if anything, meaner-looking. Yet he was as polite as any Iraqi I'd met, and seemed reasonably worldly too. That was one of problems with some of the younger translators. They'd been raised in such a censored world they knew bugger all about Iraq or anywhere else.

Twenty minutes later, we pulled up at the internet café.

'Listen, would you be interested in working as a translator and driver?' I asked. 'I can only afford $10 a day. But if you're interested, we could try.'

He'd obviously been hoping I'd ask. 'Most certainly. When would we start?'

'Do you want to come to my hotel tomorrow at about 9am?'

'Why not?'

'My name's Colin, by the way. What's yours?'

'I am Mohammed. Mohammed Kadom. Staff Colonel, Mohammed Kadom.'

'OK, Mohammed. You're hired.'

The Christian And The Holy Man

LATE ONE EVENING near the end of June, the *Standard* night newsdesk rang up. It was the first I'd heard from them in ages. The guy on the end of the line wasn't even sure if I was still in Iraq.

'You doing anything on these dead Brits then, Colin?' he said.

'Er... yeah, maybe.'

I was playing for time. I had no idea what he was talking about. Once again, I hadn't been near a TV or internet café for days. But a golden rule with newsdesks is that you never admit to ignorance of anything. No matter what your excuse, it never looks good if they know more about what's happening on your patch than you do.

'So are you going down there?'

'Er, yeah, hopefully tomorrow.'

Where?

'Excellent. It's obviously going to be a huge story, so if you can file for us, that would be great. Only if you think it's safe, of course.'

'Absolutely.'

What had I just let myself in for?

'Great. Will be you be able to get there in time for the later editions tomorrow?'

'Er, need to check with my driver first. Actually, while you're on the phone, can you just read me out the latest wire report? Just want to check nothing's changed.'

It's an old ruse. You get the newsdesk to tell you the story, while maintaining the bluff that you know it all already.

'Sure, let me just dig it out. Yeah, here we go.... Six British soldiers were found shot dead in an Iraqi police station today. The bodies of the Royal Military policemen were recovered from the town of Majar al Kabir, near the city of Al Amarah, 100 miles north of Basra... blah, blah... it is understood that the six soldiers were helping to train up the local policemen at the station... Army still investigating... picture confused... can't comment further at this point. That's about it. So, yeah, plenty of room for having a nose around there tomorrow. What are people at your end saying about it?'

'Er... well, it's all a bit unclear right now. Sounds like one of the Iraqi coppers has killed them. Inside job, sort of thing.'

'Maybe. Anyway, speak tomorrow, yeah?'

Next morning I rose at six and took a taxi straight over to Mohammed's house, a modest villa in New Baghdad. The moment I mentioned Majar al Kabir, his face screwed up.

'Majar al Kabir? That is a bad fucking place. I was there with the Iraqi Army. A very poor area, full of criminals and dangerous fuckers. Giving even President Saddam Hussein trouble.'

'Well, are you willing to go?'

'Yes, but we must take a Kalashnikov or a pistol to protect us.'

'We can't do that. We're journalists. We don't carry guns.'

'Why not? Take it from me, speaking as a military man, everyone else will have them. How else will I protect you, a foreigner?'

'Well, journalists are like the Red Cross. We're not a threat, so people won't hurt us.' From the way he looked at me, I might as well have added that journalists could also heal the sick and walk on water. 'Besides,' I said. 'It won't be dangerous down there. The British Army will be all over the town, after this incident. How long will it take to get there?'

'It is about 300 kilometres from here, let's say. Let us perform the calculations.' Mohammed went into a detailed breakdown of the various roads, speeds and potential traffic hazards and hold-ups, ticking them off as if planning the parameters of a military assault. 'So, travelling at an average speed of 100 kilometres per hour, we will arrive at around 2 or 3pm.'

'Great, that'll be in time for the *Standard* deadlines.'

We spent nearly an hour getting the Nissan fixed up with oil and water and repairing slow punctures in all four tyres. It felt like saddling up on an old nag for an epic wagon trail journey during which it would probably die. Yet the clock on the dashboard, I noticed, said only 25,000 kilometres.

'Mohammed, has this car really only done 25,000 kilometres?'

'No, 425,000,' he said proudly. 'It has been back to zero four times now. But I have put a new engine in it.'

425,000 kilometres, I worked out, was roughly 10 times round the world. I was amazed it was still running at all. As, indeed, was a fat Iraqi policeman, who stopped us at a checkpoint near the outskirts of Baghdad.

'Where are you going?' he asked Mohammed.

'Majar al Kabir.'

'In this car?'

'Inshallah.'

'Inshallah, you will, my friends. On your way.'

*****

Ten minutes later we were stopped by the roadside, nursing one definite flat tyre and two suspected ones. The puncture repairs had simply liquefied after sustained exposure to the hot asphalt. We limped into the nearest town, where, to Mohammed's astonishment, I treated him to four brand new tyres at $30 each on the *Standard*. As we waited for the Nissan to be re-shod, I rang the newsdesk for latest reports from Majar al Kabir. The news was not good. The full picture of why the soldiers had been killed was now emerging. Contrary to my earlier theory, they hadn't been the victims of a single, crazed gunman inside the police station. Instead they'd been chased in there by a mob of several hundred armed locals, who'd then apparently executed them on the spot. Relations with the British had been bad for weeks, apparently, since troops had started searching local homes for stashes of illegal weapons. And rather than flooding the town with troops, the Brits had now pulled out altogether to let things cool down a bit. If we got a similar reception to the soldiers, there'd be nobody coming to help.

Fear kicked in. If I'd known it was going to be as dicey as this, I'd have never volunteered. But it was too late to get out now. For the first time since getting to Iraq, the *Standard* newsdesk were keen for my services. I could just imagine the mutters on the newsdesk if I suddenly pulled back.

'Bloody Freeman, bloody useless idiot. Gets halfway down there, then bottles it.'

'Yeah. Should've stuck with sodding roadworks.'

As Mohammed handed over my dollars, I took a nervous piss in a ditch at the back of the garage. What was it that Mike Leese on the *Standard* newsdesk had told me? That war zone reporters got hard-ons when the action loomed? I looked down. Nothing whatsoever. Quite the opposite, in fact.

The suburbs of south Baghdad gradually thinned out, giving way to palm groves criss-crossed with ditches and swamps. Clumps of reeds stuck out like tufts of mangy hair on the desert scrub. This was the farming hinterland of the River Tigris, a fertile strip that had been cultivated since the dawn of civilisation. It followed the river as it meandered south all the way to Basra and the Arabian Gulf. After the hard-baked, faecal stink of Baghdad's unwashed concrete jungle, the difference in atmosphere was palpable. The breeze was humid, and the mere smell of vegetable matter that wasn't putrefying hit the nose like air-freshener.

It was time to read up about Al Amarah and the south. I flicked open the *Bradt Travel Guide to Iraq*. Most Middle East guidebooks no longer gave the country more than a few pages, because it had been closed to tourists for years. But Bradt, a small British travel publisher, seemed to specialise in covering those few places left on earth where even the *Lonely Planet* didn't tread. There were Bradt guides to Rwanda and Haiti, and they were working on others for North Korea and Afghanistan. The Iraq book had come out the previous year, catering mainly for UN officials, aid agency workers, and occasional parties of tourists on archaeological tours – plus, now, journalists and soldiers.

'Southern Iraq', according to Bradt, effectively meant all points south of Baghdad. The south was a stronghold of Shia Islam, the rival sect to the Sunni Islam followed by most people further north, including Saddam. The two schools had emerged out of a split in the faith over who should succeed the prophet Mohammed as spiritual leader after his death in ad632. Some said the job should go to Mohammed's son-in-law, Ali, while others argued it should be put to election. The two rival camps finally went their separate ways in ad680, after Ali's son Hussein and his followers were massacred in the desert south of Baghdad. Ever since, the faith of Shi'ism – meaning literally 'followers' – had styled itself as the champions of the oppressed. Thanks to the despotism of successive Iraqi leaders like Saddam, they'd seldom been short of a constituency.

In fact, Saddam was actually pretty secular by the standards of Arab rulers, partly because of his megalomania. He had little time for anybody, Sunni or Shia, who worshipped God ahead of him. Nonetheless, he distrusted Shias because of their religious links to neighbouring Iran, which became a Shia Islamic state when Ayatollah Khomeini deposed the Shah, its pro-American monarch, in 1979. Khomeini, who viewed Saddam as just another godless Western pawn like the Shah, then started encouraging Islamic revolution in Iraq too. Saddam declared war in 1980, with half a million lives lost on each side in the eight years that followed. Relatively few Iraqi Shias had any qualms about fighting their religious brethren across the border: they were Arabs and the Iranians were Persians, two distinct ethnic groups who'd often been enemies. But when Saddam's popularity had hit an all-time low after the crushing defeat of the 1991 Gulf War, it was the Shias of the south who'd led the uprisings. Saddam crushed the rebellion by killing tens of thousands of people, and from then on, had systematically starved the south of resources.

The view from the car confirmed we were heading into Saddam's unloved boondocks. The only sign of civilisation was small, jerry-built villages, their residents sharing space with scruffy sheep, cows and donkeys. Packs of semi-feral, lupine dogs patrolled the roadside, sniffing at the corpses of companions who'd strayed into the oncoming traffic. Fewer people dressed in western clothes, and nearly all the women wore abbayas, the all-encompassing black cloaks that hid everything but a strip across the eyes. They worked like beasts of burden, tilling the fields and travelling in the back of their husbands' pick-up trucks among the livestock, while the menfolk rode comfortably upfront. While the route into Baghdad from the west was a proper motorway, here it was a two-lane trunk road, with slow-moving tractors jostling perilously with saloon cars doing 80mph. Mohammed's overtaking tactic was to tailgate each vehicle from a nerve-wrackingly close distance, blasting the horn until it moved aside.

By 3pm we were nearing Al Amarah. A large roadside mural loomed up, where Saddam's picture been replaced by that of an elderly, white-bearded Shia cleric, frowning sternly at passing motorists. Mohammed glowered back.

'Look at these fucking bastards, they are everywhere now. First Saddam, now them.'

'Don't you like religious people?'

'Not these fuckers. These are just like the imams in Iran. Wishing to tell people what to do all the time.' He began glancing around anxiously. 'I don't like it round here. It's too quiet. People are expecting trouble. And where are the Britishers? There is no security. This is bad territory, you know. Killers, robbers, all roaming around. I was crazy not to bring a pistol.'

He rummaged in the holdall that he'd dumped in the back seat, pulling out a white hand towel and a garish checked shirt of the kind favoured by most Iraqi men.

'Wear this shirt over your t-shirt, and put the towel over your head. People will think you are a Christian.'

'But I am a Christian. Technically.'

'I mean an Iraqi Christian.'

'You have Christians in Iraq?'

'Sure, man. Maybe one million of them. They are Arabs, but just not so dark. More like you.'

I draped the towel over my head and shoulders and looked in the mirror. With my stubble, I looked like Mohammed's rather unattractive wife.

'Er... am I going to have to wear this in Majar al Kabir?'

'No, of course not. They will kill you if they see you dressed like that. Just here in the car. If some guy just looks quickly as he is driving past, it will work as a disguise.'

He stuck a cassette in the stereo. A mournful Arab male voice began singing, unaccompanied. It was quite restful, like the kind of stuff you got on post-rave chill-out tapes.

'This guy's rather good. Who is he?'

'This is the Koran, our Holy Book. The prayers of Islam. We will play it now as we go into the dangerous place. Protect our souls, by God.'

For someone who didn't like imams, he was suddenly showing a lot of faith.

Majar al Kabir was down a fork off the main highway to Basra. A small boy was sat selling cigarettes at the junction, watching us like a sentry. Mohammed pulled up, bought a packet and chatted with him.

'Ask him if there's any British soldiers down there, or any other press.'

'I already did. He says no Britisher soldiers. Press, yes, one or two came earlier.'

I felt a stab of relief. Much as the *Standard* might have liked a first 'first reporter into the town of death' exclusive, I was glad that someone else had already tested the waters.

As we hit the outskirts of Majar al Kabir, Mohammed explained that it meant 'town-near-the-large-bend-in-the-river'. A more accurate description might have been 'Hick-shithole-with-lots-of-men-wandering-around-nervously-with-guns'. In the absence of any law and order, locals had set up a checkpoint on the town's main drag, manned half-heartedly by gunmen in civilian clothes. Mohammed asked them the way to the police station. As he chatted, their initial suspicion suddenly melted and they shook his hand.

'They seem very friendly. What did you say to them?' I asked.

'Ah, just something. Never mind for now.'

'You haven't told them I'm a doctor again, have you?' He'd already used this trick once in Baghdad, much to my disapproval.

'No. I will tell you later.'

The police station was a single-storey white-brick compound overlooking a garbage-strewn square. A small crowd milled around outside.

'OK, I am going to see how the mood is,' said Mohammed. 'If the people are OK, we can stay for maybe some small time. And listen – we will have a code word. If I say to you, *The weather is getting hot*, then we go straightaway. No arguing, OK?'

'Er, yes, that's fine.'

'Remember, this is as per the military procedure. Always judging the danger. Always formulating the escape plan.'

We got out, me flashing my press badge and him flashing some Iraqi ID card. His credentials seemed to impress much more than mine. Several looked at him as if to say: 'Wow. *Really*?' What was he showing them?

'It's OK, we can stay,' said Mohammed. 'Yesterday, they were angry. Now they are scared at what the Britishers will do to them.'

The crowd ushered us into the police station, where the six military policemen had ended up besieged by the mob. Inside was an overgrown courtyard with cells running around the perimeter, most empty or derelict. At the back was the one from where the soldiers' bodies had been recovered. It had been set on fire, possibly to destroy any forensic evidence, although there were still tiny flecks of blood on the surviving paintwork.

'So,' I said. 'Can anyone tell us what happened?'

One by one various locals were put up to tell their stories. The spark for the dispute tallied with what I'd heard on the way down – that British soldiers had upset the locals during searching of homes for weapons. They were said to have barged in on lone women and used teams of sniffer dogs, creatures Muslims regarded as dirty. But everything that happened from then was in dispute. Some said the soldiers had signed a written agreement not to come into town any more, and that when they'd turned up yesterday in the central souk locals thought they were breaking the agreement. A few kids had chucked tomatoes and stones, one or two soldiers had cuffed the kids back, and a fight had developed from there. Others, however, said the soldiers had been in the police station the whole time, and that they'd just been attacked by the mob without warning. Some accounts had the troops meekly surrendering, only to be executed in cold-blood. Others had them making a last stand on the rooftops, blazing away Alamo-style until they ran out of ammo. Depending on who you asked, between four and 400 Iraqis had also died.

Conspiracy theories abounded. The men who led the attack were renegade Ba'athists, said one man. No they weren't, said another, they were Iranian agents. Whoever they were, they were all from out of town. Well, the ringleaders anyway. But it was really the fault of the British, according to Haji Sami Joni, one of the town's elders. In one breath he voiced his condolences to the soldiers' next of kin. And in the next he sympathised with those who'd murdered them. 'This has brought such shame upon us – until now we had such good relations with the British,' he said. 'But they must realise they can't come into our homes and disrespect our women like they did.'

After two hours of note-taking we headed off to a hotel in Al Amarah, a tumbledown heap of indescribable squalor that made the Al Majalis look posh. After filing a story over my satellite phone for the *Standard*, I started a more in-depth piece that *The Scotsman* had asked for. It was hard to know what to say. Even if some of Majar al Kabir's 'witnesses' were being honest, the truth was already long-buried under a tangle of hearsay and conspiracy theory. It was like the

Kennedy assassination, only with several hundred different assassins blazing away with AK-47s from various grassy knolls. In the end, my report fudged it altogether, which is usually the only sensible thing to do unless you have 10,000 words of space to work with.

'Exactly how this dirt-poor Shia town became the scene of the worst massacre of British troops since their arrival on Iraqi soil three months ago was a matter of mystery, speculation and fevered local gossip last night.'

Which was a posh way of saying, 'Sorry folks, not got a clue.'

What was clear was that despite their generally friendly demeanour, Iraqis could turn very hostile very quickly. Even to the British, who had a reputation for being friendlier and cuddlier than their American counterparts. A few ringleaders might have orchestrated the violence, but several hundred ordinary bystanders had apparently been quite happy to join in. One minute they'd been minding their own business in the marketplace. The next they were diving headlong into a full-scale armed scrap. What kind of society bred people like that?

'This is the way of the Iraqi tribes,' said Mohammed. 'In the countryside, they are very strong. You attack one, you attack them all. Just like these, what do you call them?' He made a buzzing sound.

'Bees? But I thought the Shia liked the British for getting rid of Saddam?'

'They do. But let me tell you something. In the Iraqi military, we used to say that the Shia is like the large, sleeping dog. He is peaceful until you disturb him. But when he gets angry – God help you.'

'Really?'

'Take it from me. I am a military man, knowing all the ways of the peoples of Iraq.'

True enough, Mohammed had been impressive that day. Unlike my old translator Haider, he'd taken control of the situation completely. He'd worked the volatile crowds like a master of ceremonies, lining up witnesses, cross-examining, cajoling and consoling as required. Occasionally he'd even made lengthy speeches himself, reassuring anyone suspicious of our agenda. Watching, I'd got the impression that he must have made quite a good army commander. Plus, he was bigger than just about anyone else there. Then I remembered the ID card he'd been showing.

'By the way, what was that card you kept showing everyone?' Mohammed smiled and fished it out of his wallet. On it was his picture alongside an emblem of a mosque.

'What is that?'

'My father was a Sunni, my mother a Shia. But this card shows that I was born in Khadhomiya. It is a holy Shia place just north of Baghdad. The people in Majar al Kabir are very religious, like all the tribes from the country zones. When they see I was born in Khadhomiya, they become most respectful. It is as per their custom. I tell you, they are some crazy bastards in that town, very angry. But whenever some guy was saying bad things, I would say, "Please, I am a holy guy from Khadhomiya, do not make this trouble in front of me." '

'Really?' Judging by his fondness for alcohol and knowledge of foreign swear words, Mohammed's Shia piety was not that great. His ID seemed to be a kind of religious get-out-jail-free card, accepted in Shia redneck towns everywhere.

'So the card is better than a gun, then?'

'Let me speak frankly, as a military man. Nothing is better than a gun.'

We stayed in Al Amarah the rest of the week. The British Army seemed anxious to say nothing more about the whole event. When we visited their main base outside town, a sentry on the gate told me to piss off, thinking I was an Iraqi. When I told him I was a journalist, he disappeared to consult his senior commanders for an hour. I assumed he'd return with a senior commander, who'd grant an exclusive interview by way of apology. Instead he came back with a phone number for the Ministry of Defence press office in London. They weren't saying anything either. Each day, we ventured nervously into Majar al Kabir to see if anything was going on. Newspapers back home were anxious for us to be on hand when the British Army rolled back into town again, as they'd hinted they would do. Yet even with his all-powerful ID card, Mohammed wouldn't permit any visits longer than an hour or two.

'But what happens if the British come back and we're not there? My office won't be happy.'

'You can't stay in that town all the time, man! You must understand, it is a danger place! One grenade, one pistol shot, that is enough, we will all be dead.'

Eventually he told me why he was so cautious. When the British Army had been doing the weapons searches that had caused so much fuss, they hadn't just been looking for Kalashnikovs or pistols. They were searching for serious hardware: heavy machine guns and rocket-propelled-grenades, weapons the locals had acquired while fighting Saddam in the Shia rebellion of 1991. Weapons that had once been ranged against Mohammed. For four grim years after 1991, he had been posted down here with the Iraqi Army, his tank division charged with crushing any insurrection. It hadn't been easy. Backed by the Iranians across the border, Shia guerrillas had mounted a well-organised insurgent campaign, carrying out constant hit and run attacks on the Iraqi military. Saddam responded with typical brutality, ordering that villages suspected of harbouring rebels should be razed if they didn't hand them over. But his own harsh measures were paid back in spades. One of Mohammed's own junior officers was abducted and later found with his head on a pole. Majar al Kabir was known as one of the most hostile insurgent towns. For Mohammed, it felt just as much as enemy territory as it did for the British.

'Were your own division ever asked to burn down villages or anything?' I asked him one night.

'What do you think? We were following the orders of the President of Iraq, Saddam Hussein.' I didn't feel I knew him quite well enough to ask him whether the villagers had been burned along with villages, but he seemed to sense the question. 'Some people, yes, will be saying this was, let's say, some kind of war crime. But what could you do? It was a bad, bad time. Never, though, I tell you, did I do anything that was not as per the strict military procedures.'

I wondered what he meant by that. Saddam's armies, after all, were not exactly known for their strict rules of engagement. You could stick exactly to the textbook and still get a lot of blood on your hands.

*****

Satar al Battat, a young imam at Majar al Kabir's main mosque, was not the obvious person to turn to for a spot of PR crisis management. His manner was as sombre as his black imam's robes, and when his voice screamed out of the Tannoy in the mosque's minaret, he made Ian Paisley sound like some half-hearted Anglican vicar. By Friday, though, the British had enlisted him to persuade the locals that it would be good if everyone made friends again. A senior commander invited him to the British base at Al Amarah that morning, hoping to get him to deliver a sermon of reconciliation at Friday's lunchtime prayers.

Reluctantly, Mohammed agreed that we could go and watch him preach, a move he regretted almost as soon as we hit town. A vast crowd of several thousand people had gathered for the prayer session, packing the mosque and filling a football-pitch sized area of scrubland in front of it. Boys with large water cannisters strapped to their backs wandered through the crowd, squirting a rose-scented water over bodies sweating in the midday sun. After four days of expecting to be pulverised by British warplanes at any minute, everybody was extremely jumpy. As midday loomed with no sign of al Battat's return, the elders got restive.

'They are wondering why the imam has not returned yet,' said Mohammed after chatting to them. 'They think he's been arrested by the Britishers. A trap.'

'Well, I don't think the British would do that, actually.'

'Maybe you think that. But they don't. They want to march to the base to demand his release. And they are thinking that you, the Britisher, should come with them to help negotiate.'

'Oh.'

I imagined what would happen if I led a delegation of several thousand locals to the gates of the British base. Somehow, I doubted they'd be palmed off with a phone number for the Ministry of Defence press office. Instead, a bloodbath would ensue, leading to the spread of an anti-British insurgency all over southern Iraq, as the sleeping Shia dog woke up and bit, very hard. In subsequent accounts, military historians would blame it all on me.

Fortunately, before the matter could be discussed any more, Imam al Battat turned up safe and sound. Now, though, was the worry of how the meeting had gone. Would he now preach peace, or use his address to announce a jihad on all British oppressors? Starting with that idiot Brit journalist at the back? The whole town was waiting to find out.

After an ear-splitting hum of feedback from the mosque Tannoy, al Battat's voice suddenly broke through, silencing the crowd instantly. Then, just as smoothly as they'd shut up, the crowd linked hands and broke into prayer. An awesome, uniform chant went up, loud as a football crowd but as harmonised as a Gregorian choir. Not a single voice, not even a child's, sounded out of time. I began to see what Mohammed meant about the Shia being like a big, sleeping dog. If this lot fought together like they prayed together, they'd be terrifying.

After the first prayer, al Battat began his sermon. At first, it didn't sound like the meeting with the British had gone well. In a roaring wail, he lumped the British presence with a long historical line of Shia oppressors, starting with Saddam and going right back to someone called Hajjaj, whom Mohammed said was a king from 500 years ago. People had long memories around here.

Eventually al Battat came to the point. 'The most important question now is whether there should be a jihad based on the violent behaviour of the British at Al Majar al Kabir,' he said. 'Today I tell you that the religious authorities will not yet give permission for one. There are peaceful means to get our rights.'

How very sensible, I thought. The path thus smoothed, the British rolled back into town the following afternoon, meeting no trouble whatsoever. And sure enough, we were back in Al Amarah at the time and missed the whole thing. Mohammed compensated by going on a mission to find some beer. The local booze shops had all shut down, having been grenaded the week before by Shia fundamentalists. But we eventually sourced a dozen cans via the hotel receptionist, the process as furtive as buying a dozen kilos of cocaine. We drank them in my room, Mohammed then hiding the empty cans in the car boot. 'If the Shia people here see those beer containers, they will kill us with sticks,' he said.

The next morning, as I was beginning to think about going home, he wandered into my room.

'Do you want to see who is the real power around here?' he asked.

'Er... how do you mean?'

His voice lowered to an unnecessary whisper. 'At the hotel reception today I heard them talking about a guy in Al Amarah named Kareem Mahood. They are saying he is the one who did the deal with the Britishers to let them back into Majar al Kabir. Not the imam you saw, he was not really important. Mahood has an office in town, and is going to be one of the new politicians here in Al Amarah. Maybe governor. But I know him as a different guy.'

'Yeah? Who?'

'He was the leader of the Shia resistance fighters when I was down here as an armoured officer. A crooky fucker. I spent four years of my life trying to catch him. Never did we get near him. But now maybe we can interview him, yes?'

'Maybe. What does "crooky" mean?'

'It means, let's say, a clever guy, dangerous.'

'Really?'

'He was in the Iraqi army like me, but just a warrant officer, not of high rank. Then, when the fighting with the Shia started, he joined the resistance, doing hundreds of operations against the Iraqi military. He used to disguise himself for spying operations. Sometimes as a simple farmer guy, sometimes as a businessman in a suit from Baghdad. But his favourite was to dress as an Iraqi army commander. One time he went to the Iraqi Army intelligence headquarters here in Al Amarah, wearing a fake brigadier's uniform. He made the guards let him in, and then went right into the intelligence headquarters and left a message for the head guy, Brigadier Hassan. Hassan comes in a few hours later and opens the message. Do you know what it says? "Dear Brigadier Hassan, I came by to say 'hello' but you were out. Fuck you, Kareem Mahood!"'

'Very clever.'

'I tell you, this guy was pretending to be a brigadier all the time. Once he freed a whole load of prisoners that way, another time he got hold of some weapons. But never, ever did we catch him. We did not even have a picture of him, except one aged about 15. And yet it became the military orders that every Iraqi officer had to carry this picture, in case they would recognise him if he was caught.'

'So was he Saddam's most wanted man?'

'Exactly. Eventually he had 8,000 fighters on his side.'

This was beginning to sound interesting. I could do Kareem Mahood up as the Che Guevara of Iraq... the man Saddam couldn't kill. Mohammed arranged for us to interview him at his new HQ in Al Amarah, a white-walled villa on the banks of the Tigris, opposite the British Army base where we'd nearly been frogmarched to rescue Imam al Battat on Friday.

'Just remember one thing,' said Mohammed as an armed guard patted us down outside. 'Do not say I am from Iraqi army. Otherwise they will think I am a spy and kill me.'

'This guy won't recognise you, will he?'

'No. I have never seen him, and he has never seen me. Hopes to God.'

We were ushered into a large, bare lounge. Kareem Mahood sat on a settee, dressed in a spotless white robe and headdress lined with expensive-looking gold braid. He looked as hard as nails: craggy cheekbones, belligerent eyes and a big hooked Arab nose, like a bird of prey. There was definitely something of the warlord about him. One hand, decked in heavy gold rings, clutched a satellite phone, the only one I'd seen any Iraqi carry. The other clutched a small rubber stamp, which he used to authorise letters of recommendation to various supplicants who wandered in as we waited to interview him.

The other sign that Mahood was a man of parts was that he clearly had better things to do than yack to the likes of me. Most Iraqis were only too happy to be interviewed: the tough bit was shutting them up after half an hour or so. Kareem Mahood, however, gave us no more than five minutes, which elicited nothing more than a few enigmatic one-liners.

'I'm told you were a famous fighter against Saddam? Can you tell me a bit about that?'

'He says don't ask him, ask the people of Al Amarah,' said Mohammed, translating. 'They will tell you everything you need to know.'

'Er… right. Um, what does he think of what happened in Majar al Kabir?'

'He says mistakes were made on both sides.'

'Who does he blame?'

'He says he will not discuss this. God willing, everything will be fine now.'

'What did he say to the British when he met them?'

'He says he will not discuss this.'

'Well, who did he meet exactly? Can he tell us that?'

'He is saying you ask many questions.'

We left with barely a usable quote in my notebook.

'I can not believe we met that crooky fucker,' said Mohammed as we drove back to Baghdad. 'You know, I wanted to tell him, "Hey, I am Mohammed Kadom, staff colonel of the Iraqi army. For four years I was hunting you, but always you are in disguise. Now it is me who is in disguise, and I finally find you!" '

'You should have left a message for him, just like he did for that brigadier.'

Mohammed burst out laughing.

Tribal Hassles

AFTER HIS STAR performance in Majar al Kabir, Mohammed gradually made himself indispensable, supplementing his role as driver, translator and fixer with that of self-appointed personal minder. Although I'd survived in Baghdad for nearly six weeks on my own, he was constantly warning me of the various sticky ends I would face should I make the mistake of venturing out unchaperoned.

'They are robbers, killers, fuckers, they will see you are a foreigner and fuck you through and through,' he warned.

Sometimes, when he'd dropped me off at the hotel after work, he would even park up down the road to see if I tried to sneak out behind his back. I found it quite touching. Things were going fine, in fact, until one morning at the Al Majalis, when Ali the receptionist wandered up to me with his colleague Narro.

'Mr Colin, we want to talk about your friend,' said Ali. 'The translator man.'

'Yes?'

'This guy is a bad guy, you should stay away from him.'

'What's he done?'

'He was in here looking for you this morning, when you were out. When we said you were not here, he got angry. Then he told Narro, "Give me a piece of paper so I can write a message". Not asking polite, just making an order. Narro tells him "Please be polite", and then your friend got very angry. Mr Colin, please, we don't want this man in the hotel again.'

As he spoke, Mr Omar and several of the other staff had gathered round. The usual obliging smiles were gone. They were all nodding at what Ali said.

'I'm so sorry, Ali, maybe there has been some mistake. Let me talk to Mohammed and find out.'

'Mr Colin, what do you know about your friend?' asked Narro. 'I think maybe he was a security man for Saddam, or something.'

I wandered to my room in a slight panic. I'd often noticed how Mohammed had something of a swagger, the manner of a man who was used to people obeying him. In Majar al Kabir, the presence he commanded had been useful in getting the respect of the crowds. But to the Kurdish lads at reception, perhaps that same self-confidence came across as the voice of the old regime. The kind that ordered them about and had them hauled off to prison if they answered back.

I felt both fear and guilt. In emails home I'd been singing Mohammed's praises, going on about how exciting it was to have an ex-Iraqi army colonel at my side. Now it dawned that while I found him rather racy company, a lot of Iraqis might see otherwise. Had the staff at the Al Majalis got him sussed as some cunning Ba'athist thug, who'd conned some naive foreigner into hiring him, ready for some horrible fate further down the road? Come to think of it, was he really just a colonel in the regular army, as he claimed to be? Might he have been in one of the more sinister branches of Saddam's security apparatus? The ones whose main job was arresting and torturing civilians? Unable to speak his language, and unable to verify his background, I had no way of telling.

The next day, I waited outside the hotel for Mohammed to turn up, anxious to get to him before the staff did. As he parked up the Nissan I wandered over, looking as angry as I dared. When I mentioned the row with Narro, he waved his hand dismissively.

'Don't worry, this was nothing. I had a bad morning. First the car wouldn't start. Then I got here late and you were out. Then, when I want to leave you a message, that asshole on the reception wouldn't give me a piece of paper.'

'That's Narro. He's not an asshole. He's a good guy.'

'He's a fucking asshole.'

'What's wrong with him? Is it because he's Kurdish?'

'I am fine with the Kurdish. Some of my best friends in the military are Kurdish. Just this Kurdish asshole in your hotel.'

'Well, listen, I didn't see what happened, so I can't say whose fault it was. But please just remember, this hotel is where I live, and until now they have been very good to me. And it's going to be difficult for us to work together if they won't let you in.'

He nodded sulkily. 'So?'

'Apologise to Narro. Forget whose fault it was. Just say you're sorry, you had a bad day, or something.'

The next day he told me that he'd made peace with Narro, and that the two had hugged and kissed each on the cheeks in the Arab way. Somehow I doubted that they were really now best of mates, as he claimed. But frankly, I was as keen to downplay the whole thing as Mohammed was. Just as he couldn't afford to lose me, I couldn't afford to lose him. There was no way I'd find another translator remotely as good as he was, especially on my budget.

For the next few days, though, Mohammed remained morose. Waiting at a checkpoint at the Green Zone one morning, we bumped into my British friend Omar Hadi and his Iraqi driver. The three starting chatting together in Arabic, but the conversation soon ended up as a finger-wagging monologue from Mohammed. When he went off to buy cigarettes, I asked Omar what they'd been discussing.

'Er, politics. He was saying that Iraqis who want democracy don't know what they're talking about, and that the only people who know how to run the country are the military.'

'Listen Omar, you see this guy differently because you speak Arabic. How does he come across? Am I safe with him?'

'Well, he's a Ba'athist for sure. But he seems fine with you personally. Be a little careful though, yes.'

After a few days, Mohammed cheered up again. The more I thought about it though, the more it seemed a miracle was that he wasn't pissed off all the time. After all, in the last few months, all his hard-earned blessings had turned to curses. In return for risking his life in four brutal, nasty conflicts – Iran-Iraq, the Shia insurrection and the two Gulf wars – he'd enjoyed various privileges of rank. As a staff colonel, he'd been a big shot, respected and admired in equal measure, with six bodyguards and a chauffeur. When the cops saw his car they'd close the road off to other traffic so he could speed on through. The mere mention of his rank could get him a table in the best Baghdad restaurants.

Now, instead of looking forward to promotion to brigadier or general, followed by a comfortable retirement as a distinguished war hero, he faced a future where his military record could be a liability, not a matter of pride. Under Saddam, his efforts against the Shia insurgents had won him a bravery commendation. Now, many of his countrymen saw them as tantamount to war crimes. People he once considered beneath him – like Narro – could see his downfall all too clearly. One day he mentioned how he could feel contemptuous eyes everywhere.

'It is hard to imagine the hell it is,' he said. 'After 23 years of risking your life during an army career, suddenly they disband the army, with no chance even for a pension for fighting for your country. You go from being someone to being no-one, and other people can see it. They never say anything to my face, because they know I would kill them. But sometimes you can see them thinking, "Hey, you, fucker, you're not important now." '

At least he was trying to get back on his feet. Translating and driving might not be a job commensurate with the dignity of a staff colonel in the Iraqi Army, but there was at least some prestige attached to working with a foreigner, even one who only paid $10 a day. It did beg a question though. What, exactly, were the other 400,000-or-so fed up ex-Iraqi army soldiers doing?

The official answer was nothing at all. Having ignored their president's call to commit collective suicide by resisting the US-led invasion, most, like Mohammed, had quietly deserted their posts during the war and made their way home. But unlike the old civilian police force, which had been called back into service, the army had been disbanded permanently through a decree from Iraq's new Coalition governor, Paul Bremer. On one level it made sense. Not only were Iraq's armed forces far too big, they were also very closely associated with Saddam's regime. In some parts of the country, putting them back on the streets to help restore law and order would have started riots. But scrapping them altogether left nearly half a million armed men, many of them combat-hardened, with no money, no dignity, and nothing to do all day. And that, in turn, meant no shortage of potential recruits for the growing anti-American insurgency.

Rebellion and discontent had been brewing for some time. When I'd first arrived back in May, US troops were still waved at as they drove through the streets. Nobody complained about the invasion itself, only the practical discomforts that it had brought: the lack of electricity, the looting, and so on. But as the weeks passed, the goodwill that the Iraqis had initially shown to Saddam's conquerors had gradually seeped away. How could a mighty country like America, which had sent men to the moon, take so long to get Baghdad's electricity working? Why could a country that had brushed aside Saddam, the mightiest Arab ruler of all, not deal with a few looters?

The American answer was that things just weren't that simple. The national electricity grid was on its last legs anyway after years without proper maintenance because of sanctions. It needed rebuilding from scratch, not a few sticking plasters, and that would take years, not months. The same applied to setting up a new Iraqi police service, rebuilding the economy, and nearly every other problem. Yet many Iraqis simply could not, or would not, grasp those timelines. When results failed to materialise quickly, they found it easy to assume America wasn't really interested in rebuilding Iraq, and was only really after its oil. Conspiracy theories came easily to them. Here, after all, was a people who had been fed lies and propaganda by its own government for 30 years. Why trust a foreign power?

Often I wondered what Mohammed himself might be doing now if we hadn't bumped into each other that morning. He'd have continued driving round town as a taxi driver, getting more and more desperate. Then he'd go back to a house with no proper electricity or running water, and a wife who was demanding to know how the dashing young colonel she'd married years ago was going to get his act together again. One day, maybe, he'd have a run-in with the Americans at a checkpoint, where some 19-year-old US private would yell at him. In the rank-conscious military world that Mohammed came from, being ordered about by some lowly foreign soldier would be gravely insulting. He'd go home, cursing the Americans to anyone that listened. Later, someone in his neighbourhood would take him aside for a quiet word. 'Listen, my friend, do you want to get your revenge on the Americans? And do you need to earn some money to feed your family? There is a way...'

By mid-June, attacks on US troops were rising. What was supposed to be the last, dying gasp of defiance from Saddam loyalists seemed to have gained new life. Things were particularly bad in the town of Fallujah, west of Baghdad. There'd been a demonstration there back in late April, when residents had demanded that US troops move out of a school they were using as a base. The troops claimed that some of the protesters began shooting at them, and they'd returned fire, killing about 20 people. Locals had vowed revenge, and now US patrols in Fallujah were getting shot at, rocketed and grenaded on almost a daily basis. In Baghdad, meanwhile, Humvees were finding themselves sitting ducks in the constant traffic jams, so much so that the rest of the traffic now tried to keep their distance from them. Whenever we got stuck behind a Humvee, Mohammed would predict our imminent death.

'Now are fucked through and through,' he'd say, scanning the street for exits. 'The fighters will hit us by mistake because their aim will be no good. And the Americans will think we are the fighters and shoot us.'

Things weren't helped, in my opinion, by the American approach towards gun-control. In early June they announced a new gun amnesty that sounded something like a fantasy document from their National Rifle Association. The only weapons that were to be officially banned were 'crew-operated' ones, like belt-fed machine guns and rocket-propelled grenades. Otherwise, they let people keep everything from Kalashnikovs downwards, as long as they kept it 'in a safe place' at home and didn't carry it around with them. It was even OK to sell guns to other people, as long as you didn't go commercial and set up an AKs-R-Us in the street. The policy drove a coach and horses through the British gun-control efforts in southern Iraq, where they'd been arresting anybody even caught with a pistol. The Americans justified it on the basis that it would be unreasonable, not to say impractical, to force Iraqi families to hand over their weapons while the security situation was so dodgy. Yet expecting the US tradition of responsible home gun ownership to take root overnight in a land which had quite the opposite tradition seemed, at best, naive.

If the Iraqis were getting fed up with the Americans, the feeling was mutual. The troops who'd taken part in the invasion were desperate to go home, not having had a break since they'd pitched up in Kuwait in late 2002. But the insurgent attacks, and general lack of law and order, meant their leave dates were being pushed back indefinitely. Morale plummeted. A summer that should have been spent living it up as war heroes back home, cooking barbecues with their families and being stood free drinks in their local bars, now looked like being spent entirely on the streets of Baghdad. Many troops were still living rough in bombed-out buildings occupied during the invasion, or bivouacked around tanks parked on street corners, with only stray dogs for company. Few had running water to wash off the multiple layers of sweat and dust they picked up each day. Grime streaked their faces and hands like camouflage cream and even the army chaplains, responsible for troop welfare, sounded fed up.

'We had anticipated we'd be going home in June or July, and when we heard recently that it might not be for a long time yet, we were all disappointed,' said Chaplain Jerry Sieg, an earnest-looking Methodist who I met outside the internet café in Zayuna one day. 'How does it feel? It's like waking up on Christmas morning and finding that there are no Christmas presents.'

The internet café was a good place to meet the troops, who'd brief you on their gripes and whinges as they sent emails back home. Mostly they complained not about the danger, but the boredom. Life, they said, was an endless drudge of day patrol, guard duty, and night patrols. At least getting shot at helped pass the time. Chaplain Sieg was doing his best to cheer them up. His latest wheeze was an army talent contest, although it didn't sound thrilling. His first line-up was due to feature a couple of amateur rappers, a wannabe comedian, and a 'guy who plays a pretty mean harmonica'. It was not in his gift to provide the troops with what they really wanted, which was drink and sex. With the American top brass anxious not to offend Muslim sensibilities, boozing was out. As too, was fraternising with local women, although the odd bit of discreet whoring went on anyway.

'Our commanders are kinda relaxed about it so long's you're careful,' one soldier I met outside the internet café told me. 'You get 'em coming up to you, these war widows, saying, "My husband was killed fighting against Iran and I need to feed my family". Then it's down the back of the alleyway, or inside the tank, and you do it quick while your buddies keep guard.'

Such encounters were fraught with danger. A soldier might not know until it was too late whether the said widow had a stash of explosives strapped under her clothes.

To fight the boredom, soldiers swapped books and CDs with a fervour once only reserved for each other's well-thumbed porn mags.

Many developed tastes they never knew they had. Heavy metal fans got into Whitney Houston, rap aficionados into Country and Western. One Bible Belt soldier, who played in a 'Christian-punk' band back home, told me he'd found his demo cassettes in demand for the first time ever.

Not surprisingly, such pissed off, demoralised soldiers found the task of policing the peace rather harder than the task of fighting the war. 'We did the invasion, we're the nasty guys, the killers,' said one soldier I met, who'd scrawled *Fuck Iraq* on his helmet. 'We shouldn't be doing the peacekeeping anyway. Get someone else in.'

He had a point. Many were short-tempered, with little in the way of policing skills. I personally hadn't seen any soldiers abusing or mistreating Iraqis, but I did see incidents of alarming tactlessness, where troops made enemies of people who could have been friends. One such person was Dr Faisal, the internet café's scholarly, English-speaking proprietor. He didn't mind troops being there, but one day he asked a unit not to bring their weapons in, saying it made his Iraqi customers nervous. The unit weren't quite sure what to do, so they called up their lieutenant to come down and sort it out.

I imagined the lieutenant would understand and perhaps just speak the language of the dollar. *Military orders, I'm sure you understand. Maybe we could pay a little extra?* Instead he went straight on the offensive.

'Are you the gentleman who's been trying to take my mens' weapons away from them?'

Dr Faisal stared up from his desk, clearly as surprised as I was.

'No sir, I just asked them not to bring them in here. I am sorry, but it frightens my customers.'

'My men need to keep their weapons with them at all times. That is military regulations, as you should know.'

'Sir, I know you have your rules, but you must understand, I must think about my customers.'

'Yes, and my men need to read their emails!' The lieutenant leaned forward over Faisal's desk, his voice sharpening. 'Who are exactly are you? What is your name and where do you live?'

'Please, I am not making trouble. I just say please, don't let your men in here with their weapons.'

'Why is that such a problem? Are you a supporter of Saddam Hussein?'

By this time the entire café was watching. The atmosphere was very tense. 'Excuse me, lieutenant,' I croaked. 'Aren't you just making things worse here?'

He turned toward me, trying to work out whether I was an Iraqi or a foreigner. Soldiers, I'd come to realise, saw everybody who wasn't in uniform as basically the same.

'Pardon me?' he said.

'I mean, can't you see you're frightening this man? All he's done is make a polite request to you, and now you're accusing him of supporting Saddam Hussein.'

'Do you support Saddam Hussein too?'

'Of course I don't. But this is his private internet café, and it should be up to him who comes in. You are guests in his country. So am I.'

'We are not guests in this country. We are not here at anybody's invitation.'

I shrugged and turned away. *Your call, mate,* I thought. *But if you're not guests, don't be surprised if people start shooting at you.*

Dr Faisal relented. 'OK, lieutenant, you are in charge,' he said. 'Your men can come in with their weapons. I cannot stop them.'

'That's sorted out then. Good day to you, sir.'

As the lieutenant wandered out, I glanced over to Dr Faisal. He rolled his eyes and resumed his paperwork. He'd done the sensible thing: conceding defeat, while making it clear that as a mere Iraqi, he now had no say in anything that went on in his country, not even in his own internet café. But I was seething. Didn't that idiot realise that, after 30 years of dictatorship, Iraqis might be a little nervous around armed men in uniform? Didn't he appreciate that demanding someone's name, address and political affiliation was exactly the sort of thing Saddam's spooks did? And besides, even if Dr Faisal was a die-hard Saddamist, wasn't it his right to serve who he wanted? Surely Americans, of all people, should understand that? Worst of all, this lieutenant was supposed to be the brains of the outfit, a leader of men. If a commanding officer couldn't deal amicably with the polite, educated Dr Faisal, Christ knew how a bunch of ordinary grunts would cope with an angry street mob in Fallujah.

Was it behaviour like that which was driving the Iraqis into the insurgency? The Americans insisted that most of their attackers were only doing it for the money, bankrolled by suitcases of dollars from Saddam's henchmen. An insurgent was thought to get between $200 and $500 per attack, a lot of money in Iraq. But while the Americans described it as a mercenary operation, Mohammed reckoned it was business mixed with pleasure. It was, he pointed out, far too dangerous to be just a way of earning a living. The moment you fired on a Humvee with your rusty old Kalashnikov, you were inviting retaliation from troops with laser-sighted machine guns and super-accurate missile launchers. If they didn't get you, they'd call in back-up, and if the back-up didn't get you, they'd call in helicopter gunships. For every Coalition press notice announcing the death of a US serviceman in an attack, there were scores more in which a dozen insurgents died without injuring any US personnel. Few mercenaries would take on jobs where the odds were that bad. Whoever was pulling the trigger had to be revenging some grudge.

A culture of vengeance, Mohammed said, ran deep in Iraqi society, thanks to its tribal make-up. Like much of the Arab world, the country was divided up into hundreds of different clans and sub-clans, composed of huge extended families running into tens or even hundreds of thousands of people. In many other parts of the Middle East, tribal identity had been eroded in thanks to modernisation and city living. But in Iraq, isolated from outside influences for three decades, it remained alive and well, especially in rural areas. From the way Mohammed talked about it, belonging to a tribe sounded like being in the Mafia. Your first loyalty was to them, not the government, and in return they looked after you. There was help with jobs, help with money, help if you had a brush with the law. But if one of your tribe was killed or hurt, you were honour-bound to take revenge.

'This is why the Americans are having these tribal hassles in Fallujah right now,' Mohammed explained one day. 'As you are knowing, they have killed many people outside that school one day. Now the tribes of Fallujah, they are fucking angry. And they are tough guys, good fighters. Every time the Americans kill one of them, they must kill one back.'

'Do you have a tribe?' I asked.

'Of course. The Al Obeidi tribe. Very strong, very famous tribe.'

'Have you ever been in a tribal hassle?'

'By God, almost. One day during the time of Saddam Hussein, I got a knock at my home at two o'clock in the morning. There were these six guys wearing scarves over their faces. They said, "Hey Colonel Mohammed, you are an Al Obeidi. There is some tribal hassle going on, we need you to help us." They came because they knew I was a military officer and that I was permitted to keep a Kalashnikov at home. But I did not want to be involved. I said, "I am sorry, but I will get in trouble with the army." They said, "Fuck you, this is a tribal matter", and we had some kind of argument. They left, but they said, "The tribe will hear about this, and you will be in the fucking trouble".'

'So what happened?'

'The next day I went to the sheikh of the tribe, and explained everything. Eventually he said, "OK, you are officer in the army, I understand". But it is a serious thing, let me tell you, disobeying the orders of the tribe.'

'And you didn't even know what the fight was about?'

'It is not about asking the right and wrong. Only that you must defend the tribe. Let me tell you an old Iraqi story. A guy wanders into a restaurant in Baghdad. For no reason, he takes out a gun and starts shooting, killing the customers one by one. Then one of the customers pulls out his own gun and shoots the guy dead. Everyone says to him. "Hey man, thanks God you shot this crazy fucker". But when the dead man's tribe hears about this, what do you think they say? Do they say, "Thanks God, someone killed our asshole brother before he killed any more peoples"? No, they say, "Which fucker shot our brother? Who is his tribe?" This is the Iraqi way. It is a strange thing for the foreigner to comprehend.'

'God help the Americans in Fallujah, then.'

'God help them.'

*****

By mid-July, there had been some 600 insurgent attacks on American troops. More than 30 had been killed, and several times that number wounded. US forces had done two major sweeps aimed at nipping the insurgency in the bud, arresting about 3,500 people. But still, the number of 'hostile incidents' – anything from a full-scale ambush to a man lurking suspiciously with a gun – continued at about 25 a day. In Baghdad, soldiers became paranoid about having Iraqis too near them. Dr Faisal's internet café was declared off-limits.

As the attacks grew, US commanders began to notice that the incident pins spreading across their maps in headquarters were forming a certain pattern. Most took place either in Baghdad itself, Fallujah and Ramadi in the west, or the area stretching up to Saddam's home town of Tikrit in the north. The Americans, with their flair for theatrical military jargon, dubbed it the Sunni Triangle, although it was really more a squint oblong shape. Its real defining characteristic was not its shape or religious hue, but the fact that most towns within the Sunni Triangle had large numbers of people who'd served in Saddam's security services. He'd known that in volatile tribal neighbourhoods like Fallujah, it was better to have the locals working for him rather than against him. In many towns, the state security forces had been among the biggest employers. Entire neighbourhoods of housing would be set aside for them. Deprived of income, these towns were now rebelling against the Americans.

One day, I went to do a 24-hour 'mini-embed' with a team of US soldiers in a northern Baghdad suburb called Al Adamiyah. It was Baghdad's answer to Chelsea – a stinking rich suburb a few bends down the Tigris from the city centre, full of big mansionhouses that had been home to the same families for years. Saddam had ruled that anybody who didn't have a relative born in Adamiyah before 1948 couldn't buy property there, which meant the community was long-established and close-knit. Being one of the smartest parts of town, it was also home to a lot of Saddam's top henchmen. It was here, during the war, that he had made his last public appearance, waving triumphantly at a crowd in a market place. On the US Army security maps of Baghdad, which divided the city up into 'friendly', 'compliant', and 'hostile' areas, Al Adamiyah fell into the last category.

The soldiers I hooked up with were based in one of the palaces of Uday Hussein, Saddam's eldest son. It had smart, well-designed gardens and a swimming pool in the middle of a landscaped back lawn that sloped down to the river. The banqueting suite now served as the makeshift command room for the 2nd Battalion, 3rd Artillery

Regiment, aka 'The Gunners'. The way they'd redecorated it showed you the strange inner compromises of men trained to kill in the name of freedom and the American way. On some walls were Army-issue posters extolling the 'Soldierly virtues' of discipline, courage, and patriotism. On the others were macho, hand-painted montages, showing grinning skulls hanging over atom-bomb clouds and buxom women draped suggestively around Howitzer gun barrels. The raid we were going to accompany them on that night was called 'Operation Bulldog Gangbang'.

The Gunners were no experts in counter-insurgency. They'd come to Iraq to provide artillery support during the war, blasting off massive Howitzers that could obliterate Republican Guard tanks from 20 miles away. Now, with no particular training, they were fighting a much more lightly-armed but equally deadly enemy that was forever just around the corner. Their track-mounted Howitzers stood redundant in a corner of the palace grounds, useless when it came to picking off snipers in one of Al Adamiyah's crowded alleyways. That night's raid was to try and arrest members of an insurgent cell who'd started attacking local Iraqis thought to be working as translators and cleaners at the Gunners' base. The cell had posted 'death lists' on walls around Adamiyah, giving the names of suspects and urging people to 'kill them and deform their faces'. Already, one of the Gunners' translators had been shot dead and another injured in a grenade attack.

Even among the residents of Al Adamiyah, where 'collaborators' were frowned upon, such tactics were considered a bit strong. Fighting the Americans was one thing; killing fellow Iraqis was another. Since the attacks had begun, the Gunners had had several locals wander up to their gates and give them names of alleged cell members. According to the locals, they weren't Saddamists at all, but newly-arrived fanatics from Al Qaeda, happy to spill any amount of blood – Iraqi, American, or their own – to drive home the wedge between occupier and occupied. Whether they really were Al Qaeda, or whether the locals just didn't want to acknowledge the ruthlessness of some of their own people, nobody knew. The Americans reckoned they'd killed at least a couple of thousand foreign jihadists during the invasion itself. Were more coming through already? The Gunners' Major Scott Sossaman wasn't sure.

'Several independent sources have said these people are Al Qaeda, and there is no point in them making stuff up as we don't pay for information,' he said. 'Having said that, I think people do just use whatever name they've heard in the news, because they think it'll get our attention. This week it's Al Qaeda, next week it'll be some other bogeyman. It's a bit like being back home and someone telling you there's a child molester in your neighbourhood. You'll pay attention in a way you might not for any other criminal.'

Certainly, from the description the Iraqi informants had given of him, the main target of Bulldog Gangbang didn't sound particularly impressive. He was a fat, balding bloke in his early 40s, normally seen wandering around in a scruffy, white string vest. As a poster-boy for the insurgency, he was not exactly Osama bin Laden, yet other aspects of his CV rang sinister bells. He was said to be a co-ordinator for the local Wahaabi sect, a puritanical brand of Islam from Saudi Arabia favoured by both bin Laden and Al Qaeda. He was also said to have been jailed in 1999 for bombing a Baghdad nightclub. Anybody stupid enough to do that in Saddam's time had to be a headcase.

Prior to the raid we joined around 30 soldiers for a pre-briefing staffed by Maj Sossaman's boss, a stocky young colonel. He was genial, but clearly not a man to mess about. Earlier that day, he'd been on patrol in his Humvee when a drunken Iraqi in the car behind him had started waving a pistol around. The colonel's gunners had opened fire on them, killing all four occupants of the car instantly. He told the story matter-of-factly, as if relating how he'd exchanged insurance details after a minor road shunt. 'Guy should've know better than to pull a pistol like that,' he said, shrugging. 'Ended up getting his friends killed too.'

I nodded politely. To pull a gun in the presence of group of soldiers was certainly to invite trouble. But had it really been necessary to kill all four of them immediately? What about firing a warning shot first, or just taking out the guy with the gun? More to the point, had anybody stuck around to explain what had happened? Or had the locals in Al Adamiyah just been left to draw their own conclusions? As a reporter, it was my job to ask these questions. To my shame, I didn't. That, I realised over time, was the problem with embeds: it was hard to ask awkward questions of people who were going to be looking after you during a raid in one of Baghdad's most dangerous suburbs.

We rolled out the palace gates in a squad of eight open-topped Humvees just after midnight, kicking up huge clouds of dust under a full moon. The soldiers 'locked and loaded' their M16s in unison and began a chant in the voice of Elmer Fudd from the Disney cartoons. *'We're going to hunt the wabbit, we're going to hunt the wabbit.'*

The wabbit, alas, was nowhere to be seen. The Gunners surrounded the suspect's house and rapped on the door, bracing themselves for a volley of gunfire or grenades. Instead, an elderly-looking grandpa-figure appeared in his nightgown, politely letting everyone in. The troops herded three men and several women and children into the lounge as they searched the rest of the house. The translator, wearing a mask to disguise himself, quickly concluded that none were Al Qaeda sympathisers. The only thing the Gunners found was the family Kalashnikov. The Gunners apologised, and then, to my astonishment, handed the gun back to Grandpa as we left.

'Isn't it a bit dangerous to give someone back their machine gun just after you've raided their house?' I asked one soldier.

'I guess it's their right to home defence,' he said.

'What happens if they open up on you in revenge as you leave?' He didn't answer.

*****

One hot summer morning, I was chatting with Ali the nightwatchman in the dingy reception area at the Al Majalis. He was showing me a new pistol he'd bought. Its calibre was eight millimetre rather than the usual nine, less powerful but easier to handle. He'd bought it for his mum. Suddenly he leaned forward on the counter, rotting teeth gleaming unevenly in the semi-gloom, and dropped his voice to a conspiratorial whisper.

'Did you hear about the spider of Baghdad?'

'No? What spider?'

'Everybody is talking about him. There is a spider going around, killing many American soldiers.'

'Eh? A spider? You mean like this?' I ran my hand in a tarantula-like motion towards the broken bell on the counter.

'No, no,' he said. He raised his hands as if pointing a rifle and cocked an imaginary bolt action. 'Dush! A spider!'

'Oh, you mean a sniper?'

'Yes. Sorry. This word. This spider, he was in the Republican Guard. Very good. Now he is shooting at the Americans.'

'Really?'

'Yes, Mr Colin. Killing maybe ten, maybe 20 soldiers. Making the Americans very afraid.'

It sounded like a story, so I checked it out. For once, a piece of gossip from the Al Majalis reception desk turned out to have a kernel of truth to it, although, as ever, the reality was rather more mundane. A lone assassin was indeed targeting the Americans, although his *modus operandi* was not long-range marksmanship. Instead, he would wander up behind a US soldier on a busy street and fire a small-calibre .22 pistol right against the base of his victim's skull. That muffled any muzzle crack, allowing the killer to melt away into the crowd before anybody noticed. So far, he'd killed not 20 soldiers, but two, the first as he was browsing in a CD shop, the second as he was queuing for a soft drink at a street stall. It wasn't exactly *The Day of the Jackal*, so I forgot all about it until a few days later, when I had a call from *Scotsman* foreign editor James Hall.

'Have you heard?' he asked. 'There's a British journalist been shot dead in Baghdad. A freelancer.'

'Jesus. Who?'

As ever, I was completely in the dark. There was only one other British freelancer I knew working in Baghdad, and I wasn't even sure if he was in the country at the time.

'It's not confirmed yet, but we think we know who it was. A bloke called Richard Wild.'

'Never heard of him.'

'A young guy. Not long out of uni. Was working as a cameraman for ITN. He was offering to write for us too, as it happens. Came into the office not long ago. Only been in Iraq a couple of weeks.'

'What happened?'

'Not clear yet. Seems like someone just wandered up and shot him in the back of the head. Somewhere near the Baghdad Museum. Do you want to see if you can find out a bit more?'

'Sure.'

'Listen, don't go anywhere near the museum. The guy might still be around.'

I went down to the Palestine Hotel to see if anyone else had heard anything. Sure enough, inside the ITN suite, several worried-looking reporters had gathered. From what they said, it sounded like Richard had been hit by whoever had killed the two soldiers. He'd been scouting out film locations at the museum, and had apparently been shot amid a crowd of people. Once again a .22 pistol was thought to have been involved. He'd been chatting to some American troops nearby, and was tall and fit-looking with a crew cut. Maybe he'd been mistaken for a grunt. It wasn't a particularly convincing explanation, as most insurgents must have known that US troops never wandered around out of uniform, unarmed and alone. But it was a tempting one, as the alternative was that he'd just been shot just for being Western.

The other question being pondered was exactly who he'd been working for. When freelancers came up with big exclusives, every news organisation was happy to bill them as their 'own special correspondent' or whatever. But when they came unstuck, nobody wanted to admit to having anything to do with them, for fear of the legal consequences. It was easy to imagine the questions that could be asked in Richard's case. Why was he wandering down a street in Baghdad on his own? Had he done a hostile environment course? What was he doing in Iraq in the first place? Who was responsible for him? The answer, it turned out, was nobody. Richard, like me, had come out here entirely on his own. He'd done a stint as a 'logger' for ITN back in London, cataloguing raw camera footage, but since coming out to Baghdad he'd been completely freelance. An independent TV producer named Michael Burke, who was out in Baghdad, had offered to take any decent film footage off him, and had actually suggested Richard might check out the museum as a filming location. But that wasn't the same as ordering him to go there.

As we mulled all of this over, Burke came in, looking shaken up. The American military police who'd picked up Richard's body had found a piece of paper with Burke's name and satphone number on it. They'd rung him up and asked him to identify the body. The MP was also a friend of one of the two soldiers who'd been killed in the same way. 'Not very OK Corral', as he put it.

A few hours later I was knocking out a story about Richard's murder for *The Scotsman*. Back home, the paper was unearthing details about his background. It emerged that his parents, who lived in the Scottish borders, had begged him not to go to Baghdad. It was easy to see why they thought he had other options. He'd been head boy at school, edited the school newspaper and got straight 'As' in his exams before gaining a history degree at Cambridge, fitting in a gap year of officer training at Sandhurst somewhere in between. Then it had been ITN and his plan to become a foreign correspondent. Not because he was pissed off and desperate, like me, but because it was something he passionately wanted to do. Like me, he'd been living in some down-at-heel dosshouse that nobody else had heard of. Like me, he'd been tapping up other, more seasoned hacks for advice. And, like me, he'd been travelling around in taxis and walking about on his own. Unlike me, the poor guy's luck had run out.

Richard was the first foreign journalist to be killed since the end of the war, and his death got a lot of coverage. He was written up in glowing terms, a young, idealistic guy, a future star of journalism cut down ahead of his prime. But even the pieces that sang his praises also pondered the wisdom of what he was doing. 'It is certainly the case that freelancers, working alone, are always at a disadvantage without the backup and staff of an international news agency,' said *The Guardian*. Back in Britain, news of the killing fortunately bypassed my parents. But the next day my satellite phone bleeped with a text message from Max. 'Just read bout freelancer dead,' it read. 'I know u r ok but am so worried bout u. PLEASE b care4ul.'

The next couple of weeks were tense, but saw no further assassinations. Mercifully, Richard's death began to look like a dreadful one-off. But most foreign journalists in Baghdad began taking new security precautions, as recommended by the ex-military guys retained as security advisers by the big TV networks. Rule number one was never to walk the streets unaccompanied. Rule number two was never to spend more than about half an hour in one place. This was based on the theory that most would-be assassins needed at least that long to plan their hit on you. First they had to identify who you were, and whether you were a worthwhile target. Then, most likely, they had to wander off and pick up their gun, or a friend who had a gun. Then they had to work out a getaway strategy. And, finally, they had to pluck up the bottle to do it. The longer you stuck around in one spot, the more you went into the danger zone.

For the first few days I tried to ignore the rule about not walking the streets. On my budget, travelling in cabs was only practical if you were going on longer journeys. But even wandering the half-mile from the Al Majalis to the Palestine, I no longer felt comfortable. Every time a car slowed down near me, or someone wandered up to say hello, I saw a would-be assassin making his approach. One day I was walking on the main road back to the hotel when a shabby car slowed down alongside. I watched out the corner of my eye, more to practise being vigilant than out of any real concern. The car stopped right beside me, and a large, overweight man got out, carrying some dark object furtively in his left hand.

Don't panic, it's just coincidence, he just happens to be getting out here.

Keep walking. Just check what he's carrying, though.

It's alright, it's just a... bloody HELL, IT'S A BLOODY PISTOL!

I burst into a run, charging towards the hotel as fast as was possible in flip-flops. Barging past the crowd outside the door, I cowered behind reception. 'There's a man out there with a gun!' I yelled.

Mr Omar appeared out of a back room and grabbed one of the Kalashnikovs that lay under the counter. Without waiting for further explanation, he made for the door, where the assembled company was staring towards where I'd just run from. I wandered up and peered out from behind them. Outside one of the shops, the gunman was pointing the pistol in someone's chest and yelling at them. Then he sped off again in his car.

'Is OK, Mr Colin, this man not looking for you,' said Mr Omar. 'Only some small fight about money.' He wandered back into his office. A gunfight that didn't involve his hotel was none of his business.

Mescaline Heads And Mad Folks

RICHARD'S MURDER made me appreciate just how lucky I'd been so far. Against all the odds, I'd managed to get out here, stay out of trouble and find work. Rather than ending my journalistic career, the move to Baghdad had kickstarted it. Covering the killings of the British soldiers down at Majar al Kabir had got my name known on *The Scotsman*, and helped them to remember it on the *Standard*. Occasionally I'd do stuff for the *Sunday Telegraph*, too – mainly legwork for their chief foreign correspondent, Philip Sherwell, but it still paid well.

Which wasn't to say that living in Baghdad got any easier. The electricity was still off for all but a couple of hours a day. The telephones still didn't work. The heat continued to soar. And the food remained awful. Sick of the kebabs and rotisserie chicken in local restaurants, I fuelled myself almost entirely on crisps and sweets from the corner shop: sickly Turkish-made imitation Mars Bars and Twixes, so melted in the heat you had to eat them with a spoon, and Iranian crisps that were so thin they dissolved on your tongue like communion wafers. Occasionally, I'd find a shop selling imported Pringles and have a feast, washed down with imitation Cola or a beer from the car-bonnet off licence. My entire diet could have come from a hotel mini-bar. As it was, the sheer heat suppressed the appetite. The weight fell off me. For the first time since my early 20s, I could see my ribcage, sticking out under my clammy, sweating skin like a row of railings. The sole culinary highlight in my life was US Army rations, or MREs (Meals Ready To Eat), with boil-in-a-bag delicacies like beef teriyaki and burritos. Most US troops were sick of them and would dish them out free if you asked nicely. Packed with enough calories to keep a 14-stone Marine in battle all day, my nutrient-deprived body got a palpable energy rush every time I ate one.

Fortunately, thoughts of home and its comforts didn't intrude very much. Baghdad was too intense and in-your-face for that. There was so much to see, so much to learn, and so much to watch out for that one's attention rarely wandered from the here and now. The sheer novelty of simply being there never wore off. Even three months in, I'd wake up each morning, breathe in the hot, fume-filled air, listen to the honk of horns, roar of generators and rumble of US tanks, and think, *Shit, I'm in Baghdad.* My old life, apart from emails to Max and occasional phone calls to my parents, became increasingly distant. Every now and then, I'd see items of news from Britain on the Kurdish satellite TV down at hotel reception. Footage of the Glastonbury festival, with crop-topped young women dancing in fields, electrified the couch potatoes in the lobby. It was the first time I'd seen a scantily-clad female in months and I found myself gesticulating as enthusiastically as everyone else.

I'd also acquired a raft of new skills, tricks and survival tips, some useful anywhere, others only pertinent in Iraq. There was the trick of getting a bottle of water ice-cold by sticking it in the innards of an air conditioning unit. There was the trick of fitting a two-pin plug into a three pin socket by wedging a matchstick into the top hole. There was the knack of counting through vast wads of Iraqi dinars; you stuck a wedge of notes between the middle fingers of one hand and flicked through them with the thumb and forefinger of the other, whirring away like a Colombian drug baron counting a payment. There were also precision battlefield techniques to be learned in the long-running war of attrition against the Al Majalis's cockroaches. You gave them a sharp flick with your forefinger, scooped them up while they lay stunned on the carpet, and threw them out the window. It was much less messy than splatting them with a shoe. And I became a connoisseur of the world's worst whiskies, having downgraded from Dimple to the cheapest $3-a-bottle jobs. They all claimed to be world-famous Scottish brands, although personally I'd never heard of 'Clan Vintage', 'Rob Roy', or my favourite, 'Lordian', which carried a picture of a swashbuckling Scots laird riding horseback over the glens. The label proclaimed him as a real-life Jacobean warrior, a claim undermined by the small print beneath which said 'Lebanese industrial whisky equipment'.

What made it all infinitely more bearable was having Mohammed around. I was now the envy of other journalists. Very few had a translator who was simultaneously fluent, hardworking, streetwise and good company. Occasionally, other reporters even tried to poach him with offers of better money. Touchingly, he always told them his first loyalty was to Mr Colin, the man who'd first given him a job when he'd been cruising the streets as a cabbie. Actually, it turned out he hadn't really been doing that. Over a beer one night he confessed that he'd actually been selling guns at the time. The day he picked me up, he'd had a stash of Kalashnikovs in the back of the Nissan. He said it'd been a few one off-deals to make ends meet when he'd been out of a job. That was all I could get out of him on the subject, not that I wanted to dwell on it too much anyway. After all, hadn't the Americans said it was OK to sell guns?

Despite the constant feeling that he was never quite all he seemed, Mohammed was the only Iraqi I could remotely call a friend. Spending most days with him, we worked together, got drunk together, argued together, and laughed and bitched about the world around us together. During the long hours stuck in Baghdad's traffic jams, we even got to the point of swapping musical tastes. Like most Iraqis his age, Mohammed's taste in Western music revolved around the late 1970s, the last time they'd been free to travel abroad and carouse in nightclubs in the West. His favourites were Kenny Rogers, Abba and Dolly Parton, 'that chick with the fucking huge boobs, like they are not real'. We got some cassettes to play in the car from the Friendly Ghost, a music shop where they did a CDs-pirated-while-you-wait service for two dollars a time. The only thing they had which we could agree on was the Bee Gees. Watching the Colonel grunting along to their falsettos in *Staying Alive* was always amusing, although not as amusing as the look of surprise on his face when I told him that the Bee Gees were actually all men.

'These are *guys*?' he asked. 'But they are singing with the cissy voices.'

Cissy voices aside though, Mohammed's sense of Arab machismo made him as much a 1970s man as anyone in *Saturday Night Fever*. He was forever boasting about various 'chicks' he'd slept with, and was convinced that all women found him irresistible. On our sojourns around Baghdad, he even taught me how to letch, Iraqi-style. 'Look at that ass,' he'd shout suddenly, grinding the Nissan to a sputtering kerb-crawl past some woman shrouded in a billowing *abbaya* cloak.

'Eh? All you can see is her face.'

'That is because you are a foreigner. Watch her clothes move as she walks along. See which parts move underneath, and which parts stay still. You will see she shows off the boobs. And the ass.' As he spoke he'd cup his hands, as if testing fruit for firmness in a Baghdad *souk*.

Seldom, in fact, did we drive past a woman of child-bearing age without Mohammed providing a graphic commentary of how he might enjoy sexual congress with her. His loins seemed in a constant state of arousal, veering around in search of targets like an Iraqi tank shooting up a Kuwaiti town. Occasionally, his knowledge of the appropriate vocabulary fell short. 'When I drove to the hotel today I saw this beautiful chick, with the huge tits and the ass,' he announced one morning, as I was sat with two other foreign journalists. 'I got very erect!'

I stared at him, aghast. Had he really just said what I thought he'd said?

'Er, what do you mean, Mohammed?'

'Erect! You know. Like this!' He pointed to his groin area. The assembled company probably thought Mohammed and I regularly compared erections together.

'Er, Mohammed, I don't think that's really the right word. If a girl, er, makes you feel sexy, you say she *turns you on*. As in, say, to turn on a generator.'

'Ok, good. So, anyways, this chick turns me on like a generator...'

When we got sick of the Bee Gees, we'd listen to the BBC World Service on the Nissan's radio. Like many English-speaking Iraqis, Mohammed was a great admirer of the BBC, seeing Britain as a guiding beacon of truth and reason. This was despite the fact the World Service seemed to have long ago given up preaching about Britain and Britishness. In its place, as far as I could tell, was a relentless 'what-can-we-learn-from-other-cultures?' agenda.

'This week's film slot will feature Subere Subano, the man usually described as the father of sub-Saharan film-making.'

'Today, news focus looks at the Ghanaian government's effort to attract young people back into its cocoa industry.'

'Rape – the hidden taboo of the women of the eastern Congo. What do YOU think?'

However well-intentioned the broadcasts, they didn't seem to have enlightened listeners in Baghdad. 'They should just nuke Africa,' declared Mohammed, listening to yet another report one day about the continent's AIDS epidemic. 'It would be for the best in the long-term.'

For some reason, he never prescribed the same fate for Iraq.

To wind him up, I'd sometimes quiz him on his views on some of the issues that the World Service's liberal news agenda followed. One story that always got him worked up was the split in the worldwide Anglican church over the ordination of a gay American bishop. The church's African branch, which opposed the move, was threatening to form a breakaway sect if the ordination went ahead. It was the one thing Mohammed reckoned the Africans had got right.

'There is an order in our Holy Book, the Koran, saying that the homosexual must be killed severely and under bad conditions,' he declared, torn between abject horror and schoolboy amusement. 'I can't understand how this bishop stands in church, doing the prayer and saying "Don't commit the sins". And then he goes off and gets fucked in the ass!' He started to laugh. 'Really, you foreign people, always coming in with very strange conceptions. But the most beautiful point of this story is that when this guy, or this gay – hah – makes the prayer, there is another guy at the back of the church, saying to everyone: "Hey, yes, I fucked this guy yesterday!" '

'Are there many gay imams, Mohammed?'

'Don't say that, man! They will kill you!'

In time, Mohammed would also come to admire another broadcaster – me. Every now and then, I'd pick up a bit of TV work, doing two-way interviews with news channels back home. Most no longer had full-time correspondents in Iraq, so if something big happened they'd rope me in for a 'live from Baghdad' interview. TV punditry proved surprisingly easy.

'Hi, Colin, it's X from Y TV here. Could you do a couple of minutes on our lunchtime show later? It's about those two US soldiers injured in a bomb attack in Ramadi, west of Baghdad, this morning.'

'I'm sorry, I've been out all day and I don't know anything about it.'

'Don't worry, we can fill you in with the details from the Reuters wire. Then the presenter will just ask you a few questions.'

'Er... what will they ask me about?'

'Just the stuff that we've told you.'

Two hours later, we'd go on air.

'And as we've just been hearing, there's been more violence against US troops in Iraq. Freelance reporter Colin Freeman joins us now live from Baghdad. Colin, what's happened?'

'Well, I understand that two US soldiers were injured in a bomb attack in the town of Ramadi, west of Baghdad, this morning.'

'And what's the latest?'

'We don't know much more right now, to be honest. The details remain pretty sketchy, and the Americans are saying very little at present.'

'Colin, thank you very much.'

To my astonishment, my paltry contributions to the nation's airwaves earned me anything up to £75 a time. Mohammed was highly impressed. He suggested that as I was now 'famous', I should abandon the $5-a-night Al Majalis and move to the relative luxury of the nearby Hotel Casablanca, where the rooms cost $16 a night and boasted access to a disused swimming pool. But I stayed loyal to the Al Majalis. It was now one of several ultra-decrepit hotels in the neighbourhood that were housing Westerners on low budgets. They were an eclectic mix: a few other freelance journalists, the odd Left-wing documentary maker, and very occasionally a backpacker or two, for whom Iraq was now the ultimate destination for traveller-cred. I managed to sell a story about two 18-year-old gap year students who'd travelled in on the bus from Syria, without telling their parents. One of them was the son of the Bishop of Penrith. His Grace learned of his son's exploits from a *Daily Express* reporter back in London.

There was also a small but colourful pageant of out-and-out loonies. One German girl who turned up at the Al Majalis one day cheerfully informed me that she was on 'her own private peace mission'. We never heard anything more of her. After that came a Swiss peace campaigner, who'd had a religious vision during a mescaline trip in Mexico. For some reason, the vision had told him to hitchhike his way to Baghdad as soon as possible. He saw it as some kind of messianic pilgrimage, and claimed to have won the blessing of everyone he'd met *en route*.

Equally odd was a scruffy, long-haired Japanese student, who was thought to have been in Baghdad as a human shield during the war. Nobody was really quite sure, because he spoke only Japanese and did nothing except wander the streets aimlessly. Because of his strange appearance, the US Army were convinced he was some kind of terrorist, and on at least one occasion he was arrested and banged up for a couple of days. Also briefly in residence was some weird Korean youth charity group, Paedophiles-sans-Frontiers or something. They deemed the hotel to be in such dire straits that they donated blankets and crates of bottled water.

In early August, Dominic, my former hostile environment guru, rang to say that Tracey had finally given birth to a baby girl. To mark the occasion, I had the idea of getting Mohammed to video me celebrating, Iraqi-style, by shooting a Kalashnikov into the air. Dominic had been complaining about the over-feminised atmosphere in his house wrought by endless visits of cooing female admirers bringing bright pink girl-child clothes and toys. As a 'congratulations-on-your baby' gift, a video of me blasting away with a Kalashnikov would restore his diminished sense of masculinity. Plus I'd always wanted to try firing a machine gun, and opportunities back home were fairly rare, even in Camberwell.

Mohammed took me to see his friend Colonel Saba, who'd been an army weapons instructor and had a vast collection of Kalashnikovs at his villa in east Baghdad. We went up onto the roof, where I started off by test-firing a single round. Heard close up, the bang from the muzzle was ear-splitting, like letting off a king-sized firecracker right up next to your face. Col Saba then shoved in one of the gun's crescent-shaped magazines and flicked the fire switch to fully automatic. I pointed the barrel to the heavens and opened fire, hoping fervently that the recoil wouldn't cause me to career out of control and wipe out Mohammed, who was filming nearby. The rate of fire was so high that I emptied the entire 30-round magazine in two single bursts, the gun jumping around like a stick that had suddenly come alive. Luckily it stayed reasonably on target. Only a few days later did I learn that even though the bullets were being fired directly up in the air, they were still travelling fast enough on the way back down to kill someone. Watching the footage again, I also realised something else that I should have spotted first time – that it made me look like a bit of a prat. Unfortunately, by that time the footage had already been emailed to Dominic, who in turn had showed it to all his mates at the BBC.

The Revolution Will Not Be Air-Conditioned

APART FROM INVADING his neighbours, murdering hundreds of thousands of his own people, and possibly hoarding weapons of mass destruction, one of the official reasons for getting rid of Saddam was his treatment of the Marsh Arabs. They were a unique, 5,000-year-old tribal civilisation that had developed in the swampy marshlands that abounded all over southern Iraq, as much a part of the marsh's rare eco-system as its insects and wading birds. They lived in houses fashioned from dried reeds, and hunted and fished in elegant hand-built canoes, a picturesque lifestyle which was tailor-made for the likes of *National Geographic* magazine and which won them numerous champions in the West. Wilfred Thesiger, the British explorer, spent nearly a year living with the Marsh Arabs in the 1950s, penning a celebrated book that had made them pin-ups in anthropological circles ever since. However, during the early 1990s, the marshes' more inaccessible stretches become bolt holes for many of the Shia insurgents fleeing Saddam's armoured brigades. Among them was Mohammed's old adversary, Kareem Mahood. His nickname, back then, was 'Lord of the Marshes'.

Saddam's response was typically robust. Unable to force the insurgents out, he simply drained the marshes of water, forcing their residents into squats on the outskirts of Basra, and killing or imprisoning those who refused to move. On the grand scale of Saddam atrocities, it was actually at the lesser end of the spectrum – he'd only destroyed their way of life forever, rather than wiping them off the planet altogether. Yet their plight got a huge amount of attention in the West, because it was a crime against the environment, rather than just humanity. In draining the vast tracts of swamps, marshes and reed beds, he'd destroyed an entire habitat, squeezing dry what had been a huge fresh-water sponge in the desert-bound Middle East. In Western eyes, it somehow confirmed Saddam's status as genuinely evil. Any Arab despot could kill and torture his citizens. But wrecking the planet too?

Now that Saddam was gone, there was talk of trying to help the Marsh Arabs to return to their natural habitat. Baroness Emma Nicholson, a British Liberal Democrat peer who ran a charity dedicated to their welfare, was involved in plans to get the marshes gradually reflooded. It had lots of potential as a story. However, when I asked the Colonel if we could head down there for a look, he was his usual foreboding self.

'The people of the marshes? No way, man. We cannot make interviews with them. They are gypsies, fuckers, they will rob and kill us.'

'Come off it. You say that about everyone we go to see.'

'No, this time it really is dangerous. Remember, was I not among them as an armoured officer in the time of Saddam Hussein? I know their territories very well, every small track and road. But if you drive there, you are many kilometres from any town or city. They are lawless people, they will fuck you through and through. Why do you think the Shia fighters used to hide among them?'

I mentioned Thesiger, and how he'd lived among them for months at a time. Mohammed thought Thesiger was a naive idiot who was lucky not to have ended up dead. He didn't think much better of Baroness Nicholson.

'This woman thinks these people will want to go back to the marshes? They will not, I tell you. Now they are in homes in Basra, with the TV and electricity. None will want to go back to the fishing, and the flies, and the slushy homestead in the marshes. But if she runs this organisation, why don't you ask her to take you there?'

I rang Baroness Nicholson's office at Westminster.

'Well, we have taken a few journalists out to the marsh areas,' she said. 'But we'd want some undertaking that you'd give our charity a proper mention in your piece. A few journalists we've taken there have only given us a couple of lines. We're not a travel bureau, you know.'

Any organisation that puts conditions on your coverage in exchange for their help is best avoided. I could sympathise if journalists were cynically using her charity as a way of getting access, but not with the stroppy manner in which she assumed I'd do the same. Besides, as a freelance, I couldn't guarantee getting an article in a newspaper at all, never mind one with an agreed quota of plaudits to her charity. 'Looks like we're going down the Marshes alone,' I told Mohammed.

Reluctantly, he agreed. Despite his endless security concerns he would always give in in the end, because I paid him double every day we were outside Baghdad. He also had a suggestion. 'There was a soldier in the armoured corps of which I was commanding. He was from the Marshes. Maybe we can meet his family.'

'Great, do you know where he lives?' I asked. I had in mind a rustic old reed cabin on stilts.

'Under a motorway bridge in Basra, I think, somewhere near city trash dump. They were removed from the marshes by order of Saddam Hussein.'

'Oh.' Perhaps we weren't going to get a *National Geographic* commission. Still, if Mohammed was right, we could do a piece about the Marsh Arabs preferring to live in urban squalor rather than going back to the marshes. And all because they now had telly. It would make a change from their usual picture postcard PR. And, hopefully, piss Baroness Nicholson off a bit.

The prospect of a trip to Basra was appealing for other reasons as well. Too long in Baghdad wore you down after a while. In the three months I'd been here, the city had gone from being eerily empty to the most appalling gridlock, as the lifting of sanctions led to hundreds of thousands of new cars being imported. Travelling even a few miles across town could easily take two or three hours. And the August heat, now at its very fiercest, made it all the worse. It regularly reached 50°C, and sometimes hit 60°C. At night, things got a little cooler, but it was almost impossible to sleep in the Al Majalis's unairconditioned rooms. Within an hour, the entire mattress would be soaked in sweat. In the end I took to dossing on the floor of my hotel room, although even then I tended to stay awake half the night. At around 3am, I'd finally collapse into unconsciousness from sheer exhaustion, until the onset of the morning heat a few hours later made sleep impossible again.

We left for Basra at five in the morning, to avoid the worst of the heat. Still, by 9am even at 100kph and with all four windows down, it was like travelling in a fan-assisted oven. I drank water constantly, sweating it out at such a rate that my hair dried in a tangle of salt-crusted strands.

En route, I wanted to stop off to look at the Garden of Eden. According to the *Bradt Travel Guide to Iraq*, the marshlands of ancient Mesopotamia were where the lush, fruit-filled expanses of Eden had once stood. I found it hard to believe that anywhere this hot could ever have remotely qualified as Paradise, although it did perhaps explain why Adam and Eve hadn't bothered with clothes. Legend had it that the Tree of Knowledge, from which Eve picked the apple, was still standing down at Qurnah, a small town on what used to be the marshes' northern edge. This I could buy. Somehow it seemed very plausible that the tree which sparked all the world's troubles had sprung up from Iraqi soil.

We reached Qurnah after about six hours' drive. On either side of the road, you could see what remained of the marshes, small puddles of oily swamp and the odd stagnant pond, surrounded by barren desert. The Tree of Knowledge was supposed to be next to the town's only hotel, which had been built for foreign tourists but didn't look like it had been in use for at least a decade. The proprietor directed us to a walled garden at the back where we found a withered stump of dead wood about ten feet high, with the ground around it concreted over.

'Where's the tree, then?' I asked.

'That's it,' said Mohammed.

It was good for firewood and nothing more, and given the enthusiasm with which Iraqis had looted everything else in recent months, I was amazed no one had chopped it down. Still, it was a piece of history, or at least a good pub tale. I handed the video camera to Mohammed and told him to film me while I stood beside it.

'Can you touch the tree please, Colin?' he said, peering through the lens.

'If you say so.'

'Ah, there we go. Here are you, the first English man touching this tree since maybe 25 years.'

'Maybe since Adam himself, mate. You know he was British, don't you?'

'No. Adam was an Iraqi.'

No wonder mankind is in such a mess.

*****

An hour later we neared the outskirts of Basra. It was, amazingly, even grubbier than Baghdad – built from the same drab, beige breezeblock as the capital, but more cheaply. While Baghdad looked like it had been neglected for 15 years, Basra looked like it had never been finished in the first place. Amid the rows of squat, scruffy villas were vast swathes of open earth, as if someone had cleared a spot for development and then wisely thought better of it. The place also stank – whereas Baghdad whiffed from time to time, this place had an all-pervading odour of sewage, rotting rubbish and God only knew what else. Even the Colonel, who'd been stationed here during the Iran-Iraq war, could point out only one feature worthy of note.

'You see that place over there?' he said, as we drove past a vast, Soviet-style prefab housing complex that looked like a council estate from the innermost circle of hell. 'When I was here with the army, I used to fuck a woman who lived there.'

To my horror, the heat down here was even worse than up north. Worse still, it was hideously humid because of the nearby Gulf. Up in the dry heat of Baghdad, you sweated what felt like water. Down here, you sweated what felt like maple syrup. It stuck your clothes to your skin like never-drying superglue, and it was vile.

We headed downtown to check out the hotels. Overlooking the Shatt-al-Arab waterway was the Basra Sheraton, once popular with guests from nearby Kuwait on drinking, gambling and whoring weekends. It now stood looted and empty. The other options weren't much better. The cheapest place we checked out, which didn't even have a name, was just a collection of small, windowless dormitories, with nothing save a bed, a hairy blanket, and the unmistakeable smell of whoever'd sweated it out there the night before. A medium-priced $15-a-night establishment nearby looked OK at first, until Mohammed mentioned that it had been officially contracted out to the Iraqi army during the Iran-Iraq war. One of the perks the hotel had offered was a complimentary prostitute upon production of an Iraqi army officer's card. The thought of sleeping in a bed where thousands of Mohammed's colleagues had fornicated away the stresses of battle did not appeal.

Eventually we settled on a small two-storey place called the Ibn al Haitham. At $25 a night, it was nearly double my normal accepted travel budget, but it did at least have air-conditioning. In this humidity, that was less a luxury and more a life support system. The moment we wandered into the air-conditioned twin room I'd rented, the sweat vanished in the dry air almost instantly. I wanted to stay in there and never come out.

'Is the weather always like this down here?' I asked Mohammed, as I flopped down on the bed.

'This is a special kind of weather that they have in Basra. When it is hot, the warm, wet air comes in from the sea. It lasts for two or three days and then goes away. It is terrible, filthy weather, making everyone stinky with the bad smell.'

'So do the people of Basra just get used to it?'

'No. It makes them crazy.'

The prospect of even leaving the hotel room again was pretty grim, never mind spending several days working here as planned. We stayed in for the rest of the evening, watching Arabic pop programmes on the hotel's communal satellite TV. The remote control was in the hands of the receptionist downstairs. As the evening wore on, his choice of viewing suggested he had more than just the remote in his hands. The pop programmes gave way to a succession of Italian porn channels and just as I was fearing Mohammed announcing that he was getting 'erect' again, a lorry pulled into the hotel car park, and the images of naked women gyrating to Euro-pop abruptly switched back to a religious channel playing Koranic prayer music.

'See, this is the new Iraq,' muttered Mohammed, disgusted. 'The people are watching the sexy movies, but still pretending they are religious to everybody else.'

Outside, the driver of the lorry was in a hushed conversation with someone from the hotel. On closer inspection, the lorry turned out to be a fire engine. A fire hose was unravelled and led somewhere into the bowels of the building. If this was an emergency call-out, it was a very low-key one.

'What are they doing, Mohammed? We're not on fire, are we?'

'No. The fireman is selling his water to the hotel. I heard them saying earlier that there is a shortage of water here in Basra right now. Problems with power too. Nobody is having any water unless they pay for it. That is why we are paying so much for this shit hotel.'

'Doesn't that mean that the fire engine has no water to put out fires with?'

'Yes. It is, let's say, a corrupt thing. But at least we can take a shower.'

In between trying to locate Mohammed's Marsh Arab soldier friend – we didn't even know if he was still alive – we looked into the problems with the electricity and water. After all, Basra was being run by the British, who were supposed to be much better at this sort of thing than the Americans. If they were making as much of a mess as the Americans were in Baghdad, that was news.

We went to city hall, where a new Iraqi governor had recently been installed. Snaking around the building was a long line of stationary cars, part of a queue for a petrol station nearly a mile and a half a way. Without adequate electricity supplies, the petrol pumps had gone the same way as the water. Some of the motorists had been waiting there for two days, sleeping in their cars and passing the time by swapping conspiracy theories about who was to blame. Nobody pointed the finger at the Iraqi governor's office directly in front of them. Instead they looked to the people they saw as Basra's real masters. The British.

'I've been queuing since 8pm last night,' snarled a taxi driver called Abdul Ruzak, clad in a filthy white dishdasha robe that had doubled as both nightwear and daywear. 'Every car you see here has done the same. Cut the ears off the British. We wish Saddam was back.'

Inside the town hall, work had ground to a halt after the air conditioning had conked out. Several hundred staff, sweating in suits and business dresses, sat around idly, fanning themselves with municipal documents. I asked why nobody seemed to be doing any work. 'We cannot fill out any official forms because our hands are too sweaty,' said one clerk. 'Every time you try to write something, the paper gets wet and the ink smudges.'

Eventually we got to see the deputy governor, Mezher Kherallah. As Basra's second citizen, he had one of the few rooms with a functioning fan. Even so, he wasn't in a much better mood than the motorists queuing outside. 'I haven't slept properly for two days, because there is no electricity for air conditioning at my house,' he growled, rubbing a bleary eye. 'My wife and children are suffering too. It is just one nightmare after another.'

The problem, he said, was that Basra's ramshackle electricity, water and fuel systems were all interconnected. The hotter the weather, the more people switched on their air-conditioning. The more air-conditioning they used, the greater the demand on the electricity supply. Eventually the whole thing had overloaded and crashed. That, in turn, meant more people using petrol generators at home, which, in turn, meant fuel supplies running low. Lack of fuel, for some reason I couldn't quite understand, also made it hard to pump water. It was a vicious circle, Mr Kherallah said, now building up into a perfect storm because of the appalling humidity. With every passing hour, Basra's one million people were getting hotter, sweatier, and tetchier.

'I am telling you, the people are cursing the British for this,' he warned. 'I hate to say it, because we normally have a good relationship together, but Basra will soon become another Fallujah if it goes on like this much longer.'

*****

Mohammed eventually tracked down his Marsh Arab soldier, living in a rented breeze-block building in a slum neighbourhood. Other Basrans, Mohammed said, had not welcomed the Marsh Arabs' forced resettlement into the city. The commonly-held opinion was that they were vagabonds who had only themselves to blame for incurring Saddam's wrath. It was also widely believed that they had replaced their huntin', boatin' and fishin' lifestyle with less romantic cottage industries like robbing, thieving and carjacking. Ask who'd been responsible for the post-war looting in Basra, and many people spat out the word 'madan', the local slang for Marsh Arabs. It translated literally as 'yokels'.

Mohammed's former soldier was called Salah, a 22-year-old private with a wispy, adolescent moustache. He came out of his breeze-block shack and gave the Colonel a warm hug. That cheered me up; if nothing else, it was evidence that Mohammed hadn't terrorised his own troops. After a few rounds of tea with about twenty uncles and cousins, we headed off with Salah and his father and grandfather to see their old marshland hangouts. We headed out of town, along a bumpy raised track that meandered through endless sets of empty reservoirs. It was part of a mish-mash of dykes and dams that Saddam had built to isolate the marshes into small sections. Without streams of water to feed them, said Mohammed, they'd rapidly dried out into desert scrub. Here and there were scattered remnants of the old life. There were a few remaining pools of mud with water buffalo in them, and the odd abandoned boat lying beached in the middle of a stretch of sand. Salah's father, Hussein Sabih Ali, pointed to a building on the distant horizon, shimmering in the heat. It was Basra International Airport, where the British Army now had their HQ.

'In 1990, the Ba'ath Party told us we had ten hours to leave the Marshes,' he said. 'They said if we didn't, they would start shelling us from the airport. In the end, our homes were burnt, bulldozed and destroyed like thousands of other villages. Previously our life was very good, you know. The fish was very close, the birds, the palms, the rice, all you had to was reach outside your house. Now we have no work, and we must buy all our food, not sell it. It is a miserable existence, I tell you.'

Finally, a little further down the road, we found a patch of intact marshland stretching for several acres. Palm trees and tall reed beds clustered around a lagoon of turquoise water, where a small boy was poling a box-shaped dinghy around. It was a delightful waterside idyll, Constable come to Mesopotamia. I started filming. Then Mohammed's voice cut in.

'Come on, we have to go back to Basra now,' he hissed.

'Eh? Aren't we going to see Salah's old house?'

'No. That is still several kilometres from here. But there has been a big fight this week between two of the tribes of the marshes. With Kalashnikov and heavy machine gun. Ten are dead. If we go any further, they will think we are a party of fighters from one tribe or other, looking to get revenge.'

'And let me guess, we will get fucked through and through, right?'

'Most certainly.'

We turned round and went back to Salah's for yet more tea. I talked with his father and grandfather about the plans to re-flood the marshes, and the doubts in many quarters over whether it would actually work. Critics of the scheme had pointed out that you couldn't recreate an entire complex eco-system of plants, birds and insect life overnight. Once the marshes had dried out, all the salt in the soil had been sucked to the surface. If you simply added water again, all you would get was a barren, saline slush.

Not that they were all nostalgic for the old days. Muslam Hawash, Salah's grandfather, explained how he'd left the marshes of his own accord back in 1960. 'Back then, these hands would be swollen by the water, cut to pieces by the reeds, and bitten by the mosquitoes,' he said, holding up what looked like two bunches of thick oak twigs. 'Now I have electricity, a TV, and the roof doesn't leak. I couldn't go back to that life. If I want to go fishing, I go to the port at Basra.'

Back at the hotel, I settled down to write a couple of pieces for the *Scotsman*. One was about the Marsh Arabs, the other was about how Basra's good relationship with the British was wilting in the summer heat. To my immense relief, the blanket of humid air that had smothered the city finally moved on. But by the time we headed back to Baghdad at dawn the next morning, it was back with a vengeance. We drove out of town past the same petrol queue that was still snaking around the town hall. It was now at least twice as long as it had been before.

Twelve hours later I staggered back into the Al Majalis and bumped into Jean-Philippe, a French journalist who'd also holed up there. 'Did you hear the news about Basra?' he asked.

'No. What's happened?'

'There is riots there. The people are fighting with the British. Saying they don't have electricity and petrol. It started this afternoon. Not long after you left, probably.'

I went to the internet café to find out more. Sure enough, angry crowds had attacked the governor's building and the neighbouring Coalition offices. It would have made a great dateline to have been there, but I didn't feel particularly sorry that we'd pulled out just beforehand. The pictures looked bloody terrifying.

The wire reports linked the disturbances to the fuel and power shortages. Personally, though, I reckoned the final spark was the humidity. It had nearly driven me mad, and I'd only had a few hours of it. It was no coincidence, surely, that the rioting had exploded the morning it returned.

*****

A week later I decided I needed a rest and booked a flight back to London from Amman. Mohammed treated me to a booze-up to celebrate our time together, during which he anxiously cross-examined me on whether I was coming back or not. I said I needed to get back home first and see how I felt.

'Let me know as soon as you can,' he said. 'With no job, I am fucked through and through.'

I scrounged a lift to Amman from a CNN TV crew, where I went to one of the grimy bars downtown and drank several self-congratulatory beers alone. Eight months previously, I'd been on the brink of an early mid-life crisis, my career going nowhere. Now, despite all the risks and uncertainty, it had all worked out. I'd earned enough money to pay my bills and I'd never felt happier. Working in a lawless, messed-up country, staying in a shitty hotel, and having a lunatic ex-Iraqi tank commander as my main companion had filled some odd-shaped void in my life.

When I touched down at Heathrow, my friends Max, Dominic and Neil had turned up to welcome me back. They stood outside the main arrivals area, and clapped as I walked out. They'd brought a bottle of champagne, which we drank as Dominic drove us back into London. I couldn't believe how orderly everything was. The streets seemed incredibly clean and polished, even in Camberwell. When red traffic lights loomed, Dominic actually stopped.

For the next three weeks I relaxed, treating friends and family to film shows of my video diary from Iraq. In what was surely a first for a home movie, people didn't actually fall asleep after the first ten minutes.

Then, with not much else to do, I packed my bags and prepared to head back.

Contractual Disputes

ARRIVING BACK IN Amman for the haul back to Baghdad, I switched my satphone on for the first time since leaving Iraq. There were three voice messages, all originating from a satellite phone number belonging to Jean-Philippe. He also knew Mohammed, and it turned out to be the Colonel himself, sounding even more Dalek-like than ever via the space link.

August 22nd, at 5.01pm. 'Colin, hello, I am Mohammed. When are you coming back?'

August 29th, at 2.45pm. 'Colin, hello, I am Mohammed. Man, I have no money and needing the job most desperately. Please ring Jean-Philippe speedily.'

September 5th, at 5.25pm. 'OK, COLIN, FUCK YOU! YOU ARE MY FRIEND BUT YOU DON'T EVEN RING BACK TO ME. FUCK YOU! I WILL FIND THE NEW JOB BY MYSELVES.'

What was he on about? He hadn't been short of cash when I'd left. And why was it my fault? I'd tried to fix him up with work to tide him over before I left by introducing him to a female Japanese newspaper journalist who was in town for three weeks.

I gave Jean-Philippe a ring and got Mohammed to call me. He apologised for swearing, but explained that there'd been a major crisis. The air conditioning unit in his house had broken down. That didn't sound like a *crisis*, exactly, but Iraqis have a surprising capacity to get worked up about seemingly minor things while remaining heroically stoical about major ones. Repairs to the unit were going to cost several hundred dollars, he said. Meanwhile, my Japanese reporter had taken one look at him and decided he looked too dodgy. So he'd been out of funds.

'Don't worry, I'll be back in Baghdad in a couple of days,' I said. 'You'll be earning again soon.'

'It is too late. I am going to make acceptance of a new job. Driving and translating for your friend Ryan.'

Bollocks. I should have known this might happen. 'Ryan' was Ryan Manelick, a colleague of John Dawkins and Omar Hadi's at Ultra Services. An ex-US Air Force guy who'd come out to Iraq to help with the procurement business, he was about my age, and had stayed at the Al Majalis for a while, kindly supplying me with MREs that he picked up from his various business trips around US Army bases. He was a nice, friendly guy, although I knew he'd been eyeing up Mohammed as a potential hire. However, he'd assured me that he wouldn't poach him, despite the fact that he could offer better money. Had he gone against me behind my back?

I put the phone down, cursing. Half the reason I'd decided to go back to Iraq was because Mohammed made the place just about bearable. On the kind of wages I was willing to pay, it might take months to find another good translator. During which time I'd find it impossible to earn any money. Already worried about my cash flow, I took a bus rather than a taxi back into Baghdad. It cost a mere $25, and drove all night rather than stopping at the Iraqi border and waiting for daytime. Apparently the robbers considered it beneath their dignity to soil their hands with people who couldn't afford their own cars.

I got into Baghdad and arranged to meet Mohammed at a little shebeen that we sometimes drank in around the corner from the hotel. It was a bare room behind a boarded-up shop, kitted out with a few wicker chairs and a screen in the corner playing some Lebanese version of MTV. A bloke in the corner sold cans of Turkish Efes beer, while another guy sat by the door with a pistol in case of trouble. It was the nearest thing Baghdad had to a pub. Most of the city's other watering holes, such as 'Saddoun Street Nights', a garish fleshpot near the Palestine Hotel, hadn't yet re-opened for fear of Islamist attacks.

As soon as Mohammed turned up I noticed a new swagger about him. Tucked in his waist belt was a Thuraya satphone like my own. He was wearing it like he'd have worn a pistol in his old days as an armoured officer, there for all to be in awe of. Where had he got the money for that from? He'd obviously started working for Ryan already.

'So how much is he paying you?' I asked, cracking open an Efes.

'$20 a day.'

'$20 a day? I can pay you that. By the way, did he come to you while I was away?'

'No. I will be honest. I went to him. Listen, it is not about the money. Ryan can offer me permanent job. For two years maybe. Helping to build the company. Also, in time he can employ my seven brothers. Can you offer me that? For how long will you even stay here in Baghdad?'

He had a point. The slightest thing could send me scuttling back home at any moment. Getting robbed or threatened, falling ill, a car accident, straying near a gunfight, running out of work. Or just getting plain bored. Not that I was letting him know that.

'I might be here another two or three years myself. And anyway, I thought you liked working with me? Working with Ryan will be boring. Just delivering toilets and stuff. You're a man of action. Like me.'

'Of course I am. And yes, I would prefer this working with you. But it is my family. They are saying "Mohammed, why are you accepting this employment with the journalist, when there is a job for every man in the homestead with the firm of Ryan?" They will not permit it.'

I gave in. I knew from bitter experience that once his mind was made up about something, it was impossible to change it. Especially on financial matters. 'Well, come back to me if it doesn't work out,' I said. 'I'll miss you, you know.'

He began to laugh. 'Most honestly, you are talking like some bitch who has lost her boyfriend. "Oh, Mohammed, Mohammed, please don't go..."'

'Yes, yes, alright. And meanwhile, where am I going to find a new translator?'

'For that I have already made a fixing. Two of my friends from the high-ranking military, both colonels staff. One is speaking English and can translate, the other will drive. They have not dealt with a foreigner before, but they will be adoptable to that. I have talked to them already. They will accept $10 a day each.'

'Didn't you say you had a mate who was a general who spoke English? Can't I have him?'

'I asked, but he would not accept. It is beneath him.'

We parted company and I headed back to my hotel room. My old friend the Al Majalis was shut for much-needed repairs until mid-

October, so I was staying at the Al Andalous, the place next door that stank of mushrooms. It hadn't got any more fragrant since I'd last crossed its threshold on my first night in Baghdad five months ago. It seemed like yet another sign that this trip might not be quite like the last. Was I pushing my luck a little to expect it to go well a second time?

A couple of days later Mohammed introduced me to my new workmates. One turned out to be Colonel Saba, the weapons instructor at whose house I'd filmed the Kalashnikov video. The other was Colonel Ali, a former artillery man. He'd served in the Republican Guard, the elite special force directly accountable to Saddam. To be honest, he looked neither elite nor special. He was placid and boyish-faced, with a figure like a mid-career British darts champion. But his English was good, and Mohammed vouched for his integrity. Mohammed had studied with both Ali and Saba at the Indian Military Academy, where they'd gone for further training after graduating from officer training school in Baghdad. He'd showed me old photos of the three of them in their student days, similar to the ones I had from my own time at college. While mine were of various fellow layabouts brandishing beers, his showed three fit, disciplined young men parading in smart white uniforms and beating each other up in army boxing contests. Saba, who had been the Indian Military Academy's heavyweight boxing champ, would now be my bodyguard and driver.

I flung myself into work as much as possible, anxious to test out my new team. The staples of the news agenda were pretty much as before: the insurgency, the lack of security and electricity, and occasional more upbeat pieces on life in the 'New Iraq', such as the start of the new school year, the first without Saddam as headmaster-in-chief. The *Scotsman* commissioned a 'back to school' piece, for which I interviewed a couple of teachers. They'd spent the whole summer holidays going through the school textbooks and tearing out the photos of Saddam, whose smug face was usually the only splash of colour in otherwise pictureless tracts. He typically appeared under the unassuming caption of *High Excellency, Struggler Against Zionist Imperialism, Field Marshal and Commander of All Iraq*. Flicking through the wooden dialogue passages of an English language textbook, I saw his government's efforts at brainwashing.

Librarian: 'Do you want another book on the Palestinians?'

Student: 'No thanks. I'd rather read one about the revolution of the Arab Ba'ath Socialist Party.'

Librarian: 'They're working hard for our educational programme.'

Student: 'Oh, that's great!'

Aside from set pieces like the back-to-school story, though, I kept running out of things to do. Asked by *The Scotsman*'s foreign editor to compile a list of future story ideas, I couldn't get much further than a visit to meet a fortune teller Saba knew or a feature on the start of the Baghdad cockfighting season.

Neither were going to win Foreign Journalist of the Year. But I pressed ahead regardless. Maybe at the cockfighting ring, people would be betting on two cocks named Saddam and Bush, which would give the story the news angle it otherwise completely lacked.

When we got there, we found out the season didn't start for another two months.

Saba's fortune teller, a wizened fellow in his 60s, wasn't much better.

'So what kind of things do people ask him about?' I asked Ali, handing the fortune teller a $10 consultation fee. 'Is it if they're to fall in love, that sort of thing?'

'Not any more. Now, it's mainly robberies, carjackings and murders.'

'What, he tells them if they're going to get robbed or murdered?'

'No. People only come to him when it has already happened. Then he tells them who did it.'

'How does he know?'

'He asks to the spirits. They are called in Arabic the *djinn*. Just like the whisky you drink in England.'

'But what if the *djinn* are wrong?'

'He says the *djinn* are always right.'

God only knew how many innocent people were getting wrongly accused and killed because of this bloke. Although, given what I'd seen of the new Iraqi police force, his guess was probably as good as anybody's. I was curious to know why Saba believed in such mumbo jumbo, given that he was supposedly an educated member of Iraq's military elite.

'Once, when Saba was living in a military barracks, he lost his pistol. He suspected another colonel had taken it, so he went to this fortune teller to find out.'

'And was it the other colonel?'

'Yes. The fortune teller confirmed it. And then one day the pistol just reappeared in Saba's room.'

'And did the other colonel get punished?'

'No. There was no proof. But the next year, he was jailed for six months for stealing an air conditioning unit.'

The Iraqi spirits clearly moved in mysterious ways.

*****

One day we returned from another fruitless newsgathering expedition to find the Al Andalous hotel surrounded by several US Humvees. Inside, several soldiers were stood at reception.

'Excuse me, what's going on?' I asked. 'I'm a journalist, I live at this hotel.'

The soldiers didn't look like they believed me on either count. They refused to tell me anything, but after they left the receptionist said they'd examined the guest register. 'American look for men from Syria, Yemen.' When I asked why, he imitated the sound of a bomb blowing up.

Carbombers. They'd been coming in in growing numbers ever since mid-summer, adding a new, psychotic ingredient to Baghdad's unholy mix of criminality. Unlike the insurgents, their targets weren't just US troops. They'd also hit some of the new Iraqi police stations and a string of embassies belonging to other Arab nations, warning fellow Muslims not to give diplomatic recognition to occupied Iraq. Their highest-profile attack so far had been on the United Nations' Baghdad HQ, when I was back home in August. A car bomber had driven in during a press conference, killing 19 people, including the UN's head of mission, Sergio Vieira de Mello. By the end of September, they were blowing themselves up on average about once a week, sending muffled thumps sounding across the city. *The Scotsman* normally wanted a piece from the scene, but I soon ran out of fresh ways to describe the aftermath, partly because the bodies and mangled limbs had usually been cleared away by the time I made it to the blast site through Baghdad's traffic. And even if they weren't, *The Scotsman*, like most British newspapers, wouldn't go into the gory details. The one time I filed a piece mentioning how someone's brain was spattered across a wall, they edited it out.

Little was known about who the bombers were. They travelled under false IDs, and left little for forensics to go on after they'd detonated 25 kilos of explosive underneath their car seats. But most were thought to be Al Qaeda footsoldiers who'd slipped across the border from neighbouring Arab countries, intent on derailing the US mission. Their target was not just Coalition soldiers, but anyone trying to make things better, be it Iraqi traffic cops or well-intentioned international outfits like the UN. The fact that the Americans thought my hotel might have been serving as the bombers' last stop-off point was rather disturbing,

I wondered what they hoped to find by scanning the hotel register.

Soldier: 'Have you got any terrorists staying at the moment?'

Receptionist: Yes, there's one in Room 202. A Mr Ali from Syria. Occupation, suicide bomber.'

At least the Al Andalous's terrorist residents could check out to Paradise. I seemed stuck there for good. The savage heat of summer was gradually easing, but that would bring its own problems; soon it would start getting pretty cold at night, and just as the rooms didn't have any air conditioning, they didn't have any heating either. If it rained, God knew what kind of mould and damp would kick back in.

Jean Phillipe, my French colleague, had already moved into a rented flat in a neighbourhood a couple of miles away. It was right next to a mosque, which meant you were blasted with Tannoyed prayer calls from 5am onwards, but at least it had a kitchen where you could cook your own food. I'd begun to worry about the long-term health effects of my 'mini bar' diet of crisps, chocolate, Coca Cola and beer. Right now, the only thing preventing me getting scurvy was when I forgot to remove the disgusting gherkins from the street kebabs I still occasionally ate. If I could find a flat with a kitchen myself, I figured, I could buy vegetables and chicken from the markets and knock up some sort of stir fry.

Another reason for leaving the Al Andalous was that the streetlife around the hotel seemed to be getting steadily rowdier. Gunfire was more frequent than ever, and often loud enough to make me glance out on the balcony to see if it was on our street. One day I looked down to see Hassan, the glue-sniffing local shoeshine man, curled up in a pool of blood. A man was stood over him with a pistol. He'd shot Hassan in the foot. The gunman calmly stuck his pistol back in his belt, strode unhurriedly back to his car, and drove off. As Hassan lay there clutching his foot and yelping in pain, a crowd of gathered round, more to spectate than to help. Eventually someone hailed a taxi and bundled Hassan into the back seat, counting out a wad of dinars and telling the unsuspecting cabbie to drive him to hospital. Later I learned it was a punishment shooting, possibly over a drug debt, possibly over something Hassan had said to the guy while out of his mind on shoe-polish. Whatever it was, nobody thought of getting the brave new Iraqi cops on the case. A couple of days later, Jean-Philippe told me that the flat above his was up for rent. I moved in straightaway.

The rent was $200 a month, which got me three rooms, a kitchen and a combined shower and hole-in-the-floor toilet. The lounge had a hideous mustard-yellow sofa running around its perimeter, with an ornate gilt headrests. Similar specimens snaked round the contours of nearly every Iraqi living room I'd been in, sometimes 20 or 30 feet long, like they'd been ordered by the yard. There was also a desk, a cooker, and a broken-down radiogram that didn't look like it had played a record since about 1955. The place had the feel of one of those drab, lonely flats in which British spies ended their days after defecting to Moscow, but flathunting in Baghdad was more about security than style. It was on a main road, which meant I didn't have to wander down empty side streets as I came and went. And its owner had a grocery shop directly beneath, which meant that from dawn till nightfall he had an eye on the stairwell.

The flat was also only about a mile away from the Al Hamra, which had replaced the Palestine as the main hangout for foreign journalists. It looked like a cheap hotel on the Spanish Costa: a cramped compound of not-so-whitewashed tower blocks gathered around a small swimming pool. But compared to the cavernous, impersonal blocks of the Palestine, it was almost boutique. The Hamra sold more-or-less edible hamburgers and more-or-less drinkable wine, and at nights the tables around the pool would draw in an eclectic crowd. Any newly-arrived journalist needing to dash off a quick 'life in occupied Iraq' atmosphere piece needed only to describe the evening drinking scene on their doorstep. Mingling with the hacks would be teams of Texan contractors in Stetsons, groups of Arab businessmen, US military commanders sipping diet cokes, and parties of preppy-looking Coalition officials who'd got security clearance for a night outside the Green Zone. The latter always looked rather excited, like schoolkids who'd escaped from a particularly strict boarding school. There was also a shadowy fraternity of gun-toting Westerners in what were dubbed 'combat casuals' – khaki trousers, hiking boots and dark glasses, with a pistol in a holster strapped fashionably low around the thigh. They tended not to talk to anyone else, although every now and then you'd overhear the odd intriguing snatch of conversation from their tables: *'Did I ever tell you about the armoured Volvo I had in Chad in 1984?' 'Hey, what's Afghan Bob up to these days?'* Many were just ex-military guys working as private security guards. But in most of the articles written about the Hamra poolside scene, the inevitable assumption was that they were CIA men of some sort.

Now and then I'd spend an evening at the Hamra with Omar Hadi and Ryan Manelick. I thought my line of work was haphazard, but it was nothing compared to theirs. As we'd sit drinking, their satphones would ring constantly as various deals were thrashed out around the Middle East. Where were the 200 computers for the US Army base in Tikrit? Why was that consignment of shower units still stuck at the Turkish border? Could they deliver 10 tonnes of cement from Jordan by next week? And by the way, did they know anyone who had a crane? It didn't matter whether it was a product or a line of business they knew anything about; in Iraq, all anyone cared about was whether you could supply it, or something that would pass for it.

The rewards were lucrative. Omar, who'd set up a sideline in supplying Iraqi staff to act as bag searchers at the Presidential Palace, was already rumoured to be earning six figures. But the competition was cut-throat. Most of their rivals were wily, tough operators, who specialised in working in countries with no real business laws, or at least none that couldn't be bent by bribes or threats. Many had a distinct air of sleaze. They were typically blokes in their late 40s or early 50s, often with only a hotel room, business card and satphone to their names. Their pasty, haggard faces spoke of lifetimes spent cracking shady deals in hotel lobbies, hoping to turn a profit before whichever junta they'd paid off collapsed. Omar's friend, John Dawkins, who'd worked in Russia, and Afghanistan, was used to them, but Omar himself found it a bit of a learning curve. One day, he visited an American contractor to discuss a purchase of some bulletproof vests. The door opened to reveal a hippyish figure covered in tattoos and smoking a joint. He introduced Omar first to an unfeasibly young-looking girlfriend, and then to a fully-grown eagle, which he'd bought as a pet from one of the downtown bird markets.

Most of the contractors knew each other, got drunk together, and forged *ad hoc* partnerships for business deals, but it wasn't exactly Baghdad Rotary Club. Because everyone was out for themselves, business partners had a habit of becoming business enemies when things went wrong, and they often did. It was rare to meet a contractor who didn't complain how so-and-so had ripped him off for $50,000, or how so-and-so had tried to get him framed, and how so-and-so was fucking dead if he saw him again. Occasionally, you'd then bump into so-and-so, who'd tell you exactly the same thing the opposite way round.

One episode that typified the bizarre working world of contracting was Omar and Ryan's dealings with a guy called Phil Bloom, an American who'd pitched up in Baghdad after previously working in Romania. He'd asked them to supply him with some mobile homes, which Omar, who'd originally trained as an architect, was making from scratch as another sideline. They were simple things, constructed from not much more than a few steel frames and sandwich panels, but they were in huge demand on US Army bases. Bloom had a client who wanted some, and Omar agreed to get a sample delivered to him in the Green Zone. Bloom then rang back to say he wanted it there at 9am the very next day. Unfortunately, the only sample Omar had at that time was languishing in a base in Balad, 100 miles north of Baghdad. When he explained this, Bloom threw a fit. Anxious not to let a new client down, Omar and Ryan roped in Colonel Mohammed, who pulled off a stroke of fixing that outclassed anything he'd ever done for me. Within the space of a single hour late on a Friday night, he organised a crane, a flatbed truck and a team of armed guards, who then spirited the mobile home right through the Sunni Triangle in the dead of night. Bloom then inspected it the next morning, said it wasn't the one he'd seen in the photo, and threatened to cut Ryan's balls off.

It was probably just as well that the business relationship withered then and there. Bloom ended up in jail after being convicted of fraudulently obtaining nearly $9 million in contracts by bribing US officials with cars, booze and prostitutes.

In between dodging each other, contractors also had to watch out for the insurgents, who regarded them as both the supporters and profiteers of the occupation, and, as such, even more contemptible than those in uniform. Ryan and John were particularly at risk. Ultra Services had won most of its contracts at US army bases north of Baghdad. Doing business there involved lots of travel on lonely desert roads, where insurgents might attack at any minute. Unlike the big corporate contracting firms, Ultra Services didn't have the luxury of armoured cars or US military escorts. One day, a carload of armed men chased and shot at John in his 4x4; his laptop, stashed in the back seat, ended up with a bullet in it. From then on he resorted to disguise: he dyed his hair black, stained his skin darker, grew a moustache and started dressing in Iraqi robes and headdress. Ryan and Mohammed, meanwhile, resorted to weapons. First pistols, then MP5s – snub-nosed, folding-stock sub-machine guns that could fire about 600 rounds a minute. They cost about $1,500 apiece, and were considered a status symbol among the gun-carrying classes of Baghdad. The few Iraqis who had them carried them as proudly as Prada handbags. Normally they had to be imported from Europe, but Mohammed sourced them in a couple of hours in Saddam City, a vast slum on the east side of town that was home to Baghdad's last big weapons *souk*. Mohammed got them boxed and in mint condition, and at half the price they sold for on the legal market.

Despite the dangers, Ryan was loving every moment of being in Iraq. Like me, he'd come out here to escape a broken relationship and career drift. He'd quit the Air Force a few years ago and worked variously as a bartender, a comic store shop assistant and carer to handicapped children. Being in Baghdad had plugged all the gaps in his life at once. He was seeing a bit of life, helping a shattered country rebuild itself and, hopefully, earning enough money to make maintenance payments for his three kids. I got on well with him. Unlike many other contractors, who tended to be either sleazy, or taciturn, or both, he was a garrulous, happy-go-lucky character. Too many foreigners in Baghdad played it like they'd seen it all before.

Ryan, like me, was happy to admit that it was all just a big new adventure to be relished. He'd taken a perverse pleasure in the privations of the Al Majalis hotel, he enjoyed Mohammed's eccentric company, and, in a place where people liked to give the impression that they knew what they were doing, would gleefully relate stories about the days when things didn't quite go according to plan.

He also had no shortage of absurdly grandiose get-rich quick schemes, such as his project to secure Iraq's highways by setting up a network of interconnected watchtowers every five kilometres. It wasn't actually a bad idea, but there was no chance a small outfit like Ultra Services was going to get the contract. Some people claimed to detect a Walter Mittyish quality in him, an idealism that betrayed a slight naivety about the dangerous world he was working in. Like me, he was forever getting chided by Mohammed over his own personal security. He'd think nothing of driving home from the Hamra hotel in his 4x4 late at night, handing his MP5 to Omar or whoever else happened to be sat in the front seat. He became the only Westerner in living memory to go water-skiing down the Tigris, hiring an old speedboat and some ancient waterskis from a guy who owned a marina. Mohammed pointed out that the riverbank was a popular place for people to go drinking and shoot guns, and was convinced that any reasonable-minded drunkard would naturally want to fire a few good-natured blasts at the passing speedboat. He insisted on sitting on board the boat with a pistol, scouring the horizon for trouble as if back on patrol in the southern Iraqi marshes. Ryan didn't care about the danger. 'If I get shot waterskiing down in a war zone, that is one hell of a thing to have on my tombstone,' he said. He roped in a photographer from the Hamra to take pictures, and I sent out a story. It made a page lead in the *Sun*.

Not everyone was as impressed by such stunts as the *Sun* newsdesk. John felt it was a bad idea to draw attention to oneself. It wasn't his only complaint about Ryan either. John had hired him to work in Iraq on the recommendation of Ryan's father, Greg Manelick, whom he knew from working in Russia. But after just a summer working together, John and Ryan were beginning to fall out. John, now based mainly in Istanbul, reckoned Ryan was irresponsible and disorganised. Ryan, who was the operations manager on the ground in Baghdad, accused John of taking contracts that the company couldn't deliver and leaving him to pick up the pieces. Who was really at fault, I had no idea. Fall-outs and bust-ups, it was clear, were par for the course in the contracting business.

Then, in mid-October, word got round of a mysterious incident at Ultra Services. It involved Kirk von Ackermann, a 37-year-old American who'd been brought in to work in Baghdad as a manager alongside Ryan. I'd met him only once at a barbecue at the Hamra, and all I knew about him was that he was an ex-airman like Ryan, and that he'd previously worked in counter-terrorism. There was nothing particularly unusual about that. The contracting scene in Iraq was full of ex-forces people, hired partly because they knew their way around the US military, and partly because they knew how to handle themselves in dangerous places.

On October 9th, Kirk had been on one of Ultra Service's periodic tours of US army bases in the Sunni Triangle. The journey finished with an afternoon's drive from Saddam Hussein's home town of Tikrit across a range of low hills to the northern city of Kirkuk. *En route*, he'd called one of Ultra Services' local Iraqi employees to tell him that his 4x4 had a flat tyre which he couldn't fix. Could the employee come out to help? About 45 minutes later, the employee arrived to find the 4x4 still parked by the roadside, but no sign of Kirk. His satphone, laptop, and a briefcase containing about $40,000 in $100 bills were still in the vehicle's back seat, suggesting he hadn't been the victim of a robbery. Nor was there any sign of a struggle. No bullets, no blood, not even marks in the dust. He'd just vanished.

The first I heard of this was when I went round to Ultra Services' new office in Baghdad's posh Mansour neighbourhood, about a week after Kirk went missing. Ryan was there with Charles Phillips, an ex-Harvard graduate who was another of Ultra Services' American employees. They told me that the US Army was now investigating Kirk's disappearance, but nobody was any the wiser as to what had happened. Ryan, debating whether to get me to do a story in case the publicity brought some answers, ran through the various theories. None of them particularly added up. If insurgents or robbers had come across him and carried out an opportunistic hit, why didn't they take his car, or at least the money that was in it? Likewise, if he'd been abducted, where was the ransom note? As a former counter-terrorism officer, Kirk would have been wary of strangers offering him help, and he always carried a gun. 'If anyone had tried to grab him, he'd have shot the fuck out of them,' Ryan reckoned. 'It's a real mystery. It's like he was abducted by aliens.'

A few days later, I drove with Saba and Ali up to the area where Kirk had disappeared, to ask a few questions. I'd heard that a local Iraqi police chief was on the case; perhaps he might spill some details that Ryan and Co were keeping quiet. It turned out he'd recently been sacked after some row with a rival, with none of his successors briefed about the disappearance. Later on, though, when I tracked him down to his house, I found him still in uniform with a dozen odd policemen at his disposal, running what seemed to some kind of parallel force. He claimed to know John Dawkins, and said he had turned up not long before with photocopied pictures of Kirk, asking if anyone had seen him. He directed us to the spot where Kirk had vanished. It was near the brow of a long, winding hilltop road, miles from anywhere and surrounded by rocky outcrops. A long way from any help if you got yourself in a tight spot. At the bottom of the other side of the hill, there was a US Army checkpoint, where Dawkins had handed over a copy of Kirk's photograph. But during troop changeovers, no information was passed on about the case. The newcomers were unaware of who Kirk was, or why they had his photo. In a land where hundreds were dying or disappearing each week, no one had the resources to spend time looking for another missing person.

On The Redneck Riviera

IT WAS EARLY December, and the endless monochrome blue of the summer skies had finally broken. Now the days were short and sometimes overcast, the nights cold and crisp. I was on a three-day embed with a US Army unit in the Sunni Triangle, having asked to go to one of its sharpest, most hostile corners. Sat in front of me in a Humvee was Lieutenant Colonel Aubrey Garner, commander of the 1st Battalion, 68th Armour Regiment. He was giving me a guided tour of his fiefdom, a farming province of palm trees and orange groves about 30 miles north of Baghdad, called Mashahidah. Or, as he nicknamed it, the Redneck Riviera.

Redneck because the locals were mostly rural hicks – poor, uneducated, and hostile to outsiders, especially American soldiers.

Riviera because of the meandering presence of the Tigris, along which Saddam's cronies had built numerous villas and ranch houses. They were vast, nouveau-riche squiredoms that looked like miniatures of the presidential palaces in Baghdad, mostly grace-and-favour homes awarded to people who'd done Saddam some kind of good turn. Now that their benefactor had been deposed, the landed gentry were taking revenge by paying the local peasantry to attack the US Army.

'A lot of the big homes around here are owned by ex-Ba'athists, and they stand to lose their way of life for ever if democracy breaks out,' Garner said, cradling an M4 carbine in his lap as we drove from his base towards Tarmiyah, the local market town. 'I don't think they're doing the fighting directly themselves, but I think they are the guys who are paying people to attack us, orchestrating the violence. They're rednecks in the sense of rural baddies.'

It was certainly bandit country. Every day that Garner's forces surged out along Mashahidah's country lanes, they expected to get attacked. Insurgents would fire bursts of machine gun fire or rocket propelled grenades through the cover of the date palm and orange groves, before melting back into the dense undergrowth. They did their own voodoo-style psy-ops, like leaving dead foxes in the middle of the road with a sign telling the troops to leave. And graffiti here and there proclaimed the presence of insurgent militias like Mohammed's Army and the 9-11 Brigade. 'It's like kids forming a garage band,' said Garner dismissively. 'They just think, "What's the baddest thing we can call ourselves?"'

He was less sanguine about one of their other new tricks. In recent months, the insurgents had begun to use improvised explosive devices, crude home-made bombs consisting of artillery shells wired to detonators that could be let off by remote control as a convoy went past. Small ones might be disguised as Coke cans or wrapped in plastic bags, larger ones were stitched into animal corpses to look like roadkill or buried altogether in the verge. Garner's own convoy had been both IED-d and RPG-d already, both times *en route* to or from Tarmiyah.

The ferocity of the daily hostilities in these areas had taken a long time to reach the outside world. The week before my visit, US troops in Samarra, a city further north, claimed to have killed more than 50 insurgents in a pitched battle. The scale of the clash had prompted talk back home that America was now back at war again. Yet for the troops round here, it had seemed that way for the past six months. Garner's battalion hadn't lost a man in direct combat yet, but they'd had several serious injuries and lost two men in combat-related accidents, both as nasty as anything the insurgents could have wished on them. One company commander was electrocuted when he brushed against low-hanging pylon wires as his Bradley went in pursuit of some men acting suspiciously. Another soldier died when his Humvee overturned into one of the irrigation ditches that lined the farm roads, drowning him in just a few feet of water.

As the convoy rolled into Tarmiyah, I got an idea for the first time what it felt like to be unwelcome in Iraq. Everyone stopped what they were doing to stare, even the people who were sitting doing nothing. None of the hundreds of eyes fixed on us looked friendly. And none of the kids waved in the hope of getting sweets. Garner said that if they did, they usually got a clip round the ear from the nearest responsible adult.

'How the children react is a good indicator of how the town as a whole feels,' he said. 'If the kids give you the thumbs down or throw rocks, there is a good chance you're going to get some kind of action. They generally take their cue from the adults, and if they hear the grown-ups busy cussing us, they take on that attitude too.'

Garner was a sturdy-looking guy in his late 30s, head shaved bald except for a set of dark eyebrows, which spent much of their time knitted together in a pensive expression. He seemed more worldly-wise than many US commanders. He'd done a brief stint in Bosnia, and a spell at Sandhurst, where he'd studied the British Army's tactics in Northern Ireland. Mashahidah's rolling farmlands were his South Armagh: hotter, flatter and drier, but just as deadly. Every country lane was a potential ambush site, every farmyard and shack a potential weapons dump, and every passing labourer a potential pair of eyes and ears, if not willing hands, for the enemy.

The stint at Sandhurst meant Garner was well-drilled in the importance of 'hearts and minds' strategies, and of reaching out to Mashahidah's community leaders. As well as being sheriff he was also mayor, with hundreds of thousands of dollars to spend on the area's ramshackle civic infrastructure. In theory, his cash to build new schools, clinics and police stations would easily outbid the Ba'athist war chest in winning over the locals. But in practice, it wasn't quite like that. Despite endless rounds of glad-handing and cups of tea with local sheikhs, he was sure that some of the money he was handing over for community projects was ending up in the insurgents' pockets. 'If I give money to build a school I am convinced that a certain percentage of it gets channelled into attacks on Coalition forces,' he said.

He couldn't quite prove it, and was wary of making accusations for fear of jeopardising what cordiality remained. But the feeling was there, alright, and it came across in the way he talked about the local Iraqi power brokers he dealt with. Other US commanders I'd met often took a romantic view of the whole thing, telling you how their new sheikh buddies had become their blood brothers, and exchanging Arabic greetings with high fives. For Garner, there was no Lawrence of Arabia stuff. Instead of respect towards the sheikhs, he'd begun to feel anger. Take Sayeed Jassim, a fat local sheikh whose unctuous manner apparently hid all manner of secret agendas. Garner nicknamed him Jabba the Hutt. 'I cannot prove that he is putting money into the insurgents' hands, but I suspect he is involved in planning and funding in some indirect way,' he said. 'I've really focused a lot of my own personal energy in trying to work with people like him, but I haven't got the success I hoped for by that engagement.' His battalion's first posting had been up around the partly Kurdish city of Kirkuk further north. There, his tea-drinking with local sheikhs led to invites to lavish dinners at their private homes. Round here, his social diary remained empty. He gazed out the Humvee's window, where Tarmiyah's young street urchins were wandering around hawking cigarettes and trinkets. 'This thing about tribal sheikhs caring for the poor is bullshit, as far as I can see,' he said. 'They have vast amounts of money, and yet these kids are running around with no shoes on. Some of these sheikhs do not have an egalitarian bone in their bodies.'

Jabba the Hutt was at least friendly on the surface. Some villages hated the Americans so much that they'd have nothing to do with them at all. The battalion's civil projects officer, Major Mary Graf, said that in some of the most hostile areas, their offers of help had simply been turned down point blank. 'It's frustrating,' she said. 'We really thought that we were coming here to liberate, and yet here we find people who don't want to be liberated.'

More sinister still were the sheikhs Garner seldom met, but whose names cropped up a lot in conversation. 'On the few occasions they do turn up, all the other sheikhs in the room suddenly go quiet,' said Garner. 'They are like the Mr Bigs, I guess, the Tony Sopranos.'

Whether these were the real figures behind the insurgency, Garner couldn't be sure. If there was one group of people he'd learned to trust even less than the sheikhs, it was his informants. Many of their tip-offs were malicious, motivated by the hope of getting rid of a business rival or settling a family feud. And when he did catch someone red-handed, he came up against a rural Omerta as strong as anything in the New Jersey mob.

'Recently we did a raid on a chicken farm and found a dozen remote-controlled bomb detonators,' he said. 'We arrested a guy there whom I was pretty convinced was not really the man involved. But he wouldn't admit that it was anybody else. He will probably end up in jail for 15 to 20 years because he agreed to take the rap. It's like dealing with the Mafia. But I'm not the FBI, I'm just a tank commander.'

We pulled in at Tarmiyah's new police station, a low-rise building surrounded by a wall, like a fort in a cowboy movie. Garner had paid for its construction back in September, but two days after it opened, the locals in Tarmiyah had rioted and burned the place to the ground. They'd chosen a day when they knew no American forces would be there, and had gambled correctly that the local Iraqi police would not defend the place. Rather than leaving it abandoned as a 'monument to insurgent power', Garner had rebuilt it with a permanent roster of his own troops inside. That, however, merely seemed to have convinced the Iraqi security forces that they no longer had to turn up, other than on pay day. Up on the roof, half a dozen of the new Iraqi Civil Defence Corps, or ICDC, were supposed to be keeping watch over the village. Garner found one lone sentry, standing alone, shivering and exhausted.

'Where is the rest of this man's shift?' Garner asked an interpreter.

'He doesn't know sir, he says they never turned up last night. He has been here on his own ever since.'

Garner ordered the man's commander to be summonsed for a dressing down. Yet blaming the chiefs wouldn't help that much. The new ICDC's real bosses, after all, were Garner's own battalion, who'd been training them. The problem was the recruitment material. Many of the rookie ICDC were rejects from the new Iraqi police force, which wasn't exactly known for rigorous standards itself. Some were also thought to be double agents. A few weeks earlier, Garner's forces had caught an ICDC member conducting a rocket attack on a US base.

Since bringing peace and prosperity to Mashahidah was proving so hard, perhaps it wasn't surprising that the happiest people in Garner's outfit were those doing old-fashioned combat. Down in the town of Mashahidah itself was Forward Observation Base Animal, a US outpost in an old Ba'ath Party HQ. Since they'd arrived in June, they been attacked nearly 80 times. On the map in the command room back at battalion HQ, the base was nicknamed The Carnation because it had so many coloured incident pins stuck in it. Yet inside, there wasn't a glum face. 'They have been pissed off ever since we occupied this place because it once belonged to the Ba'ath,' said Captain Brian Ridley gleefully, striding across a rooftop draped with wire netting to predetonate incoming ordnance. 'I don't think there is anybody attacked more than us. When you go on leave to our main headquarters and say you have been down here at Animal base, people go, *"Oh, shit."*'

While their boss chafed under the role of tank commander turned civic leader, the residents of FOB Animal, or the Animal House as it was affectionately known, were in their element. The 1-68 Armor Regiment were, after all, frontline combat troops, and this was as clear a frontline as you got in somewhere like Iraq. The insurgents would pop up on the distant horizon to launch gunfire or rocket attacks, and the soldiers shot back. For those manning the gun positions on the roof, it was a real-life version of the DVD games they played in their dorms downstairs, with a points score system to match. So far they'd killed five insurgents, captured more than 100, and suffered six serious injuries themselves. Up on the roof, a soldier named Mark Lopez was sat behind a belt-fed grenade thrower, a fearsome thing that could fire grenades with the accuracy of a World Series baseball pitcher and many times the range. He'd recently had three weeks' surgery back in Germany after suffering shrapnel wounds to the stomach, leg, hip and head. Yet he'd come back for more, despite being told he didn't have to. 'I wanted to,' he said. 'I know it sounds cheesy, but we have grown like a family.'

In his bedroom, where a TV sat surrounded by weapons and piles of kit, Ridley stuck on a video shot by a soldier of a mortar and gun attack on the base, involving up to 20 fighters. The footage was shaky because the cameraman kept getting thrown to the ground by the explosions. 'We are at war here,' said Ridley, staring at the screen. 'And you go up to HQ and they're doing first-aid class and jogging. But for every ten of us guys out here, there are ten back at base who want to be down here, and for every ten of them, there are another ten back in the States wanting to be in Iraq. We are in the top one per cent right now, doing the job we're trained to do.'

The opposition, it had to be said, didn't seem to be trained at all. The arrests the troops had made had turned a previously shadowy entity into a rogues' gallery of names, faces, and nicknames, mostly inspired by the amateurish circumstances in which they'd been caught. Cinderella, for example, lost his shoe as he attempted to flee a pursuing patrol. Mercedes Boy was apprehended in his flashy, easy-to-spot getaway car. Ridley couldn't remember what the pair known as Dumb and Dumber had done to get caught, but 'it sure wasn't real bright'. Then there was Snoofs, a toothless woman whose sons were suspected of organising rocket attacks, Mosaic Boy, whose only noteworthy attribute appeared to be the crazy paving in his front garden, and a half-blind man known as the One-Eyed Kamel. They even had a couple of tipsters, nicknamed Crockett and Tubbs because of their enthusiasm for Miami Vice-style secret *rendezvous*. As with most informants, though, nobody knew quite what their angle was. Among the attacks that Crockett had failed to warn them of was a recent RPG strike on the Animal House. One of the suspects for the attack was his own brother.

We left the Animal House and headed up along Ambush Alley back to HQ, constantly scanning the road for trouble. The road was dead straight, yet on the radio I could hear a constant chatter among the convoy's drivers and rooftop gunners, identifying potential hazards. Watch out for that stationary truck. Check out that guy hanging around on the edge of the field. Had someone planted something in that pile of rubbish over there? It looked different from this morning. How nerve-wracking it must be to drive this stretch of road every day, knowing that by the law of averages, sooner or later you'd get hit. I reflected that this was only 30 miles north of Baghdad, where I still felt relatively safe travelling around on my own. I wouldn't do that round here.

Later that night, Garner chatted a bit more in his room, where a poster of Saddam Hussein hung on the wall. Ever since he'd come here, Garner's mission had been to show the locals that there was a better way than Saddam's, that you could govern with carrot as well as stick. Yet some days, he'd find himself looking at that glowering, moustachioed face and wondering whether the old brute had a point after all.

'It's all very well trying to be nice to everyone, but it just seems impossible when everyone's out for themselves, skimming money and enriching themselves and their family ahead of others,' he said. 'Saddam faced the same challenges, he just went about it differently. And in some ways, he was a success at it.'

A week later when I was back in Baghdad, Garner emailed me. A rare item of good news from the Redneck Riviera. Jabba the Hutt had spent the night in jail after refusing to stop at a US Army checkpoint.

Contract Killing

AMONG THE FEW pleasant features of my new flat was a small study room with a window overlooking the main road. Sometimes in the late evenings, I'd take my laptop in there and write emails home, listening to the sound of kids playing football in the street outside. It was the closest Baghdad got to tranquillity, which meant it wasn't very tranquil at all. Every now and then, some motorist would come screaming past, driving three times as fast as normal because it was night time and they were scared of getting robbed. Then there'd be a screech of tyres and angry yells as they suddenly found themselves swerving at 90mph through the middle of a seven-a-side football match.

My emails were thick with foreign correspondent romance, about how I was typing away by candlelight with the BBC World Service on in the background and the sights and smells – and dangers – of the war-torn city just outside. Actually, the candlelight was unnecessary, because late evenings were one of the few times of day when there was electricity. And frequently I'd turn the World Service off because some tedious old doss was waffling on about why Shariah law was a great idea in southern Sudan, or whatever. But every now and then one had to self-romanticise a bit, as the reality of my new job was that it was often just an exhausting, tedious grind.

Being a freelancer in Iraq involved serious multi-tasking. You weren't just a journalist. You were also your own researcher, security consultant, IT expert, salesman and accountant. The toughest aspect of being a journalistic privateer, though, was being an employer yourself. Mohammed had been hard enough to deal with at times, but he was a lot easier than his replacements, Colonel Ali and Colonel Saba, who had become progressively more disgruntled as time had gone on. Their main complaint, not surprisingly, was their paltry $10 a day wages. Ali, in particular, kept on agitating for more, and had managed to persuade the more placid Saba that he was getting ripped

144

off too. I insisted it was all I could afford, but arguing against two was much harder than arguing against one. Eventually I turned to Mohammed for advice.

'Oh yes, you want to watch Ali, he is a crooky bastard,' he said. 'He will try to screw you out of as much money as he can. You must not show any weakness.'

'You might have told me that when you recommended him. So what should I do?'

'That is very simple. You must tell him, "Fuck you, Ali, I can get another translator anyplace", and "Fuck you, Saba, I can get another driver anyplace". Don't let those assholes think they're special.'

Other than confirming why Iraqis had never excelled at international diplomacy, this advice proved useless. Told that I'd sack him if he didn't stop asking for more, Ali simply called my bluff. He demanded $150 out of me for a three-day trip to Basra, cleverly delivering his wage ultimatum the morning we were due to leave so that I couldn't rope in someone else at such short notice. I sacked him as soon as we got back. He didn't seem bothered.

Did this sort of thing happen to John Simpson, I wondered? If so, he didn't write about them much in *Strange Places, Questionable People*, his book about the trials and tribulations of being a foreign correspondent. At no point in his accounts of Soviet-occupied Afghanistan or the collapse of Communism was there any mention of a stand-up row with an underpaid translator. Nor did he seem to spend the vast majority of his time blundering around aimlessly as I did. How would my memoirs read, I wondered?

8am: Get up with no proper plan for morning or afternoon. No carbombs this morning. Fight vague feelings of disappointment at being deprived of easy story for the day.

9am: Visit hospitals on vague tip about people selling kidneys for cash: 'Not happened since 1996', says doctor.

11am: Head to the Shia slum of Saddam City. Hope to get locals to talk about the Mahdi Army, local gang of gun-toting Shia yobbos who are now effectively the law in Saddam City. Proposed headline: 'Shia militias make us live in fear'. Surrounded within minutes by locals enthusiastically endorsing said Mahdi Army. So keen are they to voice their praise that they insist we joint them for lunch. Force-fed foul fish dish under guise of 'traditional Iraqi hospitality'.

1pm: Give up on Mahdi Army. In desperation, check out local cock-fighting scene again. Still not started.

2pm: Drive past a goat farm. Remember a fellow freelancer who once sold a story about pigs in the Balkans to Farmer's Weekly. *Wonder if they might like an Iraqi follow-up.*

*****

Tucked away somewhere in east Baghdad was a big Christian neighbourhood known only as Area 52. Nobody seemed to know why it was called that, but everybody knew where it was, mainly because it was where all Baghdad's best booze shops were. In Saddam's time, Christians had been the only people licensed to sell alcohol. The Christians who lived there were mainly Chaldean Catholics, part of the Eastern Rites, a branch of the faith that had developed entirely separately from Rome. Yet they shared many traditions that I knew from home, such as driving a Santa float round the streets in the run-up to Christmas. This year, though, Santa was packing more than just pressies. When I interviewed a local reverend who was organising the float, he showed me the silver pistol he planned to carry on the night. Santa's Elves, riding at the back of the float, were toting Kalashnikovs.

I was in for a different kind of Christmas myself. I was one of a number of freelancers planning on staying on over the festive period, tempted by various opportunities to provide cover for staff reporters who wanted to spend time at home. Christmas dinner would be in the Summerland restaurant, a dark, anonymous-looking eaterie next to the Al Hamra hotel, where the social scene that had sprung up around the Hamra's poolside had relocated itself for the winter. The Summerland almost resembled a restaurant back home: it had a small bar with beer on draft and a good range of steaks, which tasted fine as long as you didn't dwell too long on the possibility that it might be horsemeat. But like everywhere in Baghdad, it had its quirks. Often there was only one choice of wine, a petrol-bouqueted concoction called 'Mr Le Bonjour', which came complete with a picture of a beret-wearing Frenchman to remind you that were drinking wine, not vinegar. Rather charmingly, the waiter would always make you taste it first, despite having nothing else on offer.

It was easy to get to know your fellow diners at the Summerland. The same journalists from the neighbouring Hamra hotel ate there nearly every night, mainly because they couldn't go anywhere else in Baghdad after dark. By now I had my own little crowd of longer-term acquaintances. Joining Omar and Ryan at dinner in the Summerland would be Jill Carroll and Glen Carey, both Americans and both fellow freelance journalists. Like me, they lived a hand-to-mouth existence and took whatever work came their way. Glen's main gig was reporting for an oil news agency, while Jill worked for some Italian outfit that paid a pittance. They, too, had crap days and crap weeks, rows with translators and stories that fell flat. It was one of the things I liked about them; nothing was more annoying than sitting in the Summerland with some fellow reporter droning on about what a successful day they'd had.

One person who'd be absent from Christmas lunch was Ryan Manelick. He'd been in Iraq solidly since June, and was now planning to fly home to Pennsylvania to see his three young children. One Saturday night in mid-December he joined us for dinner, clearly in a good mood. Tomorrow was his 31st birthday, and the day after that he'd be heading home. He had one quick business trip to a US Army base in Balad, 50 miles north of Baghdad, and then he was off for a much-deserved break. No more sweating blood delivering contracts. No more cruising the same dangerous desert roads that Kirk had vanished on. And no more arguing with John Dawkins.

Things had got steadily worse between the pair of them since Kirk's disappearance. I'd put together a story about the incident for the *San Francisco Chronicle*, which covered Kirk's home town of Moss Beach, and Ryan and his colleague Charles Phillips had both been hinting to me that there'd soon be a dramatic follow-up story. They wouldn't go into detail, but it involved suspicions that Dawkins had been bribing a US Army contracting officer to win business for Ultra Services. Kirk had apparently found out about it, and had been planning to tell the authorities, fearing he might get implicated himself. That, Ryan reckoned, had prompted Dawkins to have him abducted and killed. What's more, he said, that was just the tip of the iceberg. 'I'll tell you the whole story in the New Year,' he promised. 'You'll be able to write a book on it.'

Yes, mate, a novel, I thought privately. I'd known John longer than I'd known Ryan, and while he wasn't much more than a casual acquaintance, he didn't seem like a murderer. Maybe he was tough as a businessman, but he was a bright guy and no thug, as far as I could tell. There were plenty of contractors in Baghdad who might bump people off, sure. But Dawkins, on my reckoning, wasn't one of them.

As Ryan and Charles got up from the table to go, we gave them the usual parting shots about taking care on the drive to Balad. Ryan drained his red wine and grinned. 'I'm in fear of my life, you know,' he said. 'It's not Iraqis I'm worried about, either. It's people from my own country.' Nobody made anything of it. Ryan could be melodramatic, after all. He wished us all Merry Christmas, and headed off with Charles in his 4x4.

As they drove north the next day, I headed south to Basra on a job for the *Sunday Telegraph*. We left at 6am, aiming as usual to get there before the road got dark and dangerous. With me was Colonel Saba, who'd stuck with me after I'd sacked Colonel Ali, and my new translator, Amir, a former chemist whom I'd met at an internet café. Around midday, we stopped at a petrol station about an hour outside Basra, a shack with a few petrol pumps in a small, remote hamlet. An attendant refuelled the car, showing not the slightest attention as gunfire crackled further down the road.

'Who's that shooting?' I asked.

'He says the radio has reported that Saddam Hussein has been caught,' said Amir. 'They are shooting in celebration. Don't worry. It's been reported lots of times before, and it's always been wrong.'

The crackle continued. I rang *The Scotsman* foreign desk. It probably was just another false alarm, but it never hurt to check. The capture of Saddam, after all, was the story everyone had been waiting for, the final chapter in his fall. I'd always told my translators and drivers to be ready for it, though I didn't really want it to happen, for fear that newsdesks might then lose interest in Iraq as a story. I got through to Chris Marks, *The Scotsman* deputy foreign editor. He was similarly trying to work out whether this was finally it.

'Hmmm... Reuters reporting Saddam "rumoured to have been found somewhere up near Tikrit",' he said, scanning the newswires. 'US military making no comment at the moment, but say they will hold a press conference midday your time.'

That was interesting. I wouldn't expect them to call a press conference unless there was something to it.

'I'll call you back the moment I hear anything definite,' said Chris, ringing off.

We sat at the roadside, wondering what to do. There was no point in carrying on to Basra if Saddam *had* been detained, but equally it would be impossible to get to Tikrit today. It was 400 miles north of where we were. I cursed. The biggest story in Iraq, and here I was about as far away as possible from where it was happening. *Please, let Saddam still be free*, I thought. It was just like being back in London eight months ago, when I'd got upset at seeing his statue come down. A while later, Chris rang back. 'They've got him,' he said.

Bollocks. When was there going to be a world event that I was actually near enough to cover?

Plied with the offer of double money, and a guarantee of at least talks for possibly treble, Saba agreed to turn the car around and head back to Baghdad. It would be a 700-mile round journey, but we'd get back in time to catch a little of the celebrations, if nothing else.

An hour into our journey back, the phone rang again. It was Omar. I assumed he was ringing to ask what I'd heard about Saddam's capture. Instead, he had news of his own.

'Ryan's been killed,' he said.

'What?'

'Shot dead as he was driving back from Balad. Some guys just drove up alongside his car and machine-gunned it. Killed an Iraqi employee he was with as well, and wounded another. His body's been picked up by the US Army.'

'Jesus *Christ*. Do they know who did it?'

'No.'

'Was Colonel Mohammed with him?'

'No idea. If I hear any more, I'll let you know.'

I felt numb. Back home, bereavement had hardly ever touched me; out here, surrounded by death, I'd often asked myself what it might be like if someone I knew was murdered. Now here was Ryan, a man I'd been dining with just the night before, shot dead in cold blood. I sat there as we drove along, braced in case overwhelming shock or grief suddenly kicked in. Time passed, and it didn't. Had it just not really sunk in yet? Or was it just that I didn't really know Ryan that well?

More pressing right now was who'd killed him. Was it anything to do with his fall-out with John? Surely not. Was it retribution for Saddam's capture? More likely. Balad, where Ryan had been visiting, was in the heart of the Sunni Triangle, and his white 4x4, as Mohammed often pointed out, would have stood out a mile. But it wasn't yet clear what time he'd been attacked. It might have been before the news of Saddam's arrest had come out. I rang Chris on the *Scotsman*'s foreign desk again.

'Chris, is there any mention of a killing up near Balad? A US contractor?'

'Haven't seen anything, mate. Why?'

'Um, well, just had a phone call to say a friend of mine has been killed up there.'

'My God, sorry.'

I didn't say any more. I knew that Chris's priority, right now, was Saddam's capture, the biggest story in Iraq since the start of the war. It would have to be mine, too. For the next week there'd be pages and pages to fill on the subject, which meant I'd be working round the clock. Terrible as it sounded, thinking about Ryan would have to wait.

The next day we drove up to Ad Dawr, the village outside of Tikrit where Saddam's hideout had been found and the stronghold of a tribe close to him. Locals directed us to the patch of wooded farmland where 'the President' had spent his last days. The site was still cordoned off, but jubilant US Army commanders were now offering guided tours to any journalists who turned up. I wasn't in the first batch of reporters to be shown round, but it didn't really matter. The story was so huge that all of the different papers I freelanced for – the *Scotsman*, the *Daily Express*, the *Standard* and the *San Francisco Chronicle* – wanted their own 'inside Saddam's spider hole' stories. In fact, the spider hole was not where he lived. It was barely deep enough to hold two coffins, and only used as an emergency bolt hole if people came looking for him. Most of his time was spent in a small thatched shack right next to it, not unlike the one he'd been raised in as a boy. The Americans had been all over it, but what was still left inside afforded some entertaining glimpses of how he'd spent his final days on the run. He'd been reduced to circumstances akin to those I'd endured in some of his country's poorer hotels. The shack had no running water and a hole in the ground toilet, and it was swarming with cockroaches, mosquitoes and flies. True to form, Saddam had deployed chemical weapons – empty cans of insecticide spray littered the shack. And to his monikers of *High Excellency, Struggler Against Zionist Imperialism, Field Marshal and Commander of All Iraq* could now also be added an extra title: Consumer in chief of Bounty Bars. Inside the fridge were at least three party-packs of Bounty miniatures, which seemed to be his favourite snack alongside pistachio nuts and cans of soft drink. His diet since the war, it seemed, had been even worse than mine. We were ushered out after about 20 minutes, although not before Colonel Saba had managed to pee in the presidential toilet and steal some of Saddam's pistachio nuts for the trip home.

The next few days were hectic, mining every possible angle on Saddam's capture, from what kind of war crimes he might be tried with through to whether there was a hangman available to execute him. There was no down-time, save for a few stiff nightcaps with Glen Carey, the American oil agency freelance, when we drank to Ryan's memory. Glen circulated an email from Ryan's father, Greg Manelick, asking if anybody had pictures or mementoes of his son out in Iraq. I sent Greg an email telling him about the *Sun* article about Ryan waterskiing and told him that Ryan, like me, had been having the time of his life out here. Whether that served as the consolation I intended, or whether it just made it all the harder, I had no idea. Either way, it was the only writing I was doing about Ryan's death. Saddam's capture was one of those monumental events that creates a 'news shadow' – a story so big that coverage of everything else stops, indeed seems almost irrelevant. Normally the killing of a US contractor would have attracted substantial attention. But in the newspapers and newswires that week, Ryan's death got not a single line.

The whole thing was as spooky as hell. For all the rumour and innuendo, nobody really had a clue who was to blame, or why, or, more importantly, who might be next. It reminded me of that old Agatha Christie murder mystery in which ten people on a holiday island are bumped off one by one, all of them suspecting each other of being the murderer. Charles Phillips left Iraq, John Dawkins stayed in Turkey, and Ultra Services effectively stopped operating, with everyone remotely associated with it keeping their distance. Mohammed was despondent. He said he'd pledged 'on his moustache' to keep Ryan safe, which was the Iraqi equivalent of pledging on your mother's life. He now blamed himself for not being there the day Ryan was killed. Meanwhile, I was left wondering about the people I had come to regard as friends. Ryan, Kirk and Co were polite, friendly types, who'd come to Iraq as businessmen, not mercenaries. Could they really all have turned on each other like this, corrupted by the prospect of big money in a land with no rules?

I felt I owed it to Ryan to investigate as far as I could. In early January, I got in touch again with Greg Manelick. He was based out in Sakhalin, an oil field in eastern Russia, where he worked as the chief security adviser for Exxon Mobil. He was distraught, desperate for answers, and suspicious of everyone. It turned out that Ryan had made a formal statement to the US Army's Criminal Investigation Division, the people investigating Kirk's disappearance. In it, he'd voiced the theory that Kirk had been killed because he was about to expose John's alleged bribery rackets. Had John then felt obliged to silence Ryan too?

It seemed impossible. John was a good friend of Greg Manelick from their days in Russia together. It was through their personal friendship that Dawkins had agreed to hire Ryan in the first place and Dawkins had given Greg his word that he'd not been involved. With no proof either way, Greg was inclined to give them the benefit of the doubt. In any case, he had another nominee for prime suspect. One that made my blood run cold.

'Do you know that Iraqi colonel who was acting as Ryan's bodyguard? A guy called Mohammed?'

'Yeah. He was my translator before he went to work for Ryan.'

'Well, I wonder if he's anything to do with it.'

'Eh?'

Greg set out his case. Mohammed had been working as Ryan's bodyguard, had he not? Yet on the day Ryan was killed, he wasn't with him, was he? Wasn't that just a bit too much of a coincidence? To my horror, I realised I'd never looked at it that way. It had never even occurred to me to wonder why Mohammed wasn't there that day. Surely not, though?

'Listen, I know Mohammed as well as I know anyone here,' I said. 'He always looked after me fine, and he was always on at Ryan to take more care. Plus, Ryan was giving him a job – what would be his motive?'

'All I know is that in situations like this, you look for people with the capability. That Mohammed, he was a former officer in Saddam's armies. That makes him capable, and that makes me suspicious of him.'

Capable, yes, I thought. *Willing, no.* Then again, Ryan's dad might not know the ground like I did but he was a security consultant for an oil firm in Russia, a place where ruthless business practice was commonplace. He probably knew a lot more about this kind of thing than I did. Was I just being naive? Was I just avoiding the idea that I might be the link between Ryan and his killer?

A week after speaking to Greg I flew home for a break. I wasn't sure if I'd be coming back again. Ryan's death had scared me, and after Saddam's capture, it felt like Iraq was over as a story. For all my talk of returning to do a big, in-depth, investigative story on who had killed Ryan, I wasn't sure I had the guts. Whoever'd commissioned the hit on Ryan might decide to kill me too. Plus, I wasn't really sure I wanted to know the answers. I'd already rung Mohammed and told him what Greg had said, and he'd denied everything. Just to be safe, though, I'd waited until I was safely back home in London before calling him.

Uprising

FULL-TIME STAFF reporters are, effectively, owned by the paper. There's never any arguing with the newsdesk, no matter how pointless or impossible the task in hand is. And if things go wrong, it's your fault – no matter if you're sent on a job late, wrongly briefed, or too overburdened with other stuff. Argue back, and you'll get a curt reminder that there are a dozen casual staff in the office who'll take your job instead, and for half the money, too. It's the downside of working in a supposedly 'glamorous' industry; the staff can be treated like shit. Members of a profession which prides itself on challenging authority put up with all manner of bullying from their bosses. Many news executives love to think of themselves as 'tough', but the only reason they get away with swearing and screaming is that their staff can't answer back. Try it on a building site and they'd get thumped.

As a freelance, I had none of that to worry about. There were no hungry young shifters lining up to work in Baghdad. If someone hired you for a job, it was on your terms and conditions; working for several newspapers at once, it didn't matter too much if things went sour with one. Iraq's uniquely dangerous reputation also helped: if you said something couldn't be done, a newsdesk would accept it, rather than accusing you of being a lazy, cowardly bastard. Not even the most pig-headed news editor wanted a dead stringer on his hands, it was too much paperwork. For the first time in my career, I felt free, in control. Afghanistan, Sudan, India… I could go where I wanted, when I wanted. As it was, I took some time off. Two months off, in fact. The only way a newspaper staff man could get more than five weeks a year was to wangle a 'sabbatical', to write a book or carry out some other self-improving project. The sight of everybody else struggling into work in the foul February weather made it all the sweeter.

I did wonder when the Baghdad news bubble would burst, though. Media interest had tailed off markedly after Saddam's capture. The British broadsheets still gave it plenty of coverage, but were less enthusiastic. Stories which might have commanded a page now got just a few columns. With Saddam behind bars nobody expected the insurgency to last much longer. I thought about trying Afghanistan instead, but as the anniversary of the fall of Baghdad was looming, I realised there'd be lots of commissions for 'Iraq, a year on' stuff. I resolved to go for a month or so, then return and look at the atlas again. Hopefully there'd be some war or military coup in some minor African nation – ideally one that was newsworthy but not too dangerous.

My flight to Jordan got in at midnight on March 14. On hearing I was headed to Baghdad, a taxi driver offered, on the spot, to drive me straight there for $150. At the border two hours later, I drained a large hip flask of whisky and bedded down on the back seat to avoid the eyes of the bandits. I woke up around dawn on the outskirts of Baghdad, feeling pleasingly swashbuckling.

*****

For Saad Faislawy, becoming a prisoner of war been the happiest moment in an otherwise inglorious military career. Jailed twice for desertion in Saddam's time, he'd been only too happy to surrender when American troops had surrounded him during the invasion. The food he'd had during his 75 days in PoW camp had been better than anything he'd got as a soldier. It was only after that, when his captors handed him a $10 bill and told him he was free to go, that things went to shit again. 'When the American soldiers told us we could leave, we all chanted, "Bush is the new father",' he said. 'But now what do we have instead? Nothing, despite Bush's promises.'

Saad was not the kind of happily-ever-after story that featured in the Coalition press releases marking the year since Saddam's fall. They talked of doctors who now had medicine, of teachers who now had books, of academics who could now write what they wanted, and of all kinds of other Iraqis now fulfilling their potential. They didn't talk of the much larger number of Iraqis without much potential in the first place, such as Saad. For him, the chance to make his own way in life was a burden, not an opportunity. Home was now a spare room in an abandoned dentist's office in Baghdad, and he earned a living by hawking bananas outside Al Yarmouk hospital, where my new ex-chemist translator Amir and I had collared him for an interview.

As we stood chatting, a boy aged about 14 wandered up to Amir, pointed to his clapped-out Datsun parked nearby, and muttered something. Amir glowered, asked me for 500 dinars, and then handed them over. It was an Iraqi version of the old 'mind-your-car-for-you-mister' scam, as I'd seen practised by Moss Side street urchins outside Manchester City's old ground back home. But I was annoyed that Amir had parted with my money that easily. Apart from anything else, his car was so decrepit that if the kid tried to scratch it in revenge for not paying up, it would hardly make a difference.

'Why didn't you just tell him to get lost?' I asked. 'He's only a kid.'

'It's not just the boy,' said Amir. 'You see that group of men over at the corner? Those are his friends. If I don't pay, we will have to argue with them, not him. And their Kalashnikov.'

'Ah, I see. That's interesting though. Do these kind of people operate here all the time?'

'Saad says they do, yes. When banana sales are down, he joins them.'

Middle-class Iraqis like Amir had a name for people like Saad, the freelance ruffians who now hustled and scammed them at every opportunity. They were *hawassim*, a word taken from the name Saddam had given to the most recent war, the *um il hawassim*, or mother of deciders. Originally, the term *hawassim* was used to describe the looted goods that turned up in Baghdad's markets after the war. But now it just meant anybody who was profiteering from the general chaos, the *nouveau riche* of the post-war world. The typical *hawassim* was someone from a slum area like Saddam City, who drove around in a stolen government car sporting a gold chain and gold rings from the proceeds of looting and robbery. Entire families of *hawassims* – or *hawassimeen* – were sending shudders through respectable neighbourhoods by squatting in houses belonging to Ba'athists who'd been murdered, arrested, or gone into hiding. Depending on how embittered you felt about things, a *hawassim* could also just be anyone who was generally doing better in life than you. The sort of people who might appear in a Coalition anniversary press release, in other words.

Among those having *hawassim* problems was Colonel Saba, Mohammed's ex-military colleague and my old driver. Towards the end of my last stint here, he'd suddenly stopped turning up for work. He'd been getting threatened by one of the former soldiers in his command, a ne'er-do-well like Saad whom he'd once jailed for going AWOL. The guy now wanted compensation, $1,500 to help set him up in a new life. He'd warned that if he didn't get it, something nasty might happen to Saba's family.

The news of Saba's misfortunes were broken to me by Mohammed himself, who I met for a beer at the Hamra one evening. I deliberately chose a neutral, heavily-guarded venue for our rendezvous. While I personally doubted that he'd had anything to do with Ryan's death, you couldn't really afford to trust anyone in Iraq that much, not even people you counted as friends. Not when there was murder involved.

The Colonel was gloomy. He'd been jobless since Ryan's murder, and still seemed to blame himself for not being there to bodyguard him that day. Now, to add to his woes, his old army mate was in trouble as well.

'Poor Saba is having the deepest of troubles,' he sat, draining his third Amstel in half an hour. 'Sitting all day in the homestead, waiting for this asshole to try to fuck with him.'

'So who is this guy?'

'He is just some simple soldier, not an officer. But he is coming to Saba's house several times, saying, "Give me this money, or be careful next time your wife goes out".'

'And why exactly does he have a problem with Saba?'

'Saba once sent him to the jail for desertifying the army. Just some small time of six months. Now his angry. But what was Saba supposed to do? He was his commanding officer. If he let all his soldiers run away, it will be Saba who end up inside the jail himself.'

I nodded. As ever, I had only Mohammed's word to go by. Discipline in the Iraqi Army, I knew, had been pretty brutal. In the Thieves Market downtown, you could buy DVDs showing errant soldiers getting serious kickings from their superiors. Saba didn't seem the type to do that but, as with most affairs involving my ex-regime chums, I had no real way of knowing. It all sounded like menaces mixed with a touch of blackmail. In the current climate, men like Mohammed and Saba were careful who they told about their pasts as senior figures in Saddam's security forces. A lot of their colleagues had been getting killed by anti-Saddam hit squads, some of whom didn't really care whether they were assassinating a real baddie or not. Just to have held the rank of colonel was enough. The soldier who was threatening Saba might be calculating that he would pay up just to keep him quiet.

'Why doesn't Saba just kill this guy, then?' I asked. Out here it seemed like the sensible thing to do, just like calling the police back home.

For once, Mohammed was the voice of conciliation. 'That maybe will cause all kinds of hassles. This guy, I think, is not just one, but part of some gang. Maybe doing this to many officers.'

'What about Saba's tribe then? Can't they duff him up, or something?'

'It is true, Saba has a very powerful tribe. But once he asks them, they will be expecting something in return. And maybe also this guy has a tribe too. It is a difficult problem. Maybe some kind of talking will help.'

He drank up and headed off, promising to drop by my flat sometime. Somehow, I no longer felt too worried at the prospect. After all, that was twice that he'd just counselled against settling a problem by force. Hopefully it was proof that, when out of uniform, violence wasn't his way. *Hopefully*.

*****

A week on from my return, I began bashing out the first of those Iraq anniversary pieces. While not quite as upbeat as the Coalition press releases being pumped out of the Green Zone, I did try to hint that things were slowly turning the corner. The signs of progress were small, and to someone like Saba, living in daily fear of his family being killed, they wouldn't be noticeable at all. But tangible improvements were there. Since my last trip out, for example, a new mobile phone network had come in, something that had been banned in Saddam's time. After nearly a year of being incommunicado from each other save for $1-a-minute satphones, it made life infinitely easier. The new Iraqi security forces also looked like they might finally be getting their act together. They now had radios, proper guns, flak jackets, and, most importantly, a semblance of purpose. Six months ago, they'd done little but lounge around in their police stations. If you visited as a reporter, everyone would gather round, and you could spend the whole afternoon drinking tea and chatting about the dreadful crime problems on the streets outside. Now, when Amir and I visited a station, the commander gave us only a hurried five minute interview in between signing warrants and investigation orders. Shopkeepers conceded that crime was down slightly. Hamid Ahmed, who ran a mobile phone shop near my flat, had downgraded from keeping two machine guns and a pistol under the counter to just a police truncheon, which he kept strapped in his belt alongside his new Nokia handset. 'When we first opened up again just after the war, I needed the guns to watch for robbers,' he said. 'Now I just have the truncheon instead. So security is a bit better – although not much.'

What really convinced me that things were getting better was the day I spent on the set of *Love Under Occupation*, the first Iraqi soap opera to be filmed on the streets of post-war Baghdad. Its star was a man called Fawzi, a jobless civil servant whose encounters with kidnappers, murderers and robbers made even *Brookside* look tame. Yet to my mind, the fact that a soap opera was even being filmed was surely a sign that life was finally heading towards normal. As the coming weeks would prove, it showed just how damned little I knew about what was really going on.

*****

While the insurgency wasn't in the news much more, it hadn't gone away. By March, attacks on US troops were back at the same level as they'd been before Saddam's capture. The guerrillas had also developed a scary new tactic called 'shark patrols'. These were carloads of armed men who cruised the highways leading out of Baghdad, doing random attacks on passing Westerners. Their job was made much easier by the inexplicable habit that many Westerners had of driving around in big, brand new imported 4x4s. They might make for a smoother ride on some of Baghdad's more potholed roads, but they stood out a mile. So many got wiped out by shark patrols that their unofficial name was 'bullet magnets'. Most journalists had stopped using them long ago, switching to more discreet saloon cars instead. But many security companies continued with them regardless, reckoning that their Western military training made them the equal to any insurgent ambush. Increasingly, it wasn't. 'A rocket propelled grenade can cripple even an armoured 4x4,' one security guard admitted to me. 'Then you're left stuck on the roadside, maybe with a couple of people injured, facing a shoot-out against people who've got numbers on their side. You've got to be very good or very lucky to get out alive.'

One lunchtime at the end of March, just as I was beginning to run out of 'Iraq, a year on' angles, the *Standard* rang up. Another two 4x4s had been attacked, this time in Fallujah.

'Sounds nasty,' said the voice at the end of the phone. 'Four Americans, apparently. Security contractors, escorting some sort of convoy. The wires are saying they got RPG-d. Unconfirmed eyewitnesses saying locals strung up their bodies from a bridge.'

'I'll check it out,' I said. 'I wouldn't get too excited yet, though. It sounds like Iraqi bullshit to me.'

It did, too. The local rumour mill always went into overdrive whenever there was any attack involving Americans. An attack in which one US soldier was lightly wounded would end up as the massacre of a dozen. A Humvee that got a tyre shot out would turn into a crippled tank. A helicopter that then flew overhead would become an F16 that strafed the area, killing civilians who'd actually died when some insurgent had misaimed his RPG. What's more, there was always someone on the scene willing to swear blind he'd seen it all. I had no doubt that if I went out to Fallujah, there'd be no end of people willing to testify on the Koran that bodies had been swinging from every lamppost in town. But that didn't make it true.

Only this time it was, with ghastly pictures to prove it. In what was one of the world's most gruesome news exclusives ever, the whole thing had been captured on film by a local TV cameraman. After being hit by several rocket propelled grenades, the two 4x4s had been surrounded by a mob who'd dragged the occupants out onto the roadside. Whether they were still alive at that point wasn't clear, although given what happened next, their relatives back in America probably hoped profoundly that they weren't. The mob had gone into a frenzy, beating and hacking at each body and torching them in petrol. One of them was tied to a car and dragged down Fallujah's main street while onlookers cheered. Then, as a crowning glory, two charred and mangled corpses were strung up from a green iron bridge that spanned the Euphrates on Fallujah's west side. By then they were almost unrecognisable, just thick black matchstick men with broken limbs sticking out at bizarre angles. The footage was horrific, yet it was no undercover job. People were dancing around in front of the cameraman like it was some macabre town fete.

Soon afterwards, US troops sealed off the town, leaving most of the foreign media hanging around on the outskirts. But by that time, the damage had been done. The film had been beamed all round the world, a potent reminder that despite Saddam's capture, the Iraqi insurgency was still very much alive and kicking. As I filed a story in my local internet café that night, the Iraqi customers watched as the footage was replayed endlessly on Arab satellite TV channels. They were as shocked as anyone. This was what you expected in some God-forsaken part of Africa, not civilised Iraq. For America, it was an unwelcome U-turn down memory lane to the infamous *Black Hawk Down* incident in Somalia ten years before, when two US soldiers' corpses had been dragged through Mogadishu in similar fashion. This was the insurgents' equivalent of Operation Shock and Awe – primitive street corner savagery, rather than hi-tech precision, but with no less capacity to frighten. 'Not for childrens' eyes,' cautioned CBS's anchorman Dan Rather. 'Human jackals' declared Iraq's civilian governor, Paul Bremer, resorting to the kind of colourful invective that Saddam used to use. Even Coalition spokesman General Mark Kimmitt, a man renowned for his mercilessly upbeat briefings, for once sounded upset. 'Somewhere out in this world there are going to be families who are getting knocks on the door from people, telling them what happened to their loved ones,' he told a press conference that afternoon, which I attended. 'It is not pleasant to be on either side of that door, I can tell you.'

Normally Kimmitt was careful to describe Iraq's baddies as just being the tiny minority. This time, he seemed to blaming the whole city. 'Fallujah just doesn't get it,' he declared. He then issued its people an ultimatum: they could either hand over the culprits now, or his soldiers would come and get them. The latter, he hinted, would see the place flattened. 'It will be at a time and a place of our choosing,' he said. 'It will be methodical, it will be precise and it will be overwhelming.'

For the rest of the week, the world watched to see how the Fallujans would respond. Would they hand over those who'd committed the mutilation? Or were they going to fight? Every newsdesk wanted their reporters to head out there and ask. That was no longer as easy as it had been. For the first time I could recall, there was active hostility in Fallujah towards foreign media. Several reporters who'd tried to go in there shortly after the killings had been threatened. One or two had been questioned in very aggressive fashion by insurgents. A rumour had apparently gone round that two CIA men had posed as a camera crew to gather intelligence. Whether it was true or not didn't matter: every foreign reporter was being treated as a potential spy.

Or so everyone said, anyway. As with any slightly dicey reporting assignment, gossip, hearsay and scare stories abounded, making it a difficult decision. The *Sunday Telegraph* was keen for a Fallujah dateline, although like other newsdesks, they were putting absolutely no pressure on me. But they didn't need to. Few newsdesks, I now realised, ever forced staff in a war zone to head into some really dangerous area. Instead, the pressure came all from yourself. These, after all, were the occasions on which you were judged. Did that encourage risk-taking? Yes. But was anybody forcing you to be there in the first place? No.

The real difficulty was making any kind of accurate assessment of the dangers. Dominic's hostile environment course stressed the importance of relying on local knowledge. But most Iraqi translators and fixers just picked up on local gossip, and right now that was that any foreigner would get hung, drawn and quartered like the security guards had. The few translators who were willing to go were the sort who just shrugged and said 'no problem' when you asked what they'd do if things went wrong.

I ended up doing what a lot of reporters did in such situations. Which was to weigh the odds up carefully, cross my fingers and plunge ahead regardless. My companion for the trip would be a new translator, Nasi, a student in his mid 20s. I'd hired him after a row with Amir, who, like Colonels Ali and Mohammed before him, had got fed up with the paltry wages he was getting. I was paying Nasi $30 a day to Amir's $20, but his English was much more fluent. He'd previously worked as a translator for a sergeant in a US Army unit, which meant he spoke like an Iraqi version of a Quentin Tarantino movie. Every conversation had an 'asshole' or a 'motherfucker' in it. Several other US Army translators he knew had now been killed by insurgents, so his family were keen for him to move into something less risky. Taking me to Fallujah didn't exactly count as that, but we set off on Saturday morning with a driver called Qaiss. He was one of the many who touted their services outside the Hamra hotel, and one of the few now willing to go to Fallujah, though only because we were paying him several times his normal daily rate. When I'd asked him for his assessment of the possible hazards, he'd shrugged and replied, 'No problem.'

We sped down along the motorway leading west out of Baghdad, nicknamed 'RPG alley' because of the amount of ambushes that took place on it. There is barely a conflict zone in the world these days without a road named 'RPG alley', but Baghdad's probably had the best claim to the title. Since it connected the airport and the Green Zone, insurgents never had to wait long for some passing Coalition traffic to shoot at. They'd hide among the palm trees and bushes on the roadside, open fire, then disappear into the residential areas beyond. Another favourite trick was to plant roadside bombs inside the curved metal barricade that ran down the central reservation. When they exploded, the entire barricade would shatter, sending out a deadly shower of shrapnel. Such was the threat on RPG alley that the Americans had re-landscaped it completely. They'd dismantled most of the barricade, torn many of the trees down, and put high wire fences on the flyovers so that people couldn't drop grenades on passing traffic. US snipers were also said to be holed up here and there, with orders to shoot anyone acting suspiciously. I sank low in the car and hid my face behind a copy of *Al Sabah Al Jadeed (The New Morning)*, an Arabic newspaper that I kept for such occasions. If the insurgents were watching, hopefully they wouldn't notice it was a month old.

As we drove, I found myself recalling the various rules about going into dangerous areas from Dominic's hostile environment course. We'd already broken about half a dozen of them, and we weren't even there yet. Was a qualified first aider present? No. Was our vehicle in good and roadworthy condition, with spare petrol and at least two spare tyres? I doubted it. Did I know and trust the driver?

Met him that morning. Did I have good contacts with local community leaders, sheikhs, insurgent commanders, who could vouch for me if I was suspected of being a spy? Negative. And, most importantly, what was our plan of action if it all went wrong? We'd shrug, Qaiss-style, and say 'no problem'.

The drawback with hostile environment courses was that it assumed that the world you were in worked as well as the world back home. Out here, unless you had the organisational capacity of CNN or the BBC, there was no way you could be prepared for every eventuality. You had to adopt a bit of the Iraqi attitude, which was to roll your eyes a bit, look into the middle distance, and declare, 'It is written.'

*****

Fallujah, for all its notoriety, is something of a one-horse town. It's an unremarkable satellite city west of Baghdad, Iraq's answer to Slough or Reading perhaps, with a population of about 300,000. Yet its drab, low-rise skyline is spiked by hundreds of minarets, hence its nickname among Iraqis – the 'City of Mosques'. Even under Saddam's secular rule, its people were known as being pious, conservative, religious types. Or, if you were being rather less polite, Koran-thumping hillbillies. They were a close-knit, insular bunch, with their own tribal dialects and a naturally jealous disposition. Saddam had kept them in check by giving them plum jobs in the security services, but now that was gone the latent religious fervour was coming to the fore. The anti-American message of foreign Al Qaeda fighters had found a ready audience here, one with no shortage of grievances against US troops already.

Ever since last April, when US troops had killed 20 Fallujans during a rowdy demonstration, the Coalition presence had been bitterly resented. I'd visited Fallujah three times since then. Each time the US military was trying a different carrot-or-stick strategy, and each time it had failed. They'd deployed civil affairs units with lots of money to lash around on new schools and hospitals. Then they'd given up and sent in heavy armour divisions. Late last summer, they'd even started paying blood money to the families of those killed or injured by US troops. The hope had been that US compensation culture and the Iraqi blood money system might make some meeting of minds. It hadn't. Part of the problem was that the locals were no longer really in control. Fallujah had become a magnet for all kinds of insurgents: foreign jihadists, Saddamists, Iraqis pissed off at the occupation for whatever reason. Because the American writ ran so thinly there, they could organise, recruit and train more freely than anywhere else.

We drove down the pot-holed litter-strewn dual carriageway that was Fallujah's answer to a main drag. Things looked quieter than normal, but otherwise not noticeably different, other than the absence of any US forces anywhere. Roadside petrol sellers were touting their business at the spot where the security guards had been attacked, and the burnt out husks of the two SUVs had been cleared away. Even so, the plan was to spend only an hour or two in town, and during that time I wasn't going to set foot outside the car. Instead, Nasi would approach people, check if they were happy to talk, and then get them to sit and chat in the back. It wasn't ideal, but it was much safer; I knew from previous visits that if you interviewed people out on the streets, you quickly attracted a big audience. Whereas in Baghdad you might attract half a dozen onlookers, here you'd have a crowd of 25 within minutes, most of them ranting angrily. Given recent events, large and volatile groups of people were something to be avoided.

We pulled over by the side of the road. Qaiss's elderly BMW had shaded glass, so only a very nosey local would have been able to tell there was a foreigner sat in the back. Nasi got out and went off to find what he called some of the 'educated people'. This was a term Iraqi translators often used when visiting Iraq's rougher areas, as opposed to the 'common people'. It didn't mean degree holders, it just meant slightly less excitable types who hopefully wouldn't whistle up a lynch mob to string me from the bridge. There certainly wasn't time to hang around for a passing professor of political science. Nasi came back with a bloke from a nearby kebab shop. Abdullah Ahmed, 29, clambered into the back of the car for a five-minute interview.

'Nobody cares about the Americans dying, but I didn't like the mutilation,' he said. 'I saw what happened and it hurt my eyes. But you must understand, it was just youngsters trying to be like men. It is now part of the ritual of manhood round here that you have to have killed an American soldier to be respected. The guys who actually killed those security guards disappeared straightaway: it was just local teenagers who attacked the bodies afterwards to try and say, "I am a man.'"

'People must be able to recognise them from the film footage,' I said. 'Will you hand them over to the Americans?'

'Nobody will do that. We will just give them a talking to and tell them, "Not again".'

Somehow, I doubted that giving the culprits a 'talking to' was going to get Fallujah off the hook. Nor was General Kimmitt going to buy the idea that because contractors were dead anyway, it was OK to wave bits of their corpses around on TV. On the other hand, it was hard to see how his demand that the culprits be handed over could really be met. Anybody who'd been on the film footage would have done a runner by now. Nor were the local police going to be much use. Relations with the US troops they were supposed to work alongside were already poor, ever since an incident a couple of months back in which a US unit had mistaken a police patrol for armed robbers. They'd opened fire, killing nine policemen, and letting the bandits they'd been chasing go free. 'If we try to help the Americans when they are under attack we usually end up getting shot at as well,' said one sergeant we spoke to. He said that when the contractors had got attacked, the cops had done nothing for that very reason. It was a stance they planned to maintain. 'The Americans don't trust us any more than the rest of the people here,' he said.

We drove back an hour later, triumphant at returning in one piece. *En route* I filed a quick 500-word story for the *Sunday Telegraph*. It didn't matter that we'd done little more than a nervous motorised scamper around town. The important thing was the Fallujah dateline, the proof that we'd been there and come back alive. I was delighted, rejoicing in the thought that all my friends at home would see how brave I'd been. The next day I looked at the paper on-line, only to see that some fool on the newsdesk had put 'Colin Freeman in Baghdad' by mistake.

*****

That was the last time anybody could go into Fallujah for a while. The following evening, more than 2,000 US Marines sealed it off, cutting off all the phone lines and starting an advance to hunt down those wanted for the killings of the security contractors. Resistance was fierce, and there was heavy fighting. Nobody was surprised. General Kimmitt's ultimatum to Fallujah last week had been the military equivalent of 'Come and have a go if you think you're hard enough.' It had presumably encouraged every jihadi in Iraq to hole up there for the battle. I figured it was part of some American master plan, to lure all the insurgents into one place where they could wipe them out *en masse*.

What nobody in US central command had anticipated was another major uprising at the same time. And this time, the gunmen were not from the easy-to-demonise alliance between Saddamists and Al Qaeda. Instead, they were Shias, the people Saddam had oppressed and who had the most reason to be pro-American. Leading it was the Mahdi Army, the Shia street militia that now effectively kept law and order in many of the poorer Shia neighbourhoods. On Sunday night, as the Marines threw their cordon around Fallujah, they suddenly launched an assault on the US Army in Saddam City, the big slum in east Baghdad. Eight US troops were killed, one of the biggest losses in a single engagement. Over the next few days, they launched all-out attacks across the whole of Shia-country, seizing control of nearly every city except Basra and Al Amarah, where British troops had managed to fend them off. Meanwhile, the rebellion in Fallujah had spread to other parts of the Sunni Triangle. In nearby Ramadi, 12 Marines were killed after a seven-hour battle with insurgents who attacked their base. There were also reports of trouble in Samarra, Tikrit, Kirkuk, and elsewhere. The newswires struggled to keep track of it all. In less than a week, the country that I had confidently predicted was on the road to recovery was back on the brink of all-out war. Ever since the killings of the security guards the week before, there'd been a tension in the atmosphere, as if a can of petrol was about to be poured on the flames of the insurgency. Now it had been.

You could feel the difference on the streets. Shops were shutting early, if they were opening at all. At the Hamra hotel, the service was even worse than normal because some of the staff had stayed at home to look after their families. The headlines back home spoke of 'meltdown', of 'Iraq in anarchy'.

My US freelance mate Glen and I had dinner one night, sitting picking at our food in the restaurant at the Hamra, feeling rather like we were stuck in the US embassy compound in Saigon in 1975. The dining room was empty, even the dreadful in-house pianist hadn't turned up. Already, some journalists were being instructed by their offices not to leave the hotel, while others were pulling out altogether. More worrying still, other journalists were starting to arrive – the hard-core combat-junkie types who hadn't been here since the invasion. Most of them had found that a bit of a damp squib after Saddam unsportingly failed to unleash his weapons of mass destruction. Now they were back, clearly hoping for some proper action at last.

'What should we do, Glen?' I asked. 'Is this really our gig?'

He shrugged. 'I've no idea.'

As ever, we opted for what seemed like the only sensible strategy: have another beer and see how things worked out.

*****

So why had the sleeping Shia dog, to use my old friend Mohammed's phrase, suddenly woken up and starting biting? And why had nobody in the Coalition noticed until now? It had, after all, been baring its teeth for a good while. I'd first come across the Mahdi Army last September, while covering a suicide bombing at a police station in Saddam City. They were the first genuinely scary-looking people I'd seen in Iraq. They billed themselves as a ghetto police force, but they looked more like a street gang from 1970s Los Angeles. Black, sleeveless tee-shirts, bad mullet hairdos crowned with bandanas, and lots of tattoos. Plenty of missing fingers and ears as well, the hallmark of pasts as petty criminals in Saddam's time. *Hawassim* central, in other words. In Saddam City, they were already a law unto themselves. At the suicide bombing that day, they'd wandered around in front of the Iraqi police with their decrepit weapons openly on display. The older ones clutched belt-fed machine guns, Kalashnikovs, and elderly Tommy guns, the more junior ones had clubs, machetes and bicycle chains, which somehow seemed much more sinister. You were, after all, never going to fight the Americans using a pick axe handle. Its only purpose, surely, would be for intimidating civilians. They were also openly hostile to Westerners, something most Iraqis tended to avoid. One of them had snarled at me to go back to 'America'. Yet somehow this new street army, said to be several thousand strong, had gone largely unnoticed by the Americans. When I'd asked about them at a press briefing in the Green Zone the day after the bombing, the US colonel in charge claimed never to have heard of them.

If the Mahdi Army's footsoldiers were an ugly bunch, they had nothing on their spiritual commander, Muqtadr al Sadr. A chubby, bearded young cleric, his face was as white and pasty as a Glasgow chipshop worker's, the result of an upbringing in Iraq's religious seminaries. He was, however, of noble birth, being the son of one of Iraq's most respected Shia clerics, Grand Ayatollah Mohammed Sadiq al Sadr. Sadr Senior had been gunned down in 1999, in what most people suspected was a Saddam-ordered assassination. His son had been the last person anybody expected to carry on his father's work. Despite all the years in seminary class, he was rumoured to be exceptionally dim. But after the war he'd unexpectedly stepped into the breach, trading on his father's name and his network of charitable institutions, which were lifelines in many Shia slums.

His rise to power had infuriated many others in the Shia aristocracy, who saw him as an upstart who was far too young – and stupid – to step into his father's shoes. In Shia religious circles, you were nobody until you were at least 70, had a three-foot beard and wore enormous bifocal specs as a result of poring over Koranic texts. Muqtadr, by contrast, was barely in his 30s, and committed a serious breach of etiquette by preaching in ordinary street Arabic rather than the distant, classical form favoured by most clerics. As such, he was seen as a rabble rouser, a Malcolm X-style street preacher who'd bring nothing but trouble. But what made him disdained by the elite made him popular with the masses. His sermons could be understood by the many, and not the few, and their fiery anti-American content went down well with the restless youth in the Shia ghettoes. In places like Saddam City, now renamed Sadr City in honour of the family name, his picture hung everywhere: on street corners, in mini-buses and even in police stations, scowling fiercely and wagging a chubby, anti-American finger.

Until recently, the Coalition had seen Sadr as someone they could work with. In the anarchy of the immediate post-war months, he'd brought some much needed order into the Shia ghettoes, setting up security patrols and stopping looting. But relations had gone increasingly sour. A few weeks ago, Coalition officials had threatened to shut down his in-house newspaper, *Al Hawza*. They'd accused it of making up stories about Americans being involved in suicide bombings, something they claimed could incite violence. The *Al Hawza* offices were just down the road from my flat. The weekend before the contractors' deaths in Fallujah, several thousand Sadr supporters had gathered outside to hold a protest demo. They'd mostly come from Sadr City, some on foot, others in big open-topped trucks, chanting 'ya-ya-Muqtada'. Yet for a rabble from the slums, they were remarkably disciplined. The moment a Sadr official declared the demo over, they headed back home *en masse*, streaming down the road like a football crowd leaving a match. Anybody who could mobilise – and de-mobilise – street muscle like that was clearly a force to be reckoned with. Yet at the time, the Americans were so pre-occupied with the threat from Sunni insurgents that they didn't seem to register the potential danger. They pressed ahead with the newspaper's closure, and then found themselves off guard when all hell promptly broke loose.

As ever, now that Sadr was tearing the country apart rather than simply protesting peacefully, the outside media was finally taking notice. Newsdesks back home wanted to know more about Sadr and his cause. Interviews with Mahdi Army footsoldiers were in demand. Their main HQ in Sadr City wasn't putting anybody up right now. But as was always the way in Iraq, Nasi was able to track down a friend of a friend of a cousin of a friend, or some such thing, who was a member. Nasi told me the guy worked as a mechanic, giving me visions of some brawny grease monkey covered in oil and tattoos. But when we got there, the garage turned out to be a posh Mercedes showroom, and our 'militiaman' a skinny teenager with a wispy adolescent 'tache. Ahmed Atklal, 19, was the showroom's juniormost carwasher, and occupied a similarly lowly status in the Mahdi Army. He turned up for the rallies, chanted a lot, and that, it seemed, was about it.

'So has he been in any fighting yet?' I asked.

'No,' said Nasi. 'But he says he is awaiting the orders. He says that if the Americans try to arrest Sadr, he will be happy to die. So will thousands of others.'

'Not much of a Mahdi Army man then is he?'

'Most of them are like that. Only a few are fighters all the time. The others are trained when they are needed.'

As we sat chatting to him, Ahmed's other workmates wandered past, wondering why the gawky kid with the squeegee was getting attention for once. Later, when we told them why we interviewing him, they laughed. In their view, Ahmed had neither the brain, the brawn nor the stomach to fight anyone.

'He's just a kid, making big talk,' said one man, who claimed to have fought in the Iran-Iraq war. 'Put him in a real fight, like I fought against the Iranians. Then we'll see.'

I was tempted to agree. Yet it was precisely the desire to be respected, to be taken seriously, and to prove one's manhood, that was drawing kids like Ahmed into the Mahdi Army in the first place. Working in the car showrooms, he'd never be anything other than the thicko kid from the Shia slums who did the valeting, the one everyone cheerfully took the piss out of. Out marching under the Mahdi Army banner, he was part of a powerful gang, someone not to be messed with. He might not be carrying a gun, but he could still have a part to play, as a flag waver, message runner, and general helper. Just like car showrooms, the Mahdi Army needed its gofers.

Indeed, from what Ahmed said about his life up until now, it sounded like the Mahdi Army was the best thing that had ever happened to him. He'd only been in Baghdad since New Year, having been brought up down south in Qurnah, the former marsh town where Mohammed and I had visited the withered Tree of Knowledge. Like most Shia towns, Qurnah had been deliberately neglected by Saddam. Ahmed was a typical product of the town: dirt poor, barely able to read or write, and with no prospects. The end of the war had offered nothing more than the chance to resume his job flogging fish by the roadside, wondering when life was ever going to get better.

Then, six months ago, something exciting had finally happened in Qurnah. A Sadr deputy, Sheikh Mohammad al-Yaqubi, had turned up in town to give a speech about the Sadrist movement and the Mahdi Army. With little else to do, Ahmed had gone along out of curiosity, as indeed had nearly every other young man in town. Maybe it was just the lack of any other entertainment in Qurnah, but they'd found it a life-changing experience. 'Yaqubi is just a very simple guy, but he loves God and he told us to do the same,' said Ahmed. 'He said that we should join the Mahdi army if we wanted to save both Islam and our own country from the Americans. Who would not want to do that?'

Ahmed had signed up on the spot, moving to Baghdad so as to be at the centre of things. And while he was still juniormost carwasher at the showrooms, I got the impression his Mahdi Army membership was actually having the desired effect on his colleagues, despite their tough talk and mockery. As we left, the Iran-Iraq war veteran who'd slagged Ahmed off suddenly reappeared. 'Don't use my name,' he said. 'You can't be too careful with this lot.'

Now, though, it looked like Ahmed's bluff might be called. Since the stand-off over the closure of *Al Hawza*, the Americans had arrested al-Yaqubi and issued a warrant for Al Sadr, accusing them of being involved in the murder of a rival cleric just after the war. The scene was now set for a major stand-off. Sadr was currently holed up in a shrine in the holy city of Najaf, surrounded by hundreds of supporters who'd vowed to fight to the death for him. And unlike part-timers like Ahmed, there seemed little doubt that they meant it.

Best go and see them, then.

*****

My travelling companion for the trip to Najaf was Richard Shears, a veteran reporter from the *Daily Mail* who'd just pitched up in Baghdad. That the British tabloids had decided Iraq was a story again was the clearest possible sign that things were going very wrong. What was less clear was why they'd sent Richard to cover it. He was normally their South-East Asia correspondent, and was based in Australia, half-way round the world from Iraq, to which he'd never been before. When I asked him why they hadn't sent someone from London, he muttered something about nobody wanting to come out here anymore.

Worse still for Richard, the *Mail* had appointed him a guide and minder to help him. Me. Their foreign desk, for whom I worked from time to time, had rung up and asked if I could help him find his feet in Baghdad. In their eyes, the fact that I'd survived a whole year in Iraq was ample qualification for the job. Personally, I felt it simply showed how close my luck was to running out. But seeing as they were paying a fee for my trouble, I wasn't about to argue.

The *Mail* foreign desk might have felt rather less generous had they watched how their new security consultant did the risk assessment for visiting Najaf. Which, as ever, was to ask the views of every other reporter who'd been there, and take some kind of average. To be fair, that took a certain skill. Some reporters, for effect, would talk the dangers up. Others, scared of sounding macho, might talk them down. Either way, a certain translation key had to be applied.

'We got stuck in a firefight on the way back to Baghdad.'

Sounds like: the car ended up riddled with bullets from either side.

Actual meaning: the firefight was two miles down the road, but the Americans put up a roadblock. The reporter concerned was then 'stuck' in the large traffic jam that developed behind.

'We were arrested by the Mahdi Army.'

Sounds like: we were arrested by the Mahdi Army

Actual meaning: asked by the Mahdi Army to sit in their headquarters while they verified our press credentials. Possibly kept for an hour or two because said militiamen cannot find commander senior enough to give the OK. Offered lunch and cups of tea.

'My office are saying it's suicide to go there.'

Sounds like: it's rather dangerous.

Actual meaning: that's what I've told my office, because I don't fancy it, frankly. And if I'm not going, I don't want anyone else going either.

'We had a little trouble, but it was fine in the end.'

Sounds like: the car developed a slow puncture.

Actual meaning: a man wandered up with a grenade and threatened to pull the pin out, but my translator talked him out of it. And I've told the tale about 100 times now, so I'm bored of it.

As it happened, the word on Najaf didn't sound too bad. Unlike their Sunni insurgent counterparts, the Mahdi Army were a fairly tractable, organised bunch, and were generally fine with reporters as long as you turned up at their local headquarters and 'registered' with them. The procedure wasn't particularly rigorous. When I'd done it in Sadr City earlier in the month, the man who'd scrutinised my press credentials to ensure I wasn't a CIA spy hadn't been able to read. But it was all about flattering their sense of self-importance. After all those years of oppression under Saddam, they loved anyone who treated them as if they were in charge. Plus, if you didn't do it, you were liable to get stopped and questioned (or kidnapped, if you preferred to describe it that way).

We left for Najaf just after 8am one morning, after protracted negotiations with Nasi about how much I'd pay him and his friend Ahmed, who'd become our regular driver. Similar talks preceded nearly every remotely hazardous assignment we did together. It always disturbed me that Nasi thought about the money first and the hazards second, but then no translator was perfect. If they weren't gung ho, they were overly timid, and neither was ideal. The sensible but courageous translator, who erred neither on the side of caution nor recklessness, was thin on the ground.

We fixed sets of cheap plastic sun shades to the rear passenger windows of Ahmed's hatchback. As well as keeping out the sunlight, they helped keep our white faces hidden, particularly useful when travelling down the road just south of Baghdad, where shark patrols were in regular operation.

Three hours later, we reached the outskirts of Najaf, the huge golden dome of its main mosque gleaming in the fierce sunlight. Up on a rooftop was the first sign of the new law in town. A black-clad Mahdi army militiaman sat in a nook, pointing a tripod-mounted Kalashnikov down the road. As sniping positions went, it was pretty useless – any US army unit could easily pick him off. But it showed all new arrivals who was now in charge.

We parked up and headed for the Mahdi Army HQ near the central mosque, mingling with the crowds of Shia pilgrims. Najaf was among the holiest cities in the Shia Islam, being home to the shrine of Imam Ali, the Prophet Mohammad's cousin. But during Saddam's reign it had been effectively impossible for most pilgrims to visit. Now, since Saddam's fall, hundreds of thousands had been pouring in every month, celebrating the end of a long period of Sunni oppression. As well as Iraqis and Iranians, there were pilgrims from all over the wider 'Shia Crescent' that stretched across the Middle East and beyond. Walking past us were Indians, Pakistanis, and even a few Mongolian-looking types, with dark skin and narrow eyes. Nasi told me they were Hazaras, a Shia minority from central Afghanistan, who came in on ancient buses that took two weeks to do the journey. Their presence gave Najaf a truly exotic feel, of a place where the Middle East met the Far East.

Hidden somewhere in town was Sadr himself, who'd been holed up here ever since the Coalition had announced the warrant for his arrest. For the last couple of weeks now, a large contingent of US troops had been massing in the desert outside town, ready to steam in and take him dead or alive when they got the orders. Rumour had it that Sadr was planning to make a last stand in the central mosque itself, gambling that the Americans would never dare attack it. His tactic had outraged more moderate Shias, who were appalled that a place of worship should be used as a military sanctuary. Yet in Iraq, religion and rationality also tended to occupy mutually exclusive space. Sadr knew that if the mosque was blown to pieces, most Shias would blame the Americans rather than him.

At the Mahdi Army's headquarters we registered with one of their senior officials, a smiling young cleric clad in black robes. He had an elfin face with skin as white as my own, a black goatee, and piercing dark eyes that seemed to stare out from a previous age. I got the feeling that if he'd been born six centuries ago, he'd have looked and dressed exactly the same.

'Wait here and I will get you a guide for your visit,' he said.

'A guide?' I asked. 'That's OK. I don't think we need one.'

'You have to,' he said. 'It is for your own safety. Otherwise our soldiers might think you are spies, yes? The guide will look after you and tell them that you are our guest.'

Richard and I exchanged glances. This was a throwback to Saddam's time, when every foreign journalist was assigned a minder who watched over them, day and night. Getting locals to speak frankly about how they felt about the Mahdi Army would be very difficult if one of their number was breathing down our necks the whole time. On the other hand, it would be a chance to finally meet a proper Mahdi Army man up close.

Ten minutes later, the minder arrived. Once again, my expectations of getting a tattooed, mullet-haired Rambo lookalike proved wrong. Nabras Fahim was a small, neatly-dressed man in his early 30s. Instead of a headband, black vest and a bullet belt, he wore smart slacks, a well-ironed shirt, and a polite smile. I half-expected him to greet us, 'Hi, I'm Nabras, and I'll be your militiaman for the day.' There was still a distinct hint of menace about him, though. On his hip was a 9mm Beretta pistol, and as he led us onto the streets we noticed he walked with a slight limp. It was, he claimed, a bullet graze picked up while kicking the Spanish Coalition troops out of town earlier in the month.

Over a quick stop at a tea stall, Nabras gave us his life story. In 1999, he'd been arrested for plotting against Saddam and sentenced to 15 years in jail. His cell was so overcrowded that his family had to pay $10 a month just to rent a floor space for him to lie down at night. Facing a life – and possibly a death – behind bars, he'd been freed when Saddam had emptied the prisons just before the war.

'It was a great day – we couldn't believe it at first, and then we just all ran out together,' he said. 'When the US came here, yes, we were very happy at first. But since then, what have we seen? Nothing.'

His decision, a year on, to take up arms against his liberators seemed like a classic example of the kind of short-circuited Iraqi logic that few Westerners would ever be able to grasp. When I asked him what it was the Americans had done wrong, his main gripe was the 'lack of security'. But when I put it to him that joining an armed insurrection might not exactly help, he refused to see the point. 'Just because their army came here to help us doesn't mean we must obey them,' he said.

'Yes, but how will starting a war improve security?'

'You are here to make interview with the people of Najaf, not me. No more questions.'

We hit the streets. Najaf was home to about 500,000 people, most of whom made their living from the pilgrim trade. Some ran hotels and restaurants, others ran souvenir shops around the central mosque, selling keyrings, posters and other memorabilia of Imam Ali and his ilk. Most of Najaf's residents, I figured, would not be overjoyed at Sadr holing up here, bringing the threat of the Americans laying siege, Fallujah-style, to the city. It was therefore surprising to see that sales of freshly-minted Sadr merchandise were doing almost as well as the Imam Ali stuff. Nearly every single shop we wandered into had a poster of him scowling from the wall, and in the CD stalls around the main central mosque, loudspeakers were playing his endless sermons at full blast.

'The watches with his face are $10 each, and the keyrings and the medallions are $1,' said one stallholder, who'd switched his entire stock to the Sadr franchise. 'We've sold lots since Sadr started his uprising.' He held up what looked, at first glance, like a Sadr beer mat. 'These circular photos do well, too – you can put them on your desk or your television.'

Nabras nodded proudly. But having your face displayed everywhere by loyal fans was no guarantee of popularity: Saddam, after all, had appeared on posters, watches, murals and even the money. That Sadr was building up a similar personality cult suggested he might be much the same kind of leader. The sort whose picture you put on your wall to stop his goons coming round and asking why you hadn't got his picture on your wall.

Once again, the will of Iraq's silent majority seemed to be bending to that of its violent minority. Everybody we interviewed said they thought Sadr was great, even those who we spoke to when Nabras's back was turned. Some even came up and told us of their own accord. I suspected some really felt this way and others were simply exhibiting that pragmatic, well-honed Iraqi instinct to swing behind whoever had the biggest guns in town.

As Richard stopped to buy a Sadr watch at a souvenir stall, a dissident voice finally rang out. Having spotted us interviewing the stallholder, a young engineer called Abdul Samed strode purposefully through the crowd, clearly intent on saying his piece. 'I think the recent violence is needless,' he said in faltering English, doing his best to ignore Nabras. 'We want to live here peacefully and not become like Fallujah. I am a peaceful man, and I think most of the people in this city agree with me.'

'Really?' I said. 'That's interesting.'

We carried on chatting for a couple more minutes before Nabras, who'd been stood there glowering, cut in. 'Don't write any of that down,' he said, frogmarching us off through the crowd. 'All that young man cares about is himself, his internet cafés and his college. Is that why he doesn't want to fight, because he's more interested in those things than freedom from the Americans?'

We wouldn't get the chance to ask him. I looked over my shoulder: Abdul was a distant – and nervous-looking – face in the crowd.

It wasn't until we said goodbye to Nabras and got a taxi back to where we'd parked the car that we finally got someone to speak their mind properly. In the privacy of his cab, the taxi driver, an elderly man named Khalid Mishbeel, described Sadr as 'the second Saddam'.

'Nobody likes him in Najaf at all,' he said. 'I earn my living from the pilgrims, but since all this trouble there have been hardly any coming here. Most people have no problem with the Coalition forces – if you don't hurt them, they don't hurt you. But I tell you, people here are afraid of Sadr, because he has all the men and all the guns. Just like Saddam. If you complain about him, you will get his men coming round to your house to question you. That is why everybody puts his picture in their shops.'

As we drove out of town, Richard and I inspected his new Sadr wristwatch. It was just a cheap Chinese import, with a tiny photo of Muqtadr printed off a computer and then glued onto the dial. Already, the photo had dislodged slightly and was now wedged against the minute hand of the watch, stopping it moving.

'There's the top line for your story, Richard,' I said. 'Sadr is quite literally holding back the progress of time'.

Arse On The Line

'YOU ARE STILL HERE, Mr Freeman? It's 10 o'clock and it's dark!'

Mr Nidal, the portly, affable manager of the al-Aweel internet café near my flat, gave a tut of disapproval as he spotted me still lurking in one of the booths at the back of his premises.

'Don't worry, Mr Nidal, I'll be fine.'

'It's very dangerous for you. These days not like before. My son and I will drive you home.'

'That's very kind, but really, it's no problem. I'm only down the road.'

I logged off and left before he could argue, and began the walk back. As ever, it was a tense 10 minute stroll, eyes swivelling for signs of trouble. My logic was that very few robbers or kidnappers would be expecting a foreigner to stroll past at any time, let alone late on a Friday night. Besides, I no longer looked particularly Western, or so I hoped. Unable to protect myself by force, I'd opted to live by the alternative law of jungle, which was to blend in with the surroundings. The centrepiece of my camouflage had been to grow a moustache, a fat, Iraqi-style number worthy of Saddam himself. It had been Mohammed's suggestion, and initially I'd been horrified at the idea, but it worked. After all, few self-respecting Iraqi men were ever seen without a moustache, just as few self-respecting Western men were ever seen *with* one. True, it made me look like a cross between a porn star and a 1980s snooker player, but as long as nobody looked too closely it helped me pass for some kind of fair-skinned Iraqi: a Christian or a Kurd, perhaps, or maybe a visiting Turk.

The 'tache wasn't the only fashion compromise I'd made. The standard war-reporting chic of combat trousers, shades, utility vests and boots was too close to what the security contractors wore, and that could get you killed. Again on Mohammed's advice, I'd started wearing Iraqi clothes bought from the local market. Again, too, it was back to the 1980s: plaited slacks, garish checked shirts, and pairs of nasty little loafers with gold bars on them. Like the 'tache, the overall effect was horrible, but they worked together quite effectively. Quite often, Iraqi police at checkpoints would address me in Arabic rather than English. My only worry was what would happen if I still got kidnapped anyway. Appearing in a hostage video looking like that, all that people back home would think was what a weird-looking bloke I was.

Starring in such a video was a horribly real possibility. It had already happened to several Westerners, most notoriously Nick Berg, a 26-year-old American who'd come to Iraq looking for telecoms work. In circumstances that nobody was quite sure about, he'd fallen into the clutches of an Al Qaeda gang during a trip up north to Mosul. They'd filmed his beheading and then downloaded it onto the internet, an act that had caused even more revulsion than the mutilation of the contractors in Fallujah. So far, most of the abductions had been opportunist, taking place only when foreigners had strayed into the insurgents' path. Yet there were warnings that they'd soon start targeting Westerners in Baghdad. Especially the few like me, who lived alone, with little proper security.

For a long time I'd resisted the idea of moving somewhere safer. For one thing, the flat was cheap. For another, I liked the kudos that went with being one of the few foreign journalists who wasn't corralled into a big, heavily-guarded hotel like the Hamra. It wasn't that living outside the wire had given me any particularly unique insights into Iraqi life, unless you counted the pidgin English chats I had with local shopkeepers. But living in your own flat in Baghdad did, I liked to think, afford one a certain street cred with the women at the Hamra's poolside parties. Although none had ever been impressed enough to want to spend the night there.

But the constant warnings from people like Nidal at the internet café began to get to me. After all, if I stood out to him as a potential target, I probably stood out to others, too. I was also now in the habit of going to his place at the same time each morning to file a round-up of the various daily mayhem for the *Standard*. That gave me a routine, which was what kidnappers looked for.

Eventually, reluctantly, I decided I had to be more sensible. Packing my bags, I moved into a hotel next door to the Al Hamra, called the Al Dulaimi.

It was in the same heavily-guarded compound, but it was much cheaper. It had doubled as a brothel in Saddam's time, and the shabby decor still retained a certain bordello quality, with cheap plaster pillars, ornate maroon settees and fine tourist-art pictures of Arab nomads practising falconry. Yet it was luxury by my previous standards – boasting air conditioning, satellite TV and internet in the rooms. The 'poor man's Hamra', as it was known, was now home to half the freelancers in Baghdad. Glen, Jill, and many others I knew were there, churning out cut-price correspondence for budget-conscious editors around the world and occasionally doing holiday cover for the bigger names at the Hamra next door. If the Al Dulaimi got bombed, the joke went, no staff reporter would be able to leave Baghdad for months.

Despite the fighting, the Hamra summer social scene was blossoming once again. Evenings by the poolside were also where the latest scare stories were bandied around, this summer in rather more abundance than last. Such-and-such had been followed by a mysterious car coming back from the Green Zone. So-and-so had been shot at driving near Fallujah. Someone's translator had quit after being threatened. Someone else had just left a police station when it got carbombed.

Gradually, more and more people I knew seemed to have had some kind of close shave. It got to the point where you felt that you were somehow missing out if you hadn't. Already there'd been a few fatalities. Two journalists working for Polish TV had been killed when their car was attacked by a shark patrol in Mahmoudiya, a redneck Sunni farming town south of Baghdad. They'd had a press sticker on the car, too: it was a sign, perhaps, that in some insurgents' eyes we were just another agency of the Western occupation.

Some correspondents who'd worked in other war zones found the hostility hard to understand. In other guerrilla wars, they'd been welcomed in by every faction, seen as neutral observers who'd air some militants' obscure grievances to the wider world. Yet the fact was that in the new multi-media age, we were no longer needed. If the insurgents wanted to get a message out, they could use the internet, as they'd done with Nick Berg, or go to the new Arab satellite TV channels like al Jazeera. Gone were the days when we Western journalists were the only ones who could tell 'their side of the story'. Now they could do that themselves, unedited and at full length.

The fact that the insurgents didn't particularly need us meant they also had no particular interest in giving interviews. Lots of translators and drivers claimed to have cousins or friends who were involved in the insurgency in some way, but when they tried arranging a rendezvous it often got very sticky. Frequently there'd be demands for money, and they were always paranoid that you were a spy. One fixer I knew tried to arrange an interview for a Western journalist with an insurgent cell via a middleman. 'The middleman told us that if anything happened to any members of the cell after the interview, like if they got raided by Americans, both me and the journalist would be killed,' he said. 'It wasn't worth the risk.'

Even if you went ahead with a meeting, there was little way of telling whether the person in front of you was a bona fide insurgent, or just a sympathiser who liked shooting his mouth off. Or, as happened in Pakistan with the murdered *Wall Street Journal* reporter Daniel Pearl, the whole thing might be a set up designed to get you kidnapped. And even if they were genuine – and willing to meet – you couldn't do much more than sit and listen to them talk. Accompanying them on any kind of "mission", as reporters sometimes did with insurgents elsewhere in world, would be utterly perilous. These people weren't, after all, fighting some other rag-tag guerrilla group, but the US Army – to whom they almost invariably came off worst, and to whom you'd be indistinguishable down a gunsight. Besides, whatever your take on the rights or wrongs of the occupation, it would be a considerable exercise in journalistic detachment for a Western reporter to sit and watch while some guerrilla cell staged an ambush on a group of Coalition soldiers. At best, your newspaper would probably be accused of treason. At worst, you'd end up in Guantanamo Bay.

The whole 'meet the insurgents' thing was fraught with pitfalls, in other words. And, of course, it took balls of steel in the first place. Balls that I didn't have, frankly, at least not as a one-man band. A few news organisations in Baghdad did develop insurgent contacts. But they tended to be the bigger outfits, who could dedicate a few fixers purely to building up the necessary trust, and who had strings they could pull if it all went wrong. I had no such resources. That was my excuse, anyway.

*****

Human life was in Iraq was cheap, but the cost of getting someone killed varied widely.

The US Army had put $25 million on Saddam's head, $15 million apiece for his two sons, and a sliding pay scale for their various henchmen. Osama bin Laden, their opposite number, was now offering 10 kilos of gold for anyone who killed Paul Bremer, Iraq's Coalition governor, and a single kilo for anyone who killed a Western civilian like me. At current gold prices, that made me worth around £7,500, about the price of a second-hand car.

Poorest payer of all, however, was one Sheikh Abdul Sattar al Bahadli, the Mahdi Army's main man down in British controlled-Basra. In a speech in mid-May, he offered a paltry $200 bounty for anyone who could bring him a British soldier. That was barely enough to cover someone's petrol costs, but right now al Bahadli reckoned he'd get plenty of takers. Especially once he'd shown people the pictures from Britain's *Daily Mirror* which supposedly showed British troops in Basra beating up and urinating on an Iraqi prisoner in a truck. The *Mirror* had printed them earlier in the week, presenting them as a British version of the American abuse scandal at Abu Ghraib. Within days, though, an MOD inquiry was revealing doubts about their authenticity. The truck in which the man was being beaten, the guns the soldiers were carrying, even the hood the prisoner was wearing over his head – none were the kind being used by troops in Basra. Soon the only people still insisting they were real were soon-to-be-fired *Mirror* editor Piers Morgan and Sheikh Al Bahadli himself, who knew they had dynamite propaganda value in his campaign to get Basra to rise up and kick the British out. On the off chance that he might succeed, the *Sunday Telegraph* sent me down there for a few days.

Having first checked that his budget bounty list didn't include British reporters, Nasi and I swung by al Bahadli's HQ as soon as we arrived in Basra. After a short wait, he summoned us into his office. He was a big, bear-like man, clad in black robes and a white turban. We'd been able to find out very little about him, other than a bizarre rumour going around town that he'd once been the drummer in a local dance troupe performing at Ba'athist weddings and parties. That had come from a Coalition press officer, who, to my delight, also told me that his nickname among the British was 'Sheikh behaving al Bahadli'. Nonetheless, he actually seemed quite affable. He laughed, rather than scowled, when asked if he'd been part of Basra's answer to Abba. 'If you had ever heard me try to sing, you would know that that rumour isn't true,' he said. Then, as we began to talk about the *Mirror*'s torture pictures, he delved into his desk and produced a picture exclusive of his own. 'Take a look at these,' he said, handing over an envelope. 'British Army soldiers, raping Iraqi women.'

I flicked through them. Whatever the shortcomings of the *Mirror* photos, they'd at least looked authentic to the untutored eye. The same could not be said about these. The naked rape 'victims' were women photoshopped from porn websites and crudely superimposed onto images of soldiers. In one picture, a woman was fellating a soldier while two of his friends looked on. Not only did she look rather too enthusiastic about the task, the soldiers she was pleasuring were in dark green uniforms. The Brits in Iraq only ever wore beige desert colours. Plus there was a mountain range in the background, even though Basra was surrounded by spirit-level flat desert. There was no MOD inquiry needed here.

I put these minor points to the sheikh, but he was having none of it. 'These are definitely genuine,' he said.

'But what about the mountain range? Everywhere around here is completely flat desert.'

'Ah no, there are some mountains near here.'

'Where?'

'Over near the port at Um Qasr. Perhaps you have not seen them.'

I'd been to Um Qasr. Unless I was being an even less observant reporter than normal, the imposing mountain range overlooking the port had somehow slipped me by. I had the feeling the sheikh knew the pictures were fake, and that he knew I knew he knew, too. But his followers, the poor, uneducated illiterates who'd never been near a computer in their lives, might be more easily fooled. Or, like him, might just ignore the fact they were fake anyway. The rationale was simple – even if the photos weren't real, such abuse was probably going on anyway. Plenty of people back home in Britain, after all, were saying that.

Those same people in Britain, however, were not planning to whip thousands of armed followers into a frenzy over the matter. 'I will be showing these pictures to my followers at Friday prayers tomorrow,' Sheikh al Bahadli said brightly. 'Why don't you come along?'

Nasi and I conferred. Such a mission was not without risk. Only last Saturday, al Bahadli's lot had been in full-scale battle with the British Army. The Friday prayers the day before had been where he'd delivered the pre-match pep-talk. Would the crowd, in venting their anti-British spleen, be able to observe the fine distinction between the British soldiers – evil crusaders of Tony Blair – and the British press – righteous crusaders for Truth?

No problem, said Sheikh al Bahadli. He scribbled on a small scrap of paper and handed it to Nasi. Written on it was his signature, along with the words 'the holder of this shall pass.'

Personally, I'd have preferred something rather more official-looking and preferably banner-sized. But round here, it was the Sadr movement's equivalent of a Papal blessing. It was as good a chance as I'd ever get to attend a Mahdi Army prayer meeting. We thanked the sheikh kindly, and said we'd see him the next day.

*****

The prayer service was an open-air affair, held on a patch of waste ground next to a canal. It was in the middle of one of Basra's many slums, a sewage-smelling shanty town from where the Mahdi Army drew many of its supporters. About a thousand people had turned up, along with ourselves and a few Arab media types. Just to be on the safe side, we got one of the Sheikh's deputies, whom we'd met at his HQ the day before, to lead us through the crowd to the small makeshift podium where al Bahadli was going to speak.

Whatever the truth about his rumoured past in a dance troupe, al Bahadli was certainly a showman. He turned up brandishing an assault rifle, which he waved around throughout the sermon along with the fake torture pictures. He ranted for the best part of an hour, the crowd screaming 'Yes, yes to jihad' in ever louder voices. Then, having knelt down to pray in front of the rifle, he left, posing obligingly for pictures. Nasi and I wandered off quickly before the crowd began to disperse, hoping to grab the first taxi that passed by.

As we turned a corner leading off the waste ground, there were two almighty bangs right behind us. I felt a sharp pain in the backside that left me breathless, as if someone had stuffed a firecracker down my trousers.

'What the hell... ?'

Turning round, I saw a man standing just a few feet behind us, holding a smoking pistol. He was skinny, about 25, and looked upset about something. Not half as upset as I was: the daft idiot had obviously been fiddling with his gun and had accidentally discharged it into the road right behind me. The pain I'd felt searing across my backside must have been from the muzzle blast deflecting off the concrete. It quickly subsided, but still, what a careless idiot. He could have killed me. Nasi was yelling at him in Arabic.

'Nasi, what does this bloke think he's doing?'

Nasi didn't reply. But I assumed from the way they were jabbering at each other, he was asking that exact question. Then, just as the bloke should have been outstretching his hand in apology, he raised the pistol again, his hand wobbling, and pointed it at Nasi. I watched, uncomprehending. Nasi swatted the gun away, still arguing with the guy at the top of his voice. Panic stabbed through me.

'Nasi! What the hell is going on?'

Nasi broke off briefly from his barrage of Arabic. 'Don't ask questions just now,' he said.

As Nasi and the pistol guy kept arguing, several other people gathered round, grabbing me and leading me around the corner. Just as I assumed they were getting me out of harm's way, one of them pushed me against the wall and spread-eagled my arms. Hands rifled through the pockets and patted down my trousers.

'Let us see inside your bag!' An English-speaking voice, not a friendly one. 'Open it yourself!'

Still facing the wall, I opened the bag up. Inside was my satphone, a notebook and a few posters of Muqtadr al Sadr that we'd bought from a stall before the demo started. The piece of paper from the sheikh, I suddenly realised, was probably with Nasi. Who was now nowhere to be seen.

The Voice again. 'Who are you? What are you doing here?'

'Moo mishkilleh, ana sahafi,' I shouted. It was pidgin Arabic for 'No problem. I'm a journalist.' Just to be on the safe side, I said it in

English as well. 'I'm a journalist! We were covering the prayer meeting. We were invited here by the sheikh! What's the matter?'

The Voice said nothing. Instead, someone half-nelsoned me and started frogmarching me back round the corner from where we'd come. Scores of other people were now gathered around. In the distance I could see the main crowd, still hanging about now they'd got wind of some commotion.

Shit.

This was it. This was the moment that every reporter in Iraq knew they might face one day. The group immediately around me seemed to have divided into two, pulling me one way and then the other. They seemed to be arguing over me, one lot convinced I was obviously guilty of something, the others yelling at them to let me go. That at least, was the charitable interpretation of what they were doing. For all I knew, they could have been arguing over who was going to execute me. Either way, I was now becoming the centre of attention of a very large Arab mob, all nicely fired up and warlike from the sheikh's speech. As if to confirm my suspicion, an Arab TV crew lurched into view on my right, filming what they no doubt hoped would be the live execution of a Westerner. What was I supposed to do? Realising it might be the last pictures the world saw of me alive, I tried to look stoic and serene. A man accepting his end with quiet dignity. Or, perhaps, some smug, smirking tosser, blissfully unaware of his imminent fate. One bystander seemed to see it that way: he made a beeline for me through the crowd and punched me right in the face. It didn't hurt one bit. Either he hadn't connected that well, or my adrenalin was acting as an anaesthetic.

Keep calm, mate. This is a Mahdi Army crowd. Not like those mad Sunni bastards in Fallujah. They have a hierarchy, a command structure. Someone will sort this out soon.

Sure enough, just as I was entertaining visions of my remains being hung over the nearby canal bridge, Fallujah-style, a 4x4 came barging through the crowd and stopped about 10 yards away. Out jumped Nasi and the sheikh's deputy who'd chaperoned us earlier. The deputy was a just a little guy, five-foot-five and not much out of his mid 20s. But he clearly had clout. The moment his presence become known, the hands propelling me forwards suddenly eased off. Then, before anyone could change their mind, he and Nasi barged through the crowd and grabbed me.

'Get in the fucking car, man,' screamed Nasi. 'Quick, fucking hurry! They're going to fucking kill you.'

The pair of them began dragging me away. Instantly, hands began pulling again in the opposite direction, a clear sign that the deputy's authority was waning. The SUV careered towards us, rear passenger door already open. If the driver stopped, the mob would close in and he'd never get started again.

I hurled myself into the back seat, spilling the contents of my bag all over the ground as I did so. Right now, I didn't really mind leaving a £1,000 satellite phone behind, never mind a notebook and camera.

To my astonishment, several pairs of hands then passed them all back to me as Nasi clambered in. I'd always been impressed by the general Iraqi sense of honesty: even when they were trying to murder you, they still wouldn't steal your stuff.

We careered off over the wasteland, scattering people right and left. The sheikh's deputy was up front with a driver, plus two other men.

'Nasi, will you please now tell me what the fuck all that was about?'

'They thought we were spies for the British military,' he said. 'That guy with the gun was going to try and kidnap us both. Did you see when I tried to stop him? He fucking tried to shoot it at me.'

Had he? I remembered the pistol waving in front of Nasi's face, but I'd had no idea what the guy's intentions had been. The whole thing had been a blur. Some war reporter I was – I couldn't even tell when someone tried to shoot my interpreter.

'If I hadn't gone and got the deputy, you'd be fucking dead by now,' Nasi said.

'I know, mate. You saved my life. Thank you.'

He was right, too. He'd made a very good call. In the pandemonium after the gunshot, it would have been all too easy for him to stick around, trying to argue with people who didn't want to listen. Instead he'd kept his head, worked out who might be able to help, and gone and found him. In a way it was just the simple, logical thing to do. But in the heat of the moment, you could have had all the hostile environment training in the world and not done it.

'The driver is asking where he should drop us, by the way,' said Nasi.

'Tell him to drop us outside the Marbad Hotel,' I said. It was the main hotel in downtown Basra. It wasn't where we were staying. But I didn't want any of the Mahdi Army people being able to find us again. Not even the deputy who'd just rescued us. We'd wait till they'd gone, then sneak back to our own hotel, pack up and then get a taxi straight back to Baghdad. Screw the story for the *Sunday Telegraph*. Staying on here would now be dangerous. Any aggro that the Mahdi Army had from the Brits in the next 48 hours would arouse suspicions that we had indeed been military spies, and that we'd passed on some kind of intelligence. I was also worried that they might change their minds at any minute about letting us go. After all, as far as they were concerned, I might go straight to the nearest British Army base and complain about them nearly lynching me. To try to reassure them, I thanked the sheikh's deputy for his help. I tried to sound as unruffled as possible, as if he'd just helped us with a flat tyre.

'He says no problem,' said Nasi.

We carried on driving in silence, me grinning away inanely and trying to collect my thoughts. For a while, I wondered whether I might go into some kind of post-traumatic shock. But the sheer relief of escaping that crowd of crazies seemed to cancel any other feeling out. On the horizon I spotted the small group of tower blocks that make up Basra's downtown, where the Marbad Hotel was. Then I realised they were getting further away, rather than nearer.

'Er, Nasi, where are we going? The hotel's in that direction, isn't it?'

Nasi spoke with the driver.

'Ah, the sheikh's deputy says we must go to his headquarters first.'

'What for?'

'He says the sheikh must see us first. He can't release us without his permission.'

Bastard. This was just what I'd feared. They were getting worried about letting us go. We tried telling him that we had another appointment to go to, but it didn't work. Looking anxious to get away would just make things worse. We'd just have to trust in Sheikh al Bahadli's common sense. Great.

Back at the sheikh's HQ, we were ushered into his office, the same one where he'd shown us the fake photos. It was empty.

'Where is he?'

'They say he's out right now,' said Nasi. 'He'll be back in half an hour or so.'

Several of the building's armed guards, I noticed, had now joined us in his office, clearly posted to keep watch. As we sat down on a hard wooden bench, I felt the pain in my backside return. Now it was a dull, throbbing ache. As I stood up to investigate, Nasi muttered something in Arabic.

'Colin, man, your fuckin' ass. Blood all over your trousers.'

Sure enough, the back of my strides was now stained dark red. Backing into the corner of the room, I lowered my trousers while Nasi took a look. As he did so, I felt a thin trickle of blood coming down from my underpants. I felt the wound and pulled away a small grey bullet fragment lodged in the back left pocket of my trousers.

'Fuck man, you been shot,' said Nasi.

'Tell these guys I need to go to the hospital,' I said. 'It's beginning to hurt. I can't wait here for the sheikh to come.'

He spoke to them. 'They say sorry, they can't let you go yet.'

'Jesus, man, I'm wounded here. Tell them I'm going to die.'

'They say is just a small wound. No problem. They say just be patient.'

I gave up. Members of the Mahdi Army were never going to be impressed by a small bullet graze to the arse. Short of missing a limb or two, I was stuck here.

'Can you ask them if I can call my office on my satphone? Just to tell them that I will be going to the hospital?'

'They say OK.'

I went outside and dialled the *Sunday Telegraph* foreign desk. I'd tell them what had happened, and let them know I was in Muqtadr Al Sadr's headquarters in Basra. If nothing else, it'd be a good starting point for where to dig for my body.

'Hello, it's Colin Freeman down in Basra here.'

'Hi Colin, how are you?' The line, fortunately, was crystal clear, with none of the burbling you sometimes got with a satellite link. Which was more than could be said for what came out of my mouth.

'Er, I'm fine. Well, sort of. I went to a Mahdi Army demo this morning, and someone thought we were British spies. A guy fired a gun behind me, and I've been shot. Er, sort of. Anyway, I'm fine now.

But we've been taken to the Mahdi Army HQ in Basra, and they're not letting us go until the sheikh turns up. Er, it'll be all OK, I think. But just in case they take us hostage, I thought you should know where we are. But probably nothing to worry about.'

'Sorry, say you've been sort of shot?'

'Yes. But just a little graze... I'm fine, really.'

I gave them a description of the Mahdi Army HQ, and than rang off as the sheikh turned up. He took one look at my backside, looked mildly horrified when he'd heard what happened, and, to my immense relief, drove us off to the Marbad Hotel as requested.

The Marbad, like most hotels used by Westerners visiting Basra, was heavily fortified, with blast walls and several sets of armed guards. We got out the car, thanked the sheikh for all he'd done for us, and scampered past the checkpoint.

As we wandered into the hotel courtyard, a TV crew came over. I recognised Ben Brown, one of the big-name reporters from the BBC. Unbeknown to me, he'd been at the demo as well and had seen what happened, although from some distance away.

'Are you OK?' he asked. 'We saw you got into some kind of trouble and then lost sight of you.'

I told them what had happened. 'I think I'm alright. Just this scratch on my backside.'

'Sounds like you had a lucky escape. We tried to buy the footage from that camera crew who filmed you.'

'Really? Did it show much?' I had visions of myself being lead item on the BBC 9 o'clock news.

'Nah, it was crap footage, you couldn't really see what was going on. And anyway, the guy who shot it was too scared to give it to us. But we made a call to the Brits when we saw you'd got whisked off, just in case something happened. I think they had a quick reaction force ready to come looking for you.'

'Bloody hell.' I had visions of hundreds of troops surrounding Sheikh al Bahadli's HQ. An armed stand-off, perhaps igniting a huge battle for Basra, and all for me. I'd have felt so embarrassed.

Stood next to Ben was a burly British guy in combat trousers and shirt. He was the TV's crew's security adviser, an ex-military type.

'You'd better let me check that wound out, mate,' he said.

We went into the hotel toilets and I dropped my underpants. He sucked his teeth. 'Don't like the look of that. You've got an entry and an exit wound there.'

'Really? Well, I was going to go to Basra Hospital in a bit, for a check up.'

'No way mate. Not with that. You need to go to the British Army base to get it looked at there.'

'Seriously, I'm sure I'll be fine just going to Basra Hospital.'

'We've already rung them, mate. They're expecting you. We'll drive you over.'

I stopped arguing. Basra Hospital, after all, was of Third World standards. I'd been there for a story once, where they'd showed me round the A&E department. They'd had half a dozen serious gunshot casualties in just that day alone, including a carjack victim who'd somehow survived having a bullet fired right through his skull. I wouldn't be a high priority.

'Are you feeling OK, by the way, mate?' the security guard asked. 'Not in shock or anything?'

'Don't think so. Just glad to have got out of there.'

'Well, here's a little word of warning. You've been through a bit of an ordeal. You're adrenalin's all fired up. It'll go away in a bit, but you might get a bit of a comedown. Perfectly natural, just be aware of it though.'

We headed off to the main British Army base, me waiting for some kind of post-traumatic stress to kick in. Nothing happened. In fact, I felt rather good. I'd had my moment of terror and lived to tell the tale. And, with any luck, sell it. I could get a good piece out of this. 'My terror at the hands of Shia militiamen', or something. Or, as the soldier manning the gate of the army base seemed to think, 'The day I got a hilariously-situated wound right in my bottom.'

'Shot in the arse, eh?' he said, guffawing. 'Hee hee hee. Get lots of 'em through here, I tell ya. Yer arse is the place for it, mind. Nowt too valuable in there. C'mon in.'

Five minutes later I was lying on a trolley in the Army hospital, being jabbed with tetanus injections, X-rayed and generally poked and prodded by several different medics. They looked far more concerned than I was, and seemed somewhat surprised that I wasn't more worked up. Then, just as I was beginning to wonder what all the fuss was about, a medic came through and handed me an X-ray photo.

'That's what we've found in your backside,' he said.

I looked. Just below the ghostly white outline of my hip bone was a solid white object. It was bullet shaped and it was lodged right in my arse cheek.

'Shit. Is that what I think it is?'

'We're going to have to operate on you, sir,' said the medic. 'That bullet will need to come out. You'll probably be in surgery later tonight. It'll need to be under general anaesthetic.'

'How come I never felt anything at the time?'

'Your backside is mainly just tissue and fat, sir. No bone or muscle there. Best place to get a wound, believe me.'

'What size of bullet was it by, the way?'

'Looks like a .22.'

'Oh.' Somehow, I couldn't help feeling disappointed. I'd assumed it was a nine millimetre, the calibre most Iraqis carried. A .22 was considered a bit of a peashooter round these parts, the sort a lady might keep in her handbag for personal protection. On the other hand, a nine millimetre would probably have killed me, or at very least mangled my nether regions. To my tremendous good fortune, I'd been shot by the only man in Iraq carrying a girl's gun.

And then I remembered the infamous .22 assassin. Could it be…? Nah, he'd been up in Baghdad. But you never knew.

'Will I be able to keep the bullet as a souvenir?'

'Of course, sir. Once we've dug it out.'

*****

Soon afterwards I was whisked off in an Army ambulance to the main field hospital at Shaibah, an old airfield about 45 minutes' drive from Basra. It was a sprawling, makeshift network of wards in long, air conditioned tents, originally set up to deal with casualties from the invasion. So far, there hadn't been anything like as many as they'd feared, and the medics spent much of their time treating Iraqi civilians. 'You'll get treated quicker and better here than you would on the NHS,' one of the paramedics told me.

The ambulance backed into an open-ended tent which was used as the A&E reception area. Then it was straight onto a trolley to the operating theatre, a team of medics staring down at me. As I drifted off under the anaesthetic, I still couldn't quite believe that I had a bullet right inside me.

How the hell could I not have noticed getting shot? Even for a reporter of my limited perceptive powers, it was quite astonishing.

Sometime the next morning I woke up in a ward with a large dressing taped round my left buttock. A medic handed me the bullet, swathed in cotton wool in a plastic tube. Oddly, it was a different colour to the piece I'd dug out myself the day before. I seemed to have three separate wounds, too. Bullets, I knew, could ricochet around the body like a pinball – there are cases of people dying after being shot in the foot after the round has bounced up into the heart. But even so, it didn't really make sense. Two different kinds of lead, three wounds... my arse was in danger of becoming a ballistics mystery akin to the Kennedy assassination.

Right, now, though, there was also the question of putting some sort of story together for the *Sunday Telegraph*. Unfortunately, I now only had a couple of hours to put it together before their Saturday afternoon deadline, while also feeling groggy from the anaesthetic. The medics found me a computer terminal, where I sat, still attached to a drip, and bashed out 800 words.

'Death stared me in the face on Friday,' went my top line. 'Or, to be precise, it delivered a nasty blow from behind.'

What followed should have been my best piece ever. Few reporters ever get shot, and fewer still live to tell the tale. But anaesthetic and deadline pressures did not mix well. The rest of the story was somewhat garbled. Much to my embarrassment, the rest of my first-hand account of violence on the streets of Basra ended up being re-written by someone in the office.

That apart, the following week was one of the most pleasant I'd spent in Iraq. Most of the time was spent in blissful forced idleness, lying around in bed feeling pleasantly woozy from painkillers. In between times I watched satellite TV, enjoyed a full English breakfast every day and wrote rehashed versions of the *Sunday Telegraph* piece for *The Scotsman*, the *San Francisco Chronicle*, and the *Evening Standard*. The Press Association newswire did a version too, culled from the *Standard* report: 'A British journalist told today how he was shot, beaten and dragged through the streets by a mob of Shia militiamen in Basra.'

Somehow they made it sound much more dramatic than I had. Even my old local paper, the *Grimsby Evening Telegraph*, picked it up, changing me in the ever-parochial way of these things from 'a British journalist' to 'a former Grimsby journalist'. By the end of the week, my arse had had more column inches devoted to it than Kylie Minogue's.

One afternoon the Army chaplain stopped by my bed while doing his ward rounds. 'Can I ask you a favour?' he said. 'I was wondering if you'd be willing to do a talk one evening on what it's like to be a civilian in Iraq. You've been here quite a while, haven't you?'

'Well, I suppose I have. But I'm not sure I'd know much that your guys don't know already, to be honest.'

'Don't count on it. Most people on this base are medical workers, so they don't do patrols like the regular soldiers. And with all this trouble, they don't go out of the base unless it's strictly necessary. Some have been here for months without ever really seeing the world beyond the fence. I'm sure they'd be very interested to hear your views. On what the Iraqis are like, how they see us, that sort of thing. Remember, you get a different perspective, not being a soldier.'

It was a sad sign of how bad things were if the British Army were turning to the likes of me for insights into Iraq. And that people were so bored that they'd give up their evenings to listen. But since they'd looked after me for a week, I owed them a favour. I spent a fruitless afternoon thinking of intelligent things to say, then gave up in the hope of ad libbing it. It'd only be the chaplain and a few of his *Guardian*-reading chums from the officers' mess, anyway.

It wasn't.

Packed into the briefing room were at least 150 soldiers, most of them squaddies. And, as it quickly became clear, *Mirror* readers. They sat politely while I waffled away, but in the Q&A afterwards, it was clear why they'd really come. They wanted to take a member of Her Majesty's Press to task about the fake pictures controversy. Why had the *Mirror* printed them if they knew they were fakes? Didn't they realise it could put everybody's lives at risk? And wasn't it all just to get front page news stories and sell more papers?

The only question I had a real answer to was the last one.

'Most people who buy a paper turn first to the sport, then to the telly pages, and then to the ads,' I said. 'Then, if we're very lucky, they might read a bit of the news. I tell you, I'd be very happy if news sold papers, but I'm afraid it doesn't. If you want to sell papers, you write about Big Brother.'

That shut them up.

*****

By the end of the week it was time to have the wound closed up properly, resealing the incisions the surgeons had made to dig the bullet out. It needed another spell under general anaesthetic, this time courtesy of a Territorial Army surgeon on loan from a teaching hospital in the Wirral. Like the chaplain, he had a favour to ask.

'When I get back to the Wirral, I'm going to be giving my colleagues a talk about my time out here in Iraq. Would you mind if I took a picture of your buttocks for a slide show presentation? It's a good example of a gunshot wound.'

I stared at him, momentarily dumbfounded. Reporters had never been popular with the military, and less so since the Mirror scandal. I suspected that the photos would also end up on the dartboard in the officers' mess; on the other hand, the idea of a group of learned physicians discussing my arse was quite amusing.

'Er, if you think so, why not, yes.'

I woke up the next day in a blissful, painkiller-induced high. He'd obviously bunged me up with some sort of morphine, and there was now about an inch and a half of stout stitches on the main wound, running across my backside like a railway line. The only problem was that my muscles felt so relaxed I couldn't pee. When one of the nurses escorted me to the toilets, I stood there groggily for a few minutes with nothing coming out.

'It's your bladder muscles, love, they sometimes go a bit strange after anaesthetic,' she said, as she led me back to bed. 'We'll have to get you a penis catheter.'

'A penis what?'

I wasn't quite sure what a catheter was. But frankly any device that involved the word 'penis' was bound to be painful.

'It's a tube that goes up inside. It can be a bit uncomfortable at first. But it'll allow you to pass water and relieve the stress on your bladder. Don't worry, love, we'll get a male nurse to do it.'

'Um, OK.' I nodded half-heartedly, unconvinced that this would make the experience more pleasurable. Two minutes later a male nurse arrived, armed with a sinister array of tubing that looked like a miniature home brew kit. Inserting penis catheters, it turned out, was one of his most regular assignments. Given that his patients were mainly homophobic British squaddies, he'd developed a kind of matey patter to help them get over the fact that a grown man was handling their private parts.

'That's right, I'm the chap who's going to stick something up your nob, mate,' he said cheerfully, rapidly assembling the contraption round my nether regions. 'I get all the nice jobs round here. Might hurt a bit when it goes in, but I'll give you a local anaesthetic straight after.'

Half a minute later he'd got everything in place, his repartee never faltering. I didn't look too closely, but suddenly I felt the pressure easing off my bladder for the first time in hours. It was glorious, almost as good as the morphine. The next morning he came back to empty it, and we chatted together like old friends. You had to hand it to the British Army, they were very professional. Who else could stick something up your nob and make you want to buy them a beer?

The Curse Of
The Al Dulaimi Hotel

'YOU'RE DOM'S MATE who got shot in the arse, aren't you?' The girl who'd wandered up to me in the bar grinned over her beer bottle. 'Gonna show us your scar then?'

The female nurses had said this might happen. Women loved men with war wounds, they said. All the better if you had one in an intimate place. A chat-up line for life. Unfortunately, this particular lady was not alone. Stood right beside her, also swigging drunkenly on a bottle of beer, was her husband. Who was equally keen for a look. 'Go on mate, trousers down,' he roared. 'Let's see that arse.'

It was early September, nearly three months after I'd been shot, and I was at Dominic and Tracey's wedding. It was being held in a small town in Italy where Dominic's father had grown up, a beautiful little place just north of Rome. The bride and groom, who were due to get married the next day, had invited us all out for several days of feasting and drinking. For some guests, though, the wedding seemed to be a sideshow to the main event: seeing the bloke with the bullet-scarred bum.

Such was my new minor-celebrity status since returning home to London in August. The hospital had patched me up so well that I'd stayed on in Iraq to work for another couple of months, proudly bearing a British Army medical certificate saying 'Gunshot wound left buttocks'. Much to my delight, in the box where the medics had to describe the nature of the injury, they'd put 'Enemy action.'

If I ever had any grandchildren, I'd be able to show it to them one day. They'd learn that had the bullet hit Granddad a few inches further to the right, they'd never have been born.

Yet despite it being a close call, the fact that I'd been shot in the backside made the whole thing seem a bit of a giggle rather than a terrifying brush with death. Any hopes that I might acquire some sort of new gravitas as a war reporter were rudely shattered by emails I got from people back home, all packed with arse-related puns. 'What's the bottom line... you're twice the arsehole you were... so you like it up the bum, eh?', and other witticisms. Even my mum, who can normally be counted on to worry about nearly anything, had seen the funny side.

As a result, the guests at Dom's wedding knew me not as Colin Freeman, Distinguished War Reporter and Doyen of the Iraqi Frontline. Instead, I was Dom's Mate Who Got Shot in the Arse. Which, by rights, meant I ought to be willing to bare it at any minute, like some kind of performing baboon. I hardly even recognised the couple who were now demanding I dropped my trousers in front of them. The bloke I vaguely remembered as a mate of Dominic's who I'd not met for years. His partner I'd never met in my life. Yet neither seemed willing to take no for an answer. Only after I'd politely demurred several times did they eventually wander off. 'Later on, mate,' said the bloke, in the tone of a man who wasn't going to give up easily. 'We're definitely seeing it before we all go home.' Surely Martin Bell of the BBC didn't get drunkards demanding to see his war wounds when he got injured in Sarajevo? Then again, he'd had the good sense not to get hit in the bum.

*****

My final two months back in Baghdad had been uneventful by Baghdad standards.

Nasi had started carrying a pistol everywhere we went, saying the trouble down in Basra had shown we needed protection. 'Anyone make problem for us now, they fuckin' dead, Colin, believe me,' he told me when I got back. He'd lifted his shirt to reveal a Czech-made 9mm pistol, tucked into his waistband alongside his mobile phone. He'd bought it in some gun market for $200, the bonus I'd given him for the trip to Basra. The Americans had trained him up in how to use a pistol when he'd worked for them as a translator. I pointed out that if he'd pulled it on the man who'd attacked us in Basra, we'd almost certainly both have wound up dead. To my mind, carrying a firearm anywhere in Iraq was crazy, given that anybody not in an US Abrams tank was nearly always likely to be outgunned. There was also the small ethical question over what would happen if we shot someone while out reporting. The National Union of Journalists, of which I was now a freelance member, didn't explicitly mention it in their code of conduct but I was sure it would be frowned upon.

Nasi refused to listen. 'Remember, Colin, I was making translation for the US Army before working for you, so many insurgent guys, they want me killed,' he said. 'Also, is dangerous for me working with the foreigner like you. This protection for me, not just you.'

He had a point. I had no right to dictate to him how he protected himself. 'I suppose so,' I said. 'But think before you pull it on anyone, won't you?'

'Don't worry. I trained by the Coalition force. Hey, you want gun as well?'

'No, I most certainly don't.'

Luckily the dilemma didn't last long. A couple of weeks later, I had a call from Nasi saying he wouldn't be coming into work for a while. He was ringing from a police station, where he'd been detained after an argument with a traffic policeman at a checkpoint. He and Ahmed had been pulled over because of the stick-on sunshades on the rear windows that I used to hide behind when travelling in the car. The cops, worried that terrorists were doing the same thing, had now banned the use of sunshades on pain of a 15,000 dinar fine (about $10). Nasi's protests that it was to stop me getting kidnapped and beheaded had fallen on deaf ears.

'They arrested you just for that?' I asked.

'Sort of, yes.'

'What do you mean, sort of?'

'I made an argument with the police lieutenant.'

'How do you mean?'

'He was showing a real bad attitude, getting very angry with us. So I told him he was a fuckin' asshole. Then he pulled his gun on me. So I pulled mine on him.'

'Jesus Christ, are you mad?'

'Lemme tell you, Colin, this guy was fucking crazy. He going to take me away and kick my ass just for making trouble with him. There was no choice.'

'Then what happened?'

'We just kept standing there, him with his gun at me and me with my gun at him. Both shouting "Drop the fuckin' gun!". The lieutenant's friends, they had their guns on me, too. But I told them, "If you shoot me, I will pull the trigger on your lieutenant first". Man, I swear, we were like this for about ten minutes.'

A *Reservoir Dogs*-style ending had only been avoided when other Iraqi cops had arrived on the scene. Nasi had recognised one of them as a police captain from the US Army base where he'd worked, and surrendered on condition that the captain, rather than the lieutenant, arrested him. He now faced a week in the cells followed by an appearance in court. I turned up for the hearing, in case any kind of character reference was needed, but the judge let him go anyway. In Baghdad, any crime that didn't leave someone dead or seriously injured wasn't worth bothering about. The judge did, however, confiscate his pistol.

I also showed leniency. For one, I owed Nasi after he'd saved my life down in Basra. And while I couldn't really condone pulling a gun on a policeman, I could understand why he might have done so in panic. The new Iraqi cops, long ridiculed as the weakest kids on the block, were now getting a reputation for being as mean, if not meaner, than the criminal fraternities they were fighting. There was a lot of rumours of police brutality going around, although generally the public didn't care as long as they got results.

Leading the new police force was an outfit called the Major Crimes Unit, a new elite force that had been set up back in February to deal with Baghdad's worst kidnap and terrorist gangs. It was a kind of cross between M15 and the Flying Squad, made up of ex-Saddam-era detectives rather than rookie recruits. Some were rumoured to have pretty dodgy pasts, but given that much of the insurgency was made up of their ex-workmates, they were considered ideal poachers-turned-gamekeepers. After protracted negotiations with the new Ministry of Interior, Nasi and I arranged to go on a couple of raids with them one morning.

We turned up at dawn at their HQ, a disused military base in west Baghdad. These days, you could tell how important an individual or organisation was in Iraq by the number of times they'd been attacked. Outside the gate to the Major Crimes Unit were the carcasses of no less than four carbombs, which suggested they were doing quite well. Inside, a team of about 40 heavily-armed policemen were gathered in a courtyard along with a detachment of the new Iraqi Civil Defence

Corps, who were there to provide back-up. It was the first time the two units had been out together, the idea being to get Iraqi security forces working on their own rather than relying on American back-up. Unfortunately, neither side trusted each other very much. The cops viewed the ICDC as incompetent rookies, the ICDC viewed the cops as Saddamite thugs.

There was probably a bit of truth in both, and the morning's raids did little to divest either side of their prejudices. At the house of the first suspect, the only arrest the police made was of an ICDC soldier who was caught leaving the house with his pockets full of stolen jewellery. At the house of the second, the police beat up a passing taxi driver who tried to drive through the cordon they'd set up. In full view of a photographer who was working with me, they dragged him out of his car and started pelting him with steel truncheons.

It was clearly all part of a day's work to the cops, but to the ICDC it was all too reminiscent of the bad old days. 'What the fuck are you doing – we're not in Saddam's time any more!' screamed one of the ICDC captains, as the cabbie writhed under a sea of batons. Guns that were supposed to be pointed in one unified crimefighting direction were then levelled at each other. The captain cocked his Kalashnikov and aimed it directly at the police. The police started drawing their own in response. It was like a group version of Nasi's stand-off with their colleague in the traffic department. Only the efforts of the ICDC captain's fellow soldiers, who managed to wrench the gun out of his hands, prevented the cream of Baghdad's new police force being wiped out.

With different arms of the law busy wrestling with the other, it wasn't surprising that security wasn't improving. Bombs and mortars now shook the windows of the Al Dulaimi hotel every few hours. The 'Baghdad Orchestra' – the round-the-clock gunfire that provided a constant background music – took on new, more sinister rhythms. Before, it had been a sporadic crackle, the sound of people testing weapons, firing in celebration, or doing one-off robberies and murders. Now it was prolonged exchanges lasting an hour or more at a time, the rapid treble of small arms fire chiming with the slower, heavier baritones of US Army .50 calibre machine guns. Now and then there'd also be the whistle and drum of a rocket propelled grenade. Some gun battles led to entire sections of the city being sealed off for hours, creating even worse traffic jams and making it impossible to get around. Journalists also remained in the firing line. The week after I got shot, two Japanese cameramen were killed in another shark-patrol attack down in Mahmoudiya, where the two Polish TV reporters had died in March. The perils of reporting in Iraq had become a story in itself. Nobody, it seemed, could remember anywhere that posed so much danger on so many fronts. Kidnappers, robbers, insurgents, car bombers, Al Qaeda, the Iraqi police, and nervous, trigger-happy US troops... if one lot didn't get you, another lot would.

It was seriously affecting the ability of the foreign press to report what was going on. Nearly all the cities in the Sunni Triangle were now effectively off-limits to Western reporters, as were many Sunni-dominated areas of Baghdad. I stopped travelling around in taxis altogether, and rarely strayed from the hotel compound without Nasi and Ahmed. Even that, though, was more than some people were able to do. For months now, reporters working for the BBC and many other outlets had been effectively confined to their compounds, unable to go out unless they'd got security clearance first. Their security advisers were generally pretty good, but inevitably it complicated an already complex task, and often meant that reporters got out only once every few days.

Such policies came not from the reporters themselves, but from head offices back home, for whom a Baghdad operation was becoming increasingly difficult to square with the health and safety obligations incumbent on any big employer. To their way of thinking, an operation like mine was probably verging on the irresponsible – the proof being the new scar in my backside. Yet to my mind, only allowing reporters out in the company of professional security advisers was setting a bad future trend. It took away your own sense of self-responsibility, and prevented you learning any streetcraft to survive alone, skills you never knew when you might need, be it in Iraq or elsewhere. More importantly, it deprived journalists of any casual contact with the world they were reporting on, which often provided just as many insights as the big set-piece stories. I still listened to *From Our Own Correspondent* on the World Service, a show widely considered to be foreign journalism at its finest, where many of the pieces revolved around encounters with taxi drivers, shopkeepers, and the everyday. Such experiences soon would be thin on the ground if head office deemed them too risky.

Having said that, I doubt that *From Our Own Correspondent* would have been run an episode entitled 'The night I got shitfaced in the Green Zone and wandered around in Baghdad in the dead of night.' Which was exactly what I did, shortly arriving back from Basra and vowing to be more careful in future. Another British journalist – I'll call him 'Dave' – invited me to a party being held by a friend of his who worked for a private security firm based in the Green Zone. It was a typical security firm bash – a more-or-less all-male disco, lots of warm lager and a deplorable buffet, by the end of which we were both drunk. Dave, considerably the worse for wear than me, then decided it would be a good idea to get a taxi home outside the Green Zone's gates, rather than taking up his pal's offer of spare beds in the Green Zone. With the strange, intuitive logic that only the drunk have, I decided he might have a point.

'Don' wanna sleep 'ere,' Dave slurred, as we lurched off uncertainly down one of the main roads that led through the Green Zone. 'Need to wake up in my own bed. Gonna have hangover.'

'OK, but keep your voice down,' I said. 'And try to walk straight. If the American soldiers round here see that you're pissed, we'll get arrested.'

'Daah, fuck 'em,' muttered Dave, raising his voice, and making a vaguely rude gesture in the dark to nobody in particular. 'Fuckin' Yanks! Fuckin' tossers!'

'Dave! Shut it, for Chrissakes!'

Some US soldier manning a sniper point was probably picking up the whole thing, watching us through the crosshairs of his infra red nightsights. I half-expected a shot to ring out and a voice to shout at us through a megaphone.

Somehow, despite getting lost several times, we managed to stagger our way through the world's most heavily-guarded military installation and get through one of the main checkpoints onto the deserted road. I then rang the Al Hamra to ask them to send a taxi, only to be told they'd all knocked off for the night. *Bollocks*. Now we were stuck outside. The rule at the Green Zone was that visitors were allowed to leave at night, but never to enter. And even if they had let us back in, the soldiers would have spotted Dave was drunk during the body-search and nabbed him straightaway. Not that Dave seemed bothered by our predicament. He was now curled up on the roadside, trying to go to sleep.

'Jesus, Dave, wake up. You can't go to sleep here! We'll get killed!'

'S'fine. Can't be arsed. G'night.'

As he lay comatose I scanned the street up and down. This particular gate of the Green Zone was just next to the bridge that ran over the Tigris into downtown, the area full of derelicts and muggers. It was hard to think of anywhere more dangerous to be stuck in. It being well past midnight, however, there wasn't a car on the streets anywhere.

'Hello meesta.'

A young kid wandered over from a building across the road, where there was a light on. He looked about 12, and his tousled hair gave him away as one of the glue-sniffing street urchins who hung around trying to bum money off the soldiers. I asked him if he knew anyone who could drive us home.

'Taxi? Wayn taxi?'

He shook his head, then broke into giggles as he smelt the alcohol rising off Dave's prone figure.

'Hee, hee. Meesta Whisky. You Meesta Whisky.' Then he vanished.

I began to panic. Being patronised by a glue-sniffing street urchin was bad enough. But for all we knew, he might be heading off to tip off the nearest kidnap cell. The insurgents were thought to have lots of spies stationed around here, watching the coming and goings from the Green Zone. If we got abducted now, it would be extremely embarrassing. I could see the headlines now. 'Drunk Brit journalists kidnapped as they sleep in Baghdad gutter... Missing pair acted "like lager louts in English market town", says US commander leading search.'

There was only one thing for it. We'd have to find somewhere to hide and sleep rough for the night. I pulled Dave to his feet and we staggered off in search of a derelict building. Luckily, in Baghdad that was never far away. We found an open doorway in between the nearest row of shops, wandered into an empty room, and flopped down on the bare concrete.

Several hours later we woke up, discovering in the dawn light that we had been sleeping in a corner that doubled as an informal toilet for the neighbouring shopkeepers. We staggered out the doorway, covered in filth and nursing severe hangovers, and hailed a bemused-looking taxi driver to take us back to the Hamra. A silence fell on the way home, neither of us quite able to believe how daft we'd been, or that we'd got away with it.

Later that day Dave rang up. 'Er... I think we'd better keep that one quiet. I told a couple of people earlier about it, thinking it was rather funny, but I suspect the office might not see it that way if they hear.'

Alas, the planned news blackout came too late. Word had already reached several other journalists at the Hamra, including Richard Shears, the *Daily Mail* journalist who I was supposedly advising on safety matters. 'First you get shot, and now this,' he said, smirking. 'You're sacked as my security director.'

*****

That particular escapade was now just one of my large repertoire of Baghdad pub tales. They were trotted out many times over the days and nights of drinking at Dominic's wedding. One had to be very careful not to turn into a 'war bore'. But, frankly, I couldn't help revelling in it. Like many middle-class British men of my age, I'd always been aware of living a rather sheltered, cosseted life. The closest I'd come to danger in Britain was a fight in primary school. Short of becoming an MI5 agent or passing the SAS officers' selection course, being a reporter in Iraq was about the only job I could do that had a bit of worldly glamour. The problem was that if it went wrong, it could go very, very wrong. So far, I'd got away with it, be it wandering around Baghdad while pissed or getting a bullet in the only part of my body that didn't hurt. Others hadn't been so lucky.

The phone call had come from the *Standard* newsdesk early one morning, about a fortnight after I'd got back from Iraq.

'Do you know a journalist in Baghdad called James Brandon?'

'Er, yeah. Why?' Already I was sat bolt upright in bed. Something nasty had obviously happened to him.

'He's been kidnapped down in Basra. Grabbed from his hotel by a big gang of armed men.'

206

'Oh, my God... '

'We're doing a quick profile of him now. Can you help us with any of it? Good if you can make some calls too.'

I told them what I knew. That he was a fellow resident of the Al Dulaimi hotel, another Brit like me. That he was also a fellow freelancer who'd gone to seek his fortune in Iraq. And that he'd taken over my stringing job at the *Sunday Telegraph* after I'd left. I knew they'd sent him down to Basra on some story. If I'd still been out there, it would have been me instead.

Things got worse as the morning passed. First, there were rumours that he'd been shot in both legs during the kidnap. Then the gang holding him released a video tape, showing James stripped to the waist with a masked man holding a gun to his head. He hadn't been shot, but the gunman said he would be unless the US Army withdrew their troops from Najaf, where they were now fighting a major battle with Muqtadr al Sadr's forces. The gunman gave a 24-hour deadline. Shia militants hadn't really gone in for killing kidnap victims in the same way as the Sunnis and Al Qaeda had, but there was always a first time. Besides, on this occasion they'd actually gone to the trouble of nabbing James from his hotel. Nobody would do that unless they were really serious. I put James' chances of survival at almost nil.

I followed the news on his kidnapping all day. And, a freelance to the end, earned myself a few fees by doing the rounds of various TV stations, pontificating about the dangers of self-employed reporting in Iraq. Asked about 'the James Brandon I knew', I had to be careful not to use the past tense. I didn't mention how, on the night I'd left Baghdad, I'd been at a party with him at the Al Hamra hotel, where we'd joked about how the best way to generate stories as a freelancer would be to make our own fake kidnap video. It seemed less funny now that he was in one for real, staring at me from the monitors in the TV studios. Luckily for James, Muqtadr al Sadr himself came to the rescue. When the kidnappers declared that they were acting on his behalf, he made it clear that he wanted nothing to do with it. He was apparently worried that hostage taking might sully his good name, such as it was. Fearing Muqtadr's wrath, the kidnap gang then released James unharmed later that day.

Worse was to come. A week after James was abducted, three more journalists based at the Al Dulaimi hotel went missing. Micha Garen, an American, was snatched down in the southern city of Nasiriyah, and held for a week. Then Georges Malbrunot, a French freelancer who stayed in the room opposite mine, vanished along with a French colleague, Christian Chesnot, *en route* to Najaf. There'd been little news on what had happened to them, but their car was thought to have been stopped somewhere on the road south of Baghdad. I was only on nodding terms with Micha, but Georges I knew quite well. We'd done several trips together earlier in the summer, pooling the cost of hiring translators and drivers. He was a clever, friendly guy and not a bad Arabic speaker, the sort of person you felt glad to have along on any dicey job. Once again, it felt like a case of there but for the grace of God. Had I still been in Baghdad, I might well have been splitting the cost of that trip to Najaf.

In the wake of the latest kidnappings, a slight air of panic had struck the other residents of the Al Dulaimi hotel. First there'd been me getting shot, then four other guests all getting kidnapped. Was there some connection?

The Agence France Presse News Agency seemed to think so. A couple of days after Georges went missing, they filed a story entitled: *'Kidnapped reporters: the curse of Baghdad's Dulaimi Hotel'*.

It told how all four kidnap victims had 'stayed in the same eerie Baghdad hotel', and speculated on whether it was simply a 'disturbing coincidence', or whether the hotel management had been colluding with the kidnap gangs in some way. On the face of it, there was no realistic way they could have done. All four kidnaps had taken place in different parts of the country, hundreds of miles from the hotel, each time in completely different circumstances. It had also been a long-established security rule among most reporters that they never told anyone where they were going in advance. The hotel's owner, Hamza al-Dulaimi, denied everything. 'Micah went to Nasiriyah 20 times from my hotel and it was always fine,' he told AFP. 'Georges and Christian were the first foreigners to stay here after Saddam was toppled. I consider them friends.'

Such was the air of paranoia by now, though, that nobody was taking any chances. The French consulate sent a delegation to the Al Dulaimi advising all French guests to move out just in case. Most of the other reporters shipped out too. AFP quoted a French photographer, Jerome Sassini, as he was packing his bags in room 18. 'There's no way I'm staying here,' he said.

It summed up the madness that Baghdad had become. The odds of the hotel being complicit in the kidnappings was about as high as the odds of it being cursed. But ration and reason were no match for the instinct for self-preservation. I knew that if I'd still been out there, rather than swilling and bragging away at Dominic's wedding, I'd have been right behind Jerome, maybe even ahead of him. And right now, there was no way I was going back. I'd had enough of Iraq for a while. I was going to try Afghanistan instead. There were elections there in October, the first in God knew how long, which would give me something to write about. I'd already bought my plane ticket, and I'd be heading off there as soon as I got back to London from Dominic's wedding.

And as soon as I'd finally agreed to bare my war wounds for Dom's fellow wedding guests. After the wedding reception, as we sat drunkenly in a bar in the town square, the couple who'd accosted me two nights before suddenly reappeared. This time they'd recruited half the rest of the wedding party to their cause.

'Show us yer backside!' they roared in unison.

It was no good. If I'd refused at that point, I'd have looked like a miserable spoilsport. Plus I was rat-arsed. Leaning up against the square's clock tower, I dropped my trousers, to roars of approval. And, as I later found out, the lens of Dominic's camcorder, which was recording the wedding party. Right now though, I could think of worse amateur videos to be appearing on.

A Short Trip To The Hindu Kush

IT WAS LATE AFTERNOON in the bar at Kabul's Mustapha Hotel, and the skinny American guy sat just down from me had just ordered another vodka and coke. He looked like some sort of CIA man who'd forgotten to leave after helping the mujahideen to kick out the Russians. He wore a battered tweed sports jacket, an Afghan-style domed felt cap, and a chequered kheffiya scarf wrapped round his neck like a cravat. At his side was a small pistol, and in his hands was a chocolate bar-sized lump of hash, pliant as toffee.

'Everyone in town's after this stuff, man,' he droned on in washed-out Californian tones to an identically-dressed companion. 'Really smooth, better than anything else I've come across here.'

I earwigged in from further down, trying to gauge my new surroundings. It was my first evening in Afghanistan and I'd just checked into the Mustapha, where the bar was a known expat gathering point. Despite their appearances, my two fellow drinkers weren't ex-CIA men turned drug smugglers. The one with the pistol was some sort of aid work consultant, his friend was a journalist like me. They dressed like a lot of the Westerners out here, a sort of ethnic-boho look that was half aid-worker, half-mujahideen. Yet judging by their plans for the night, Kabul was not a place where anybody really needed to pack guns. To my astonishment, they were about to head off to Kabul's newly-opened Croatian restaurant, the latest addition to a social scene that belonged more in Islington than a war zone.

It was all set out in a magazine I'd found lying on the bar, called *Afghan Scene*. There was caviar and Cuban cigars on offer at Kabul's Gator Club, and imported lattes at the Flower Street Café. The Elbow Room bar was good for cocktails and beef carpaccio salad, while at the German-run Deutscher Hof a mini-version of the Munich Oktoberfest had just got under way. All that was missing was a Kabul branch of All Bar One.

It was a world away from the kebabs and Mr Le Bonjour on offer in Baghdad, and it was certainly wasn't what I'd expected in

Afghanistan, where just three years ago the Taleban had been busily winding the clock back to the Middle Ages. The customers, however, were not locals, but the vast numbers of UN and NGO workers, who were here in ever greater numbers now that Iraq was effectively off-limits. Amid the columns, and restaurant and bar reviews, *Afghan Scene* even had its own 'society' page, with snapshots of charity workers, UN officials and diplomats attending functions, book signings and restaurant openings. It was a kind of *Hello!* magazine for the aid world.

Flicking through it, I felt vaguely crestfallen. It wasn't that I disapproved of aid workers carousing. I would be exploring the bars and restaurants myself over the coming weeks, and just because you worked for a charity didn't deprive you of the desire to get pissed every now and then. It was just that, after Baghdad, Kabul felt a bit too civilised, too safe, to be anything other than an anti-climax. Character it certainly had. The city sat surrounded by beautiful ochre mountains, with a pleasant smell of woodsmoke rising over streets that were even more bullet-scarred than Baghdad's. My room at the Mustapha, one of a row of tiny punishment cells reserved for guests who could only afford $20 a night, overlooked a courtyard where a 12-foot marijuana plant flourished. But it was clear the moment I took a taxi from the airport that the tempo here was a lot more relaxed than Iraq's. Italian and German soldiers from the NATO-backed Coalition were driving around in unaccompanied white SUVs, stopping at local shops. Doing that would earn them a death sentence in Iraq. Just how much quieter it was, though, had only come out when I'd got to the hotel and asked another guest, an American photographer, how careful one had to be here.

'Sure, pretty careful.' he said. 'You hear about the carbomb?'

'No, when was that?' I gestured at my watch, wondering if it was worth going to the scene.

'About a month ago,' he said.

The relative peace was great if you just wanted to sit around getting stoned. It was not so good if you were a freelance journalist, used to getting at least part of your income by dashing off quick and easy news stories about carbombs, kidnappings and other daily mayhem. It had the feel of a place where the action had all taken place three years ago. Osama bin Laden was still showing no sign of being caught, and the routed Taleban were yet to get their act together again. Instead, as the weeks passed, I was reminded time and again that Iraq was still the big story. Every time I wandered past the TV in the hotel dining room, the lead bulletins on CNN International and BBC World were from Baghdad, never Kabul. I'd figured the Coalition might have got the uprising under control by September, but as ever, my predictions had proved woefully wrong. Fallujah, having been besieged once already by the Americans, was now completely out of control again, effectively an insurgent city-state. The kidnapping campaigns against Westerners, meanwhile, had got far worse. Georges Malbrunot and his friend were still missing (they were kept for 124 days before being freed) and the sword of Abu Musab Al Zarqawi, the leader of Qaeda in Iraq, was hanging over the head of a British contractor, Ken Bigley. Late in October, he was beheaded, footage of his execution again downloaded on the internet. Just when Iraq looked like it couldn't get any worse, it had.

By mid-November, after just eight weeks in Afghanistan, I felt myself running out of things to do. I'd covered the elections, and interviewed an aptly-named former Taleban warlord called Mullah Rockety. I'd written about playing golf on Kabul's only golf course, where Russians were still banned from joining because they'd parked their tanks on the greens during the Soviet occupation. I'd got drunk in the Elbow Room, L'Atmosphere and pretty much everywhere else in town, and narrowly avoided being pictured in *Afghan Scene* magazine. I'd tried, and failed, to pull various female aid workers, despite Kabul's male-female ratio offering much better odds than Baghdad's. And, perhaps in slight pique, I'd penned a slightly hypocritical yarn about 'Islington on Kush', asking whether it was really right that aid workers should be out gallivanting with the likes of me when there were lives to save.

Just as I was wondering how my hotel room would cope with the Afghan winter, where temperatures plunged down to minus 20C, the *Sunday Telegraph* rang up to ask if I was interested in doing some shifts on their foreign desk. I flew straight back to London, planning to work there until New Year, when I'd go back out to Iraq again for the elections at the end of January. Yet the more I inquired, the more it now sounded like a very different place to the Iraq I'd left. The kidnapping campaign that had begun during the summer was now an epidemic. There'd been several more abductions of journalists. Kidnappers were lurking in the streets right outside the Hamra.

'It's pretty fucking grim out here, mate, not like it was in the old days,' said Jason Howe, a freelance photographer I often worked with. Like me he'd come out to Afghanistan for a change of scene, but had gone back to Baghdad to fill a vacancy at the *New York Times*. He now realised why they were struggling to get staff. A few weeks before, another photographer at his agency, Paul Taggart, had been abducted for 24 hours by a Shia gang in Sadr City. He was doing a job Jason might have done had he not gone to Afghanistan first. Surprise, surprise, Paul was also another former resident of the Al Dulaimi hotel.

'So what's it like for getting out and about?' I asked.

'Pretty bad. Everyone's terrified of getting kidnapped all the time. We're travelling everywhere by armoured car, with armed guards and another car tailing you at the back in case something goes wrong. You can't really do much on the streets. Most people are just doing embeds. But even that's getting dangerous. I've just been out on one where our convoy got hit by a roadside bomb. Gives you a hell of a shock, I tell you. You coming out?'

'Maybe. If I think I can do it without getting kidnapped and beheaded.'

'Well, that is a bit of a problem. Other than that, it's absolutely lovely.'

'Cheers. I'll buy you a beer if I get out there.'

I put the phone down, the paranoia already kicking in. Jason wasn't prone to exaggeration. And he had the whole *New York Times* operation behind him as well. They had something like 80 staff in Baghdad, complete with their own heavily-fortified compound, dozens of highly-trained drivers and translators, plus armoured cars and a retinue of trained ex-military security guards. I would have Nasi, Ahmed and his hatchback saloon.

The more I learned, the scarier it sounded. Baghdad was now crawling with armed gangs looking to kidnap Westerners. It wasn't just all the jihadist cells, but many of the ordinary criminal gangs too. The terrorist cells had put word out that they'd pay good money to anybody who could bring them a Westerner. Gangs would snatch the first person they could find, and then sell them on via a kind of hostage market through various intermediaries. Americans and Brits fetched the most – Ken Bigley had been sold for $250,000, apparently, riches beyond the wildest dreams of the average group of Baghdad thugs. The kidnappings weren't just motivated by politics but by profit, encouraging a free-market efficiency that made it much more dangerous. For every one jihadist cell offering cash for foreigners, there were dozens of kidnap gangs out looking on their behalf. People were saying it was worse than Chechnya in the 1990s, than Lebanon in the 1980s.

One night, lying in bed, I suffered a bad paranoia attack, becoming seriously frightened about what lay ahead. The prospect of being kidnapped by the likes of Zarqawi's mob was so utterly horrifying that it was all but impossible to imagine. Even if you were released, you might end up being traumatised for life. Yet I couldn't tell myself, *Don't worry, it won't happen*. The risk was real, not theoretical, and to pretend otherwise was foolhardy. The number of Westerners now living outside Baghdad's Green Zone was now probably no more than a few hundred, and the fewer there were, the more you stood out.

It also made it more dangerous for Nasi and Ahmed. They could get killed as collaborators just for working with me. Worse still, they could get bribes from kidnap gangs asking them to deliver me into their clutches. I trusted Nasi not do that, after he'd saved my life down in Basra. But it wasn't just about money. If a bribe failed, the gang could simply threaten his own family. If it came to a choice between them and me, I was pretty sure where his loyalties would lie.

Even if I didn't get kidnapped, I had visions of being absolutely terrified out of my wits the whole the time I was there. I began to wonder, frankly whether I could handle it.

*****

The kidnappers weren't the only malign presence to worry about. Whoever'd killed Ryan Manelick – and probably Kirk von Ackermann, too – was still at large, and probably thinking they'd got away with it. The US Army's Criminal Investigation Division didn't seem to be making much headway, and with Iraq in the state it was now that wasn't surprising. Up in the Sunni Triangle, where Ryan had been killed and Kirk had disappeared, US forces were now barely able to protect their own bases, never mind go out conducting a complex murder and missing persons inquiry.

But I was planning to stir things up again, by finally doing a more in-depth piece about what had happened. Throughout the past year, I'd been kept in touch with Greg Manelick, Ryan's father, on the progress of the investigation. Things had moved on a bit, despite the difficulties. The case had now been taken over by an outfit called the Major Fraud Procurement Unit, which dealt with matters such as theft and corruption within the ranks. They had 20 agents on the case, which suggested they were taking the claims that there'd been some kind of financial skulduggery at Ultra Services seriously. Scores of people had been questioned, including a US Army major who was John Dawkins' old military contact when he'd first turned up in Baghdad. The agents weren't saying much, but the suggestion was that the major had been quizzed over allegations that John had offered to buy him a BMW in return for getting contracts.

Greg, however, was beginning to despair of getting any real answers. The agents leading the inquiry kept on getting assigned to the other duties, and he was being kept largely in the dark as to how things were going. The longer things dragged on without any arrests, the more convinced he was that the US military weren't interested in unearthing the truth. They already had enough on their plate with the Abu Ghraib abuse scandal. The last thing they needed was a nice juicy tale of US Army officers being involved in corruption and murder. It was all too easy, Greg reasoned, to get the case stamped 'unsolvable in the present circumstances.'

'I know they are in the middle of a combat zone – I've been there and done it myself,' he said to me in an email. 'But that shouldn't prevent them putting in the maximum effort on the death of somebody in their own backyard who was trying to make their own lives more bearable.'

Back in April, Greg had started investigating on his own. He'd recruited a team of ex-Russian special forces soldiers, and had made plans to come to Iraq to ask some questions. But as his team pitched up in Turkey, planning to head south across the border, the insurgency had begun to kick off big time. He realised it would be impossible to do anything. He went home an angry man, fearful that the riddle of what had happened to his son – and Kirk too – was going to lie unsolved forever on those dusty desert roads around Tikrit.

'My son came out here to support the U.S. Army, not with his mouth or from a bar stool, but with his back and his brains,' he said. 'Somebody then blew them out. I think the least they can do is find out who it was.'

Greg was now happy for me to write more about the case, keen to keep it in the public eye. But in order to do it properly, I had to put some of the allegations to John Dawkins. It wasn't a prospect I relished. In 10 years of journalism, I hadn't often had to ask anyone 'are you a killer?', save for the odd doorstep of some dodgy type who'd got off a murder charge on a technicality. This was different. This was somebody I actually knew as a friend. I tracked John down via an old email address, and he agreed to answer written questions.

He sounded like a broken man. For much of the last year the CID had been all over him, interrogating him relentlessly and putting him through endless lie detector tests. 'You cannot imagine the nights that I woke up with my heart racing like never before, imagining being framed and put in jail,' he wrote. 'I was very scared about giving false positives during the lie detector tests and it was the worst experience I have ever had in my life. But I underwent them willingly because I wanted to cooperate and most importantly, clear my name with Ryan's father Greg, who I consider one of my most beloved friends.'

Right now he said he was in the clear, although the CID had said there'd be more grillings to come. Meanwhile, his reputation as a businessman had been ruined. There was little to show for the $11 million in contracts that Ultra Services had won out in Iraq, and he was finding it all but impossible to get new work. People were treating him as a 'radioactive criminal'.

So who then, I asked him, was behind Ryan's death and Kirk's disappearance? John said he couldn't be sure. But like Greg, he was putting his money on Mohammed as a likely culprit. Mohammed, he said, had been skimming money from the company. Whenever Ryan gave him cash to buy goods in Baghdad's markets, Mohammed would add a fat commission on to the price, something that Ryan turned a blind eye to but which Kirk kicked up a fuss about when he arrived.

'Ryan knew about it but let it happen,' he said. 'I think Kirk gave the message that that would stop and Mohammed took it into his own hands and had his brothers, or someone connected to him kill Kirk. Later, he likely killed Ryan – likely Ryan knew too much or asked for money or had info that could lead them to Mohammed. That is the most likely thing. Or else, they were both careless and in the wrong place, wrong time.'

He admitted things had got a lot more bitter between himself and Ryan than I had realised. He described the dead man as a 'dysfunctional' and 'paranoid' individual and said their professional relationship had deteriorated to the point where Ryan had threatened to beat John up if he ever saw him again. 'For two months he hated me so much that he would only say "Fuck you, I hate you",' wrote John. 'I stayed clear of him... He went so far as to find out if he would be legally liable in the US if he "kicked my ass in Iraq". One time he asked to fight me; I calmly told him that I don't fight unless it is self-defence and considered myself civilized enough to find other ways of resolving issues.'

Getting John's version of events was important, but it left me little the wiser as to what had really happened. He sounded sincere, but I was sceptical about the business of Mohammed skimming money from the company. Ryan had often told me that he suspected Mohammed took a premium when he went on buying trips, but figured that the company still got value for money. Only an Iraqi could get truly decent prices from another Iraqi, he reckoned, a Westerner would get ripped off senseless. The odd percentage here and there that went into someone's back pocket on any given deal was just the way business was done: Mohammed was simply charging an unofficial fee for his negotiating skills. Ryan made it clear he had no problem with it. Could that really lead to murder?

After several weeks of research, I finally put together an article for the *San Francisco Chronicle*, who were interested in a follow-up story to the original one they'd run about Kirk's disappearance. It was a long piece, although frankly it didn't shed much new light on what had happened. One problem was that the US military investigators were playing their cards very close to their chests. From my own perspective, I was particularly interested to know if they were treating Mohammed as a suspect. After all the innuendo about why he hadn't been with Ryan at the time of the killing, he'd subsequently told me that, on the morning in question, his brother had been ill in hospital with some kind of kidney complaint. Mohammed had spent the day at his bedside. The hospital, he said, had been able to verify that claim. I asked CID if they could confirm that to me off the record, and told them that, as a personal friend of his, I wanted to know if there was any reason why I might best avoid him. But they still wouldn't say a thing. Nor would they comment on John's claim that he had passed all the lie detector tests.

The *Chronicle* were planning to run the piece sometime in the New Year, when I would be back in Iraq. One of the emails from a *Chronicle* editor, Gail Bensinger, voiced a worry that was already going around in my own head. "Will publishing this piece prevent you from going back to Iraq or put you in specific danger if you do return?" she asked. "Would anyone connected with this come gunning for you?"

I said I hoped not. But with no idea who'd really killed Ryan, or why, it was hard to be sure.

*****

I was tempted not to go back to Iraq. Nobody was insisting on it. But I'd already told the *Sunday Telegraph* and several other newspapers that I was going to cover the elections. If I chose not to, it would be a failure of my nerve. Part of me wanted to find out for myself just how frightening it had got, and whether I could handle it. Besides, my fellow freelancer Jill, who'd likewise left during the summer, was planning on going back too. We chatted about it on the phone. 'One or two staff reporters have told me that it's not safe for freelancers any more, but I don't really see how it makes much difference,' she said. 'If you get kidnapped, you get kidnapped.'

If Jill could handle it, so could I. I booked a plane ticket for January 4th. Yet as the weeks and days counted down, I felt myself getting ever more nervous, far more scared than the first time I went out there. It was a nervous tension that got stronger every day, with no real way of release. For once, there wasn't a comforting voice at the back of my mind going, *Don't worry, it'll all be fine*. I couldn't afford not to worry. Not worrying could get you killed. I even thought about making a will.

Matters weren't helped by the constant advice from everyone around me. This time round, nobody was patting me on the back and congratulating me on my spirit of adventure. Instead, they just repeated a single phrase, *ad infinitum*.

'Be careful,' said my parents.

'Be careful,' said the news editor at the *Sunday Telegraph*.

'Be careful,' said some stranger I met at a party.

'Be careful,' said some person in a call-centre in Tyneside whom I rang to sort out my phone bill.

It was just a well-intentioned, throwaway comment, but it began to drive me nuts. *Be careful?* I wanted to scream. *What do you think I'm going to do?*

Was I losing it already, before I'd even gone? My mind began to play tricks on me. I wasn't superstitious by nature, but I started seeing omens everywhere – ridiculous ones, but they freaked me out nonetheless. One night round at Dominic's, I accidentally knocked over his 18-month old daughter's alphabet building blocks. They came up spelling the word 'DED', like some Ouija board scene in *The Exorcist*. And on the night before I left London, the watch I'd had for five years suddenly stopped. Was my time finally up?

Paranoia

EVERY TRANSLATOR I'd ever worked with had his favourite songs to play in the car. With Mohammed, it was the Bee Gees. Amir, more refined and thoughtful, drove around to Ravel's *Bolero*. Nadim, who filled in for Nasi when he was arrested, liked Barbra Streisand's *Woman In Love*, which we'd sung along to together. Nasi's friend Ahmed, behind the wheel right now, veered schizophrenically between cheesy Lebanese pop ballads and American rap. He particularly liked Coolio's *Gangster's Paradise*. It boomed out of the stereo now as we swung out the front checkpoint of the Hamra hotel, heading out on yet another skittish jaunt round town. '*As I walk through the shadow of the Valley of Death...*'

Sat in the back, I hummed along inaccurately to Coolio's lyrics, pretending I was centre stage in some action movie – *Colin Freeman: Straight Outta Baghdad* – with a gritty, gangsta rap soundtrack. It was a rather pathetic fantasy that I sometimes indulged in to make life out here seem more glamorous and romantic. Frankly, I doubted Coolio would ever have been seen dead in Ahmed's dented, white hatchback, with its Donald Duck sticker on the side. Mind you, in some way it was a study in authenticity. There was Nasi up front, shoving a magazine into his new pistol, a big fat Colt .45 that he'd bought to replace the one the police had confiscated back in the summer. And there was me at the back, staring at every car driving up alongside us and wondering when we might fall victim to a drive-by. In many ways, a quick blast of machine gun fire would be preferable to getting kidnapped. But right now, Westerners were worth far more alive than dead. Especially if you believed the reports about Georges Malbrunot, my former neighbour at the Al Dulaimi. He'd been released just before Christmas, for what the French press claimed was a $5 million ransom.

Every time we headed out of the Hamra hotel complex, I found myself wondering if I'd ever see it again. The first few minutes after leaving the entrance was the worst. That was when you broke cover, when you drove past the hidden spies that everyone assumed were keeping a discreet eye on the place. Thanks to the Iraq's new mobile phone service, they could now tip off their paymasters straightaway. *'Hello, yes, there's a Westerner has just left. Yeah, that fool who doesn't used an armoured car. He's in some crappy hatchback, thinks we don't notice him. Can you believe it? Have Abdul get his guys ready.'*

They'd have their snatch squad in place further down the road, ready with a couple of BMWs full of armed men. One to swing in front and block the way, the other to pull up behind, grab you out of the car, and stick you in the boot. Then that would be it, the final reel in the long-running action movie *The Life And Times Of Colin Freeman*. Save perhaps for an epilogue with me staring blankly into the lens of a jihadist's video camera.

It was a sequence that my mind had rehearsed, replayed and rewound a hundred times in the weeks before coming out here.

A blue BMW, coming up behind us. Two men up front, one in the back. Were they looking at us? Not really. But they wouldn't make it obvious, would they? They hovered alongside in the slow-moving traffic, some other saloon lurking not far behind. Now Nasi was eyeballing them too. Just a casual glance, because he didn't want them – or me – to know he was watching. But I could see his hand checking that his gun was beside him, in the little plastic holster thing that he'd fitted beneath the car stereo. Where, in happier times, Ahmed used to keep his Coolio CD. A twist of mounting, helpless apprehension gradually wound up inside me, loosening off into a nasty shudder of relief as the BMW finally pulled away.

We stopped at a set of traffic lights. A pick-up truck full of men in balaclavas forced their way through the chaotic traffic at the junction, waving their Kalashnikovs at anybody who didn't get out of their way fast enough. Not a group of insurgents, but the Iraqi police. Too scared to stop in case they present a sitting target for an RPG round, and too scared to show their faces for fear of being identified. It was a new tactic since I'd been away, prompted by the insurgent campaign against 'collaborators' in the new security forces. Insurgent spies would loiter near checkpoints and police stations, clocking officers' faces, gleaning names and addresses. Hit squads would then lurk outside the policemen's homes, gunning them down as they left for work. Or, if they were high-ranking or plain unlucky, abducting them for questioning, torturing, and beheading. The head to be delivered back to their families in due course. It had happened to hundreds of Iraqi police already, so the balaclavas were the only option. The problem, though, was that it made Baghdad look as if it was being run by terrorists. Which, in many people's eyes, it was.

We carried on down the road, heading towards the university. The plan was to interview some students and a couple of academics about how they felt about the forthcoming election. It was less than four weeks away, the first properly democratic contest in Iraq's history, but you wouldn't know it from driving around. Hardly any candidates had put up posters, because Al Qaeda had vowed to kill anyone taking part. Instead, the most frequent picture I'd seen so far was wanted posters of Zarqawi, the Al Qaeda figure now leading the insurgency. Zarqawi was also the man putting up the big wads for kidnap gangs to capture the likes of me. A huge mugshot of him wearing a black Islamic skullcap stared down from several of the big flyovers, the only terrorist I'd ever seen whose face genuinely frightened me. Someone had splashed paint over one of the posters, like they did with the Saddam ones just after the war. This time, though, it wasn't over his face, but over the mobile phone hotline number inviting people to dob him in and claim a $25 million reward.

We pulled up at the university, and headed onto the campus after a 10 minute discussion with a security guard who wanted to know why I was there. Who was I? Did I have press credentials? Who were we seeing? Did we have permission from the university's dean? How about a letter from the Education Ministry? One of the joys about working in Iraq until now had been that with no functioning government, there was no bureaucracy. Now things had moved on, gravitating, as ever, to the worst of all possible worlds. The new government was barely operational, yet was back to its old habit of insisting that everything needed written permission. That, however, involved hours and hours of hanging around at ministry offices, where every self-respecting insurgent group had look-outs on the payroll. Like, quite possibly, the man taking such a close interest in us now. For all we knew, he might be on the phone to someone as soon as we were out of sight.

We told him we were just here to see some cousin of Ahmed's, and paid him 1,000 dinars (about 50 pence) to forget about the paperwork. I looked at my watch. We'd spend one hour in the university, max. Any more than that and word might have spread that a foreigner was around. Even one hour was too long really. The ex-military security advisers generally recommended no more than 30 minutes. But in all practicality, that was never anywhere near enough to get any work done. Take the two professors we interviewed, for example. Not only were they both tedious, long-winded bastards who took forever to answer a simple question, everything they said then had to be translated into English by Nasi. An hour and a half had already passed by the time we were done, with barely a quote worth using in the notebook. As ever, the safety rule book went out the window. We blithely assumed that nobody was following us and carried on to interview some students in the university refectory.

The refectory was a big 1970s dining hall, with a few greasy kebab stalls and a place selling tea and coffee in paper cups. We sat down, and started chatting to a group at a nearby table, but after a few minutes I began to feel uncomfortable. Not only were we violating my safety rule on time, we were also violating my safety rule about avoiding places where we were visible to large numbers of people. I'd done the maths already. The insurgency had an estimated 50,000 active and passive members. Which, in a population of about 20 million, meant about one in 400 people. So in a refectory with roughly 200 diners in, there was a 50 per cent chance that someone in here right now was an insurgent sympathiser who might tip someone off to our presence. True, we weren't in Fallujah, so the odds might be less than that. On the other hand, universities tended to attract the odd dizzy radical, so they might be a bit higher. But this wasn't about statistical accuracy. It was about working out the vague likelihood of whether this was a sensible place to be in. It wasn't. We left.

As we drove out of the campus, I could feel myself tensing yet again, wondering whether the security guard we'd chatted to earlier had tipped off some pals. He hadn't, of course. But the fear was always there regardless. We drove off down to Karrada district, home to the Al Majalis hotel, where I'd spent my first few months in Baghdad. It was one of only a handful of neighbourhoods that was safe enough to go to now. Yet even here, we had to take the same precautions as we'd taken in Fallujah back in the summer. There was no interviewing people on the street any more. Instead, Nasi would get out of the car, wander into some shop, and engage the shopkeeper in conversation. If he seemed reasonably level-headed, Nasi would then ask him if he was happy to speak to a foreign journalist. If he was, we'd nip in and chat for ten minutes. Our hit rate wasn't very high. Most punters were scared of talking to Westerners now, or scared of talking about certain subjects. It was like being back in Saddam's time. 'I'll talk to you, but not about politics,' said one supermarket owner. Not much good when there was an election three weeks away.

The only remotely successful exercise of the day was the visit to the Honey Market. It was over in Area 52, the Christian district, a small, discreet shop no bigger than a Spar mini-market, packed with imported Western foods and, more importantly, a few crates of half-decent wine. Stepping inside was like wandering into a black marketeers' lock-up in World War Two. The place was stacked floor to ceiling with highly-priced, highly-desirable comestibles unavailable elsewhere. Alpen for $6 a packet, Italian pesto for $6 a jar, Heinz Baked Beans. Even some packets of dubious-looking bacon, illegal for any Muslim to buy. In Saddam's time, UN staff had been the shop's main customers, keeping themselves well-stocked in food and wine while the rest of the country starved under UN sanctions. Now the Honey Market's main customers were the ever-dwindling band of Westerners living outside the Green Zone. As ever, the shop had adapted to the times. Until recently, the booze section had been proudly displayed in a front window. Now it was blacked out, the booze kept hidden in a secret cellar in a back room. Even then, if the staff didn't recognise you, they'd often deny the cellar existed.

'Can I see some of your wine?' I asked.

'Wine?' asked the man at the counter.

'Yes, you sell wine, don't you?'

'I don't think so sir, no.'

'Well, you definitely had some last time I was here, during the summer. In through that door over there, I think it was.'

'Well, let me go and have a look. Why don't you come with me?'

He opened the door, headed down a corridor and turned into the small windowless room where the booze was kept, changing as he did so from bemused cashier to knowledgeable sommelier. 'The Chilean Merlot is $10 a bottle sir, very good. And the Lebanese Chateau Kefraya $15, also good. In this corner here, please, also champagne...'

We paid up. Enough Alpen, frozen chicken breasts, pasta and pesto to keep one Western journalist in the monotonous manner to which he had become accustomed. Plus a couple of crates of Heineken and a crate of wine. And, strictly for emergency purposes only, two bottles of my old friend the Clan Vintage whisky. There was no telling when Baghdad might erupt into all-out anarchy, necessitating emergency supplies of hard liquor as the hotel came under armed siege.

En route home we got stuck in a large traffic jam. Directly in front of us was a lorry that decided it wanted to turn round. As ever, nobody gave him the slightest quarter. I slid down low in the back seat, waiting for the traffic to move again and trying not to let anyone in the cars either side take too good a look at me.

'Irja! Irja!'

Suddenly a young, tousled-haired guy with a Kalashnikov was stood in front of us, pointing the barrel directly at the windscreen and screaming his head off. We all froze, then Nasi and Ahmed starting yelling at him in Arabic. First I simply wondered what was going on, then, for a horrible moment, I thought he was the advance gunman of a kidnap gang. I froze completely. *Please, Nasi, don't go for your gun mate*, I thought. *You'll get us all killed.* Then I remembered that irja meant 'turn around'. The guy was the lorry driver's armed escort, and was trying to make space as it U-turned. He was worried it might get robbed if they stayed stuck in traffic. Thank God for that. There were more polite ways of clearing the traffic, but right now he was welcome to it.

Back at the hotel we went in a different route from the one we'd gone out. The idea was to vary your route in and out as much as possible, although I doubted it made that much difference. Everybody suspected that there were spies working inside the Hamra as well as outside, tipping people off as to our whereabouts. The hotel complex itself now resembled a miniature Green Zone, in steady retreat behind an ever-expanding buffer zone of concrete blast walls and gun emplacements. There were two main entrances, each a ziz-zagging chicane of checkpoints designed to slow the path of any suicide bomber. Hopefully by the time he'd got halfway through, the guards would have emptied half a dozen machine gun magazines into his windscreen. Their job was as much a suicide mission as those who might attack them. The moment any car bomber knew he'd been rumbled, he'd detonate his load, most likely taking them with him. Yet they were paid no more than a couple of hundred dollars a month. It was not unreasonable to wonder whether some of them might be persuaded, either via a threat or a bribe, or both, to look the other way on a given occasion.

Within the compound were seven different hotels, all tightly bunched together on what was previously a couple of narrow streets. I was now staying in one called the Al Musafir, opposite the Al Dulaimi, which had remained virtually empty since late summer. While everyone insisted the curse was nonsense, nobody wanted to prove the point by being the first reporter to move back in there.

*****

Carbombing hour in Baghdad was usually between seven and eight o'clock in the morning. Exactly why the bombers preferred to make their appointment with Paradise at that particular time was a secret they took to the grave. But there were several theories. The first, and the most prosaic, was that there was less traffic on the roads. The second was that the soul was its purest just after dawn prayers, and would therefore make a better impression as it dined with Allah that lunchtime. A third, probably the most likely, was that it was the best time to hit long queues outside police stations and government buildings.

The carbombs came almost every morning now. It was as ritual a sound as the clanging sound of the cooking gas man passing through the streets in his horse and cart, swapping full cylinders for empty. A boom, sometimes muffled and distant, sometimes loud enough to wake you up. Sometimes a slight rattle of the windows, sometimes a plume of smoke rising. Then, one day, the sound came, right outside my hotel window.

A carbomb close up doesn't just sound loud. It also sounds *big*, as if the normal world has been re-wired through a 1,000 foot-high speaker. It's in a different league altogether to anything our ears are used to, and it plays tricks on the mind.

The force blew my window in and showered me and my bed with glass. I shook the shattered fragments off the duvet, staggered out of bed, and wandered over towards the blown-out window frame, now hanging skewed into the room. My mind was already braced for what it expected to see – a massive pile of rubble where the main tower block of the Al Hamra used to be. Yet nothing had changed, other than the armed guards running around beneath. How could that be? The sound my ears had heard was so loud that it had to have been right outside. But there was nothing. I left my room, and walked over to the other side of the hotel. Nothing there either. Just the Al Dulaimi and the neighbouring Summerland restaurant, sporting torn curtains hanging out of their shattered window frames like trouser suit pockets turned inside out. Where the hell had the bomb hit, then? Eventually, I noticed a crowd gathering at the eastern checkpoint, staring at a spot on the main road, hidden from my view by another hotel block. I went down to join them, picking my through the broken glass in the lobby. Out on the main road, I finally the saw the plume of smoke. A car bomb had tried to hit the building on the far side, a derelict eight-storey office block known as the Australian Embassy building. It was at least a hundred yards away from my hotel, with several other blocks in between, yet it had sounded so loud that I'd been convinced it was right outside my window. Christ only knew then what it had sounded like up close.

The building was an observation point for a bunch of Australian soldiers, who were there to guard a few Australian diplomats based in one of the hotels in the Hamra compound. The soldiers lived in the top couple of floors, machine guns and radio antennae bristling out of the windows to provide cover whenever the Australian diplomatic convoy came and went from the hotel. The carbomber had aimed directly for them, no doubt hoping to bring the entire building down, but had got fouled up in the series of concrete barriers strewn around the bottom. All he'd done was blast his way through a couple of them, his explosive charge tearing a gaping hole several feet deep in the concrete. A crowd of journalists began gathering with the locals around the burning debris of the car, the first time many of them had been able to photograph a street scene for months. I stayed well back. If the attackers had any sense, they'd know a large crowd of foreign journalists was about to descend. It would be all too easy for an accomplice to open fire on them, or for a second bomber to mingle in the crowd wearing a suicide vest, blowing himself up live on TV. Besides, attacks like this weren't news any more. As I walked back to the hotel, I wandered into the Al Dulaimi to inspect the damage they'd suffered. I took the stairs up to the sixth floor, where my old suite of rooms had overlooked the main road. The walls were still intact but the room was wrecked, glass and broken furniture strewn everywhere. If I'd been in there, I could have been seriously hurt.

Thank God I'd heeded the curse.

*****

The carbombing that day – which made all of three lines in the *Standard* – was just a tiny lick of what the rest of Baghdad was tasting in the run-up to the election. The Sunni insurgents and Al Qaeda were doing their best to stop it going ahead, escalating their campaigns of general mayhem in the hope that the UN, which had come in to supervise the process, would declare the country in too much chaos to have a chance of a proper vote. Election workers were getting threatened and killed, and on numerous street corners around Baghdad the graffiti threatened of dire consequences to anybody who even participated in the vote. Nasi had pointed some out to me in Karrada. 'If anyone goes to the elections, he will die,' it read. Shortly before Christmas, three election workers had been dragged out of their car and shot dead in broad daylight as they drove down Haifa Street, a known insurgent hangout in downtown. The execution had been filmed by an insurgent cameraman and released on the internet as a warning to others. Since then, many of the election officials in charge of delivering voter registration forms had quit.

The Sunni insurgents' case for de-railing the elections was simple. If it went ahead, the Shias, having two-thirds of the population, would gain a natural majority, putting them in power for the first time in nearly 100 years. The Sunnis feared they would be treated as second-class citizens – not without reason, given that that was how they'd treated the Shias during their 30 years of rule under Saddam. Their allies in Al Qaeda, meanwhile, just didn't approve of elections full stop, saying that it meant rule by man rather than by God. Getting the polls de-railed or postponed would be a major victory for both groups, and a massive setback for the Coalition. Everyone was expecting the violence to reach horrendous proportions as polling day, January 30, got nearer. A full-scale uprising, or a terrorist atrocity of some catastrophic September 11 kind was not being ruled out.

Despite the threats, a bewildering 250 different parties had registered to take part in the elections, almost one apiece for every single seat on the new 275-member Iraqi National Assembly. Talking to them wasn't easy. The smaller ones often didn't have headquarters or campaign people, and were hard to track down. The bigger ones found their offices constantly getting car bombed, and wouldn't let you in without a prior appointment, which was the one thing you couldn't risk. All it needed was for news of your visit to leak out to the wrong person, and a kidnap gang could plan a leisurely ambush. The recommended strategy was to ask the politician concerned if you could just drop by any time one particular day. But no matter how politely you tried to put it, that translated roughly as, 'I'd love to come and see you, but I'm afraid I don't quite trust you not to kidnap me.' The only outfit that did run an open office was the newly-reconstituted Iraqi Communist Party. Maybe it was the only way they could get an audience for their unreconstructed brand of Marxism, but they paid a heavy price. The day we went to see them, a party official mentioned that two of his bosses had been abducted, tortured and murdered a few days before.

In the end, during three weeks of trying, the only political interview I managed to get other than with the Communists was with a bunch called the Iraqi Omar Party. Who sounded very similar to the Omar Democratic Party and the Omar Promise Party. We bumped into them in a queue at the new Iraqi Electoral Commission's office in the Green Zone, where they were complaining about the confusion.

'Please remember, we are just the Omar Party, without any added bits,' said one of their officials, Makki al-Said. 'Unfortunately, there are now three different parties with this name, and it is causing many problems for us, because whenever the other two say anything in the newspapers, people think it's us.'

I suspected that the differences were not very great. Nearly every Iraqi party I'd seen so far had near-identical permutations on the same slogan. If it wasn't 'Justice, Freedom and Unity', it was 'Freedom, Unity and Justice', or 'Unity, Justice and Freedom'. Concrete proposals to help the voters choose were either non-existent or a closely-guarded secret. One group, the Islamic Democrats of Mesopotamia, or the Mesopotamian Muslims for Democracy, or something, had refused to tell journalists what its policies were at all. Their spokesman was worried that rival parties would 'steal' them. The election might be a democratic milestone in Iraqi history, but an informed, rational joust of ideas it was not.

Even Mr Al-Said wouldn't be drawn on the Iraqi Omar Party's policies, saying all questions had to be directed to the party leader. Eventually, after being persuaded that the voice of the humble party worker was the essence of grassroots democracy, he launched into an impromptu press conference.

'We want a clear separation between religion and state and for people to always put Iraq first,' he said. 'That means Iraqi Kurds, not Kurdish Iraqis. Iraqi Shias, not Shia Iraqis, and so on. In any sentence, Iraq must come first.'

Most Iraqi politicians said similar stuff. The only Omar Party policy that really marked them out from anyone else was that they wanted an end to the ban on members of the Ba'ath Party holding public office of any sort. Which, no matter how much they said they weren't, marked them out as Ba'athists in many peoples' eyes. That, as far as I could see, was the conspiratorial way that post-Saddam Iraqi politics would work. Parties wouldn't be judged by their stated agendas, but by the secret ones that their opponents suspected them of harbouring. Pro-religious Shia parties would bring in an Iranian-style theocracy. Pro-secular parties would bring back the Ba'athists. Pro-Western parties wanted the Americans to stay forever, and so on. No amount of 'Justice, Freedom and Unity' slogans were going to change that.

*****

In the days immediately before the election, Baghdad felt more like it was facing the outbreak of war, not democracy.

The shops were nearly all shut and the streets almost deserted. People stocked up on food and stayed indoors, Kalashnikovs handy, just like they'd done ahead of the invasion in 2003. This time, though, they seemed prepared to use them. Things felt very tense indeed. To add to my own problems, Nasi then dropped by unexpectedly.

'Hey Colin, I got a problem,' he said. 'I won't be able to work for the elections.'

'Why not?' I asked, aghast. The elections, after all, were the whole point of coming out here.

'Lemme tell you. Two nights ago, after you and I finish work, I was driving through al Mansour neighbourhood with my cousin and my uncle. Me in my car, my uncle and cousin in theirs. A car came up beside us and started shooting. They killed my uncle and wounded my cousin.'

'Jesus Christ. Why?'

'I dunno. I think maybe 'cos my uncle a policeman. Maybe they know that. I'm not sure.'

'My God, I'm sorry. But how about you? Are you OK?'

'Yeah. I fine. Don' worry 'bout me. But I need to tell you, I need to stop working for maybe two weeks, just to stay low. I got all this strange things going on in my head after my uncle get shot. I afraid to go outside. I don' wan' stay here talking to you even now. I try find you some friend who can work with you as translator for elections. I won't be answering my phone.'

'Er, yeah, sure, no problems. Just give me a call when you feel better.'

I watched him leave, not quite sure what to think. For one, I didn't know whether to believe him or not. If his uncle really had been killed, he seemed remarkably calm about it, especially since he'd seen it happen. Then again, this kind of thing happened every day now, and in a way I felt guilty for even doubting his word. I had a nagging suspicion, though, that he'd been poached by some foreign TV crew, just arrived in town and willing to pay enormous rates for a few days. He didn't have the heart to tell me, so he was making up a story instead. Nearly every Iraqi I knew now had some tale of losing a friend or relative in a carbombing, kidnap or murder. Bereavement was as common an excuse for taking time off work as illness was back home.

To put him to the test, I quickly rang Nasi's home phone number. His father and his brother, I knew, spoke a little English. I'd bring up the subject of the uncle being killed, and see if they knew what I was talking about or not.

A relative, I couldn't work out who, answered the phone. His English was pretty faltering, but my talk of the dead uncle made no register whatsoever. Instead, he said something else, which, to me anyway, was even worse.

'Yes, Nasi very sorry. He can no make work for you. The terrorist send him a threat paper at his home.' The phone went dead.

A 'threat paper' was an anonymous warning from some insurgent group. Sometimes it would be pinned on someone's front door, sometimes it was left on their garden wall with a bullet as a paperweight. In Nasi's case, it would have said that they knew he was working as an interpreter, and that he should stop forthwith if he valued his life. True, they might have just picked up on some old, outdated gossip that he was still working with the Americans. But it was equally likely that someone had found out he was working with me. The idea that our partnership might have come to the attention of some insurgent nosey-parker made me feel deeply queasy. I tried ringing Nasi again to question him further, but his phone wasn't being answered. To be honest, I wasn't sure I wanted to know any more anyway.

*****

Election day dawned. I pooled a translator with Toby Harnden, the *Sunday Telegraph*'s chief foreign correspondent, who was here to cover the elections alongside me. The plan was to go to the polling stations when they opened at 8am to watch the first voters casting their ballots. If anybody turned up, that was. Police and army checkpoints were everywhere, and private vehicles had been banned for a three-day period as a precaution against suicide bombers. But everyone expected the insurgents to make their presence known. It wouldn't take much: a few gunmen opening up on queues of voters, or a few people with suicide vests, and many folks would stay indoors.

We headed onto the main road outside the Hamra complex just after 7.30am. Rather than joining throngs of eager would-be voters, we found ourselves strolling down the four-lane carriageway completely alone. I began to regret not wearing my *Sunday Telegraph* issue flak jacket, which I'd brought with me for this very occasion but which I'd left in the car. Until now, I'd never used it other than on embeds, as it drew attention and made you look like you were expecting trouble. But here we were, sitting ducks for any insurgent snipers: I started ziz-zagging. That probably made me stand out all the more.

A mile down the road, we found our first polling station. Like most of them, it was a school building, chosen ahead of government offices in the hope that it'd be perceived as a 'neutral' venue. Now, though, it was now indistinguishable from a police or army base, covered in concrete blast walls and rolls of barbed wire. Yet waiting ahead of us at the search point was a small queue of people – our first glimpse of real, live voters.

By the time we got through the security, we'd missed the person who'd cast the historic first ballot. Instead we got Sabah Khadom, 72, who was about the 20th, even though he'd deliberately turned up early in the hope of getting pole position. 'This is my great happiness to do this today – I am not scared of car bombs,' he said, dressed in his best clothes of a smart grey dishdasha and a tweed jacket. 'This is my chance to choose who I want in government to bring us a comfortable future.'

'So who's that then?' I asked.

'I'm not telling you,' he said, grinning. 'It's my right to keep that to myself, you know.'

I was about to congratulate him on his sound grasp of the principle of the secret ballot when a loud explosion sounded in the distance. Rather than the boom of a car bomb, it was the 'crump' of a mortar landing. Insurgent mortars were, by their nature, inaccurate beasts, being little more than bombs fired out of upturned tubes in the knowledge that gravity would ensure they would land somewhere a few miles away. But they made a hell of a noise, and were ideal for frightening voters into staying at home. Several more sounded as Mr Khadom tried to speak again, drowning his words out. Unsurprisingly, the queue behind him seemed to be dwindling. Other than die-hards like him, who'd turned up before the polling station opened, the floating voters were clearly staying away.

We headed off for another polling station in downtown Karrada, walking down Abu Nawas Street next to the Tigris. By this time the mortars were as loud and sustained as the thunderclaps in the furious rainstorms that hit Baghdad in spring. Whenever they sounded too close, Toby and I would stop and take shelter in a doorway. Once again I wished I had my flak jacket with me.

We reached the second station, just round the corner from the Al Majalis on the main shopping drag in Karrada. I felt a pang of nostalgia. It was nearly two years since I'd wandered round here freely, back when Baghdad seemed a relatively safe, hopeful place. There was the kebab shop I used to eat in. There was the goat's milk yoghurt stand where I'd soothe my stomach if the kebab made me ill. There was the stairwell where you could buy beer during the fasting month of Ramadan, when Karrada's booze shops were shut. And there was the polling station, bereft of any voters now that the early birds had gone.

As we wandered over, we were greeted by a small, elderly man, dressed again in election-day best tweed jacket, this time with a waistcoat and tie. He proffered a tray of boiled, wrapped sweets, the kind most Iraqis kept on their coffee tables at home.

'I am Adnan Mahid Al Salah, agent for the Iraqi Communist Party,' he announced cheerfully, ignoring the mortar barrage as it sounded yet again. 'The sweets are for free for those who comes to vote today – not just for our party, but for all.'

He shook his box of sweets and chanted slogans, a lone preacher shouting the odds in a deserted street amid the crescendos of ordnance around him. It was a surreal image. An old-style Communist had become the sole beacon of democracy in US-liberated Iraq.

Toby and I headed on to the Palestine Hotel, where I did a quick TV interview. I was hoping vaguely that a mortar might sound while I was on camera, which I figured would hugely impress anyone who knew me at home (assuming they were watching at 6.30am on a Sunday). But they died down almost as soon as I wandered into the studio, and by the time we left the Palestine half an hour later they'd stopped altogether. Whoever had been busy blasting away had either run out of bombs or been bombed themselves. And as the silence lasted, the polling stations began to fill up again. By 1pm, the polling centre at the Lebanon Primary School, another in Karrada, was a textbook operation, with patient, orderly queues of hundreds of cheerful-looking voters. Some had even felt safe enough to bring the wife and kids along.

'It's important for the children to see what is happening,' said Zainab Sadiq, who'd made it a family outing with her two brothers and their young daughters. Like every other voter, she sported a bruise-like splotch of indelible purple ink on her forefinger, a simple anti-fraud measure to prevent anyone voting more than once. 'We do not have any choice but to come anyway. If we want a better life, this is the only way to do it.'

By mid-afternoon there was a festive atmosphere, a palpable euphoria at having defied the terrorists' threats. Impromptu football games broke out on the streets, taking advantage of the traffic ban. People sat around chatting, showing off their purple forefingers. Previously, many had been reluctant to tell you whether they'd vote. Now they were vying to take the credit for being the first to hit the polls.

'The rest of my family was too scared to go, but I said, "Oh, come on". In the end, the whole street followed us.'

'No they didn't, they followed us...'

And so on. It was the first time I'd seen smiles on peoples' faces for a long time. Even the weather obliged. It was the sunniest and warmest afternoon of the year so far, providing journalists everywhere with a handy metaphor about Iraq's new democratic spring. Meanwhile, the election officials sat back and watched, feeling quietly empowered at pulling it off against all the odds. Yes, the army and the police had helped. But for once it felt as if the day belonged to them, the ordinary civilian officials, the people who'd long been bottom in Iraq's macho, gun-obsessed political culture.

Watching with bewilderment were a group of US soldiers from the Arkansas National Guard. They'd dropped their normal defensive posture and were chatting at the roadside with some locals. I hadn't seen that in a long time. 'We got to Baghdad on April 1st last year and we have never had a day like this,' said Specialist Aaron Loftin. 'Everybody just seems to be very happy today. It's kinda weird.'

We headed back to the hotel on a high. True, it wasn't quite the 'Purple Revolution' that George W Bush would later hail it to be. In some Sunni areas, the turn-out was minimal; many polling stations hadn't opened at all. But overall, turnout had been something like 60 per cent, and in places like Karrada, at least, the gloom and paranoia had lifted. The intensive security measures, banning all private cars and swamping the streets with cops and soldiers, had done the trick. If only there could be elections every day.

*****

The euphoria didn't last. Within a few days of the election, carbombs and killing were the norm again. And while the election itself had been a cause for celebration, the results it produced were less so. The religious Shia parties won an overwhelming majority of the seats, thanks to Iraq's seniormost Shia cleric, Grand Ayatollah Ali Al Sistani, declaring that voting was a religious duty. Some people took that to mean that they would burn in hell if they didn't, leading to turnouts of nearly 100 per cent in religiously observant areas. That compared to turnouts of almost zero in some Sunni areas, where people had either boycotted the vote of their own accord or been threatened into doing so. As a result, the balance of power in the new parliament was even more skewed against the Sunnis than expected. Even the Shia political parties realised that, to non-Shias, it threatened any notion of representative government. They began private talks with the Kurds and few Sunnis who'd won seats, aimed at giving each group a few ministerial posts each. But the process was soon mired in squabbles. The Sunnis said they should have more posts than they were being offered because the insurgents had threatened their voters, the Shias responded that they were lucky to get anything at all. A week passed, then a month, with no sign of any agreement, not even on who would be prime minister. Already, the government's glowing democratic mandate had the tarnish of smoke-filled rooms.

It was back to normal for the Western reporters in the Hamra, confined to life inside the complex except for the odd expedition. Now that the elections were over, the number of journalists staying there dwindled further. There were a few individual staff reporters from the main British and American newspapers, a few TV crews, and just three freelancers: myself, Jill and Dave Enders, a young American guy not long out of college. The days when the Hamra had a social scene were over. Some TV crews were under orders not to leave their rooms other than for reporting assignments – even the hotel restaurant was out of bounds. Other newspapers rented entire corridors of rooms and put up grilled metal doors at the end, hoping to buy a bit of extra time should the much-feared assault by a group of jihadists ever take place. The place now had all the charm of a medium-security prison in lockdown. You could walk through at any time of day and not see a single other guest. What little socialising there was took place in each other's suites. I spent much of my time hanging around with Jill in the suite rented by the *Christian Science Monitor*, for whom she now had regular work. Some previous reporter had installed a dartboard in there, on which I became an expert. When conventional darts got boring, I invented 'turbo darts'. Rather than hitting the dartboard, you simply picked one of the hotel room's clapped-out fittings and aimed at that instead.

It was a strange, lonely existence. Movement was so restricted that people got unfit due to lack of basic exercise. Some reporters jogged up and down the Hamra's stairwells. I bought a skipping rope and did a boxer-style workout for half an hour each night. Another reporter brought in his own miniature trampoline.

On the rare occasions that people met up, personal safety routines became a constant point of conversation. Yet no amount of discussion ever seemed to arrive at satisfactory answers. Should one go armed or unarmed, for example? Journalistic convention was never to carry any kind of weapon, in the hope that one's neutrality would be respected like that of a clergyman or Red Cross worker. Yet the Red Cross's Baghdad HQ had been carbombed 18 months ago, killing a dozen people: *nobody* was treated as innocent round here. Instead, in a land where guns were the norm, going unarmed could simply identify you as the weakest link, the easiest kidnap target in the hotel.

On the other hand, short of hiring a posse of ex-SAS men, the chances of outgunning a bunch of determined kidnappers was pretty limited. At best, you'd end up killing or wounding one of the kidnap gang before they overwhelmed you, which wouldn't do you many favours long-term. I did toy with the idea of getting a gun to keep in the room, in case a group of insurgents tried to storm the hotel some night while everyone was asleep. Everyone feared Zarqawi's lot might try something like that as a 'spectacular'. The prospect was so awful that some reporters did keep pistols handy, on the basis that it would be better to fight than surrender. In the end though, it reminded me rather too much of Hitler in his bunker, so I settled for wedging a chair and a table against the door each night. If someone came knocking, it'd hopefully buy me enough time to clamber down the balcony, which was only on the first floor. Similar debates went back and forth on the use of 'tail cars' – a back-up vehicle that followed you at a discreet distance. If someone attacked you, they'd either try and ram them off the road, using the element of surprise, or just stay well back, watch, and then raise the alarm, giving the police a description of the car that had bundled you off. It was better than nothing. But it meant widening the circle of people you worked with, and increasing the chances of some kidnapper getting to them.

For Jill and me, such debates were largely academic anyway. As freelancers, neither of us had the money to afford either armed guards or tail cars. So we just tried to keep a low profile, hoping that neither of us looked important enough to be worth kidnapping. While I stuck to my 'tache, tracksuit trousers and quilted car coat – a stylish innovation for winter that left me looking like some Scouse drug dealer – she went out in a black abbaya that covered everything but her face. Since she had black hair, it was an ideal disguise. If she needed to, she could wear a veil that covered everything but her eyes. Sometimes I wished I could wear one myself. Yet no matter how much we told ourselves that the terrorists would prefer to kidnap some big-shot staffer from the *New York Times*, we knew we were both vulnerable. The fact was that a lot of the time, the kidnap gangs didn't really know who they were nabbing. They picked you up, waited for the TV to announce who you were, and then sold you to whoever they thought would pay most. Occasionally, we'd joke about forming our own armed faction, the Jaish al Sahaf (Journalists' Army). We'd abduct jihadist hostage takers and make videos of them being forced to drink beer and watch porn.

With so much time indoors, it wasn't surprising that readers back home were beginning to think that we'd given up totally on trying to cover the horrors outside. Robert Fisk, the veteran Middle East correspondent for the *Independent*, wrote a piece denouncing what he described as 'hotel journalism'. Baghdad-based hacks, he alleged, now rarely witnessed first-hand what they were writing about. Having a Baghdad dateline was now virtually meaningless, and effectively a fraud on the reading public. There was a kernel of truth in his comments, and seeing as he'd done a fair few stints at the Hamra himself he knew what he was talking about. But many people back home took it to mean that working in Baghdad was risk-free. That wasn't so. The greatest danger of kidnap was not necessarily when straying into some insurgent haven, but simply in coming and going from the hotel. The fact was that you didn't need to go to the frontline in Baghdad. Instead, it could come to you. The pressure never quite went away, and that was what made it wearing.

*****

The reporters weren't the only ones thinning out. Foreign security contractors, who'd once frequented the Hamra complex in large numbers, were also a rare sight now. Since the killings at Fallujah last April, they'd gradually all either relocated to the Green Zone or pulled out of Iraq altogether. The only group still at the Hamra was a joint Western-Iraqi outfit, a bunch of Scots supervising a few dozen Iraqi footsoldiers. They were only here on odd occasions, but when they did they stayed in the same hotel as me, the Al Musafir. I'd never spoken to them. Security contractors were a taciturn bunch at the best of times, and after all the 'mercenary' headlines that had arisen from the Fallujah incident, they were especially wary of reporters.

Wandering into the Summerland restaurant one night, I saw the Scottish lads huddled in a corner. They'd obviously just come off some long trip, and the beer and whisky was flowing. As too, was the talk about their next mission, which seemed to involve escorting a load of supply trucks to Al Asad, a US Army base way out west past Fallujah. I was surprised. One thing you never, ever did these days was talk in public about your planned movements. A few of the other diners in the room had also overheard, and were casting discreet, uneasy glances at the Scottish table, as if some taboo had been breached. It reminded me of those Dracula films where everyone at the village inn goes quiet at the mention of the word 'vampire'.

I pretended not to listen, but I was all ears. Al Asad was in the heart of bandit country, a whole day's drive through the worst parts of the Sunni Triangle. Any security company going out there must have some good tales. And also be completely nuts. This lot would make a great human interest story for the *Scotsman*, if they'd talk: the last security company still working in Baghdad, or something along those lines. Maybe I could even go on a run to Al Asad with them. As I left the restaurant, I stopped by their table and introduced myself, bracing myself for a polite, or not so polite, brush off. The mention of the *Scotsman* did the trick. Straightaway a chair was pulled up, a beer opened and a fat whisky poured on the side.

The guy who seemed in charge was called Stevie. He was about my age, tough-looking, with a skinhead haircut. Tattoos spilled out from underneath the cuffs of a denim shirt. If I'd seen him in a pub in Scotland I'd have been wary, but he couldn't have been more friendly.

'Bloody dangerous parts of the country you're going to,' I remarked. 'Al Asad's right on past Fallujah.'

'Yeah, we've had a few moments,' he said, sipping a Scotch and coke. 'Contacts, firefights, the lot. I did eight years in the Scots Guards, spent time in South Armagh. A nursery compared to this place. And here, you're out on your own. The Coalition won't come and help if you get attacked.'

'I don't envy you there,' I said.

'The only advantage we've got is that we're working with locals. Some from up here in Baghdad, some from Basra. When we're travelling around, they can stop and ask what's going on, find out if there's any trouble.'

'Yes, I do the same. You need Iraqi eyes and ears. A lot of Western security people never seemed to bother with that.'

'And what about you? What sort of security do you have?'

'None. Just me and my Iraqi translator and driver.'

'What, nobody armed?'

'Nope. I just try and stay low-profile.'

'I don't envy you, either.'

Stevie and his crew weren't working the next day, so when the restaurant shut, we carried on boozing over in one of their rooms at the Al Musafir, sat in amongst piles of guns and radio equipment. He asked nearly as many questions about my job as I did about his: it was as though neither of us could quite believe the other was daft enough to do what he was doing. As the night went on, his life story came out. It was a tale many of the contractors out here could probably have told. He'd done a stint in the infantry, tried joining the SAS but not quite made it, and then quit the Army to join the more lucrative world of professional bodyguarding. Stevie had already spent a lot of time in the Middle East looking after various Arab royal families. For him, Iraq was an obvious career step. The same could not be said of some of his colleagues. They, too, were ex-Army, but several had spent the subsequent years working as painters and decorators, dustmen, and the like. Stevie didn't think they were all match-fit, and he hadn't been happy about the loose talk at dinner.

'They're good lads, but some haven't really got the experience for this kind of thing,' he said. 'Been out the game too long, but they're mates of the guy in Kuwait who owns the outfit, so that's the way it goes. Same with some of the Iraqis. The boys from Baghdad are very switched on, but the ones from Basra aren't so good. It's much quieter down there. They're out of their depth up north. Tell you the truth, I'm not really happy with the whole outfit. Not enough money being spent, not enough control over what's going on.'

I spent several more evenings with Stevie and co over the next couple of weeks. It was an insight into a scary world, full of all kinds of incidents that never seemed to make the news. Stevie had stories of security teams getting ambushed by teams of up to 70 insurgents at a time, of firefights that lasted for hours with no help from the Coalition. He personally claimed to know of at least 15 or 20 contractors who'd been killed or seriously maimed. They never made the papers because the firms they worked for kept it quiet. They also knew that if they got caught alive, an even worse ending was in store. Insurgents saw hired guns like them as mercenaries, profiteers of war, worse even than the occupying troops, deserving of no mercy whatsoever. A videotaped beheading would be getting off lightly. Torture and mutilation was more likely. A Western security guard Stevie knew had been found with his head squashed flat, where his captors had driven a car over it.

'How do you cope?' I asked. 'I mean, if you get caught, you'll get beheaded for sure. At the very least.'

'I know. Some of the lads have watched those beheading videos, Bigley and that. I haven't myself, but I know it's not one clean swipe, it's someone hacking away with a kitchen knife. Horrible. Most of the time I just blank it out. But we're under no illusions. If we get a serious attack, it's a fight to the death.'

That, though, was something Stevie's crew were well-prepared for. His best friend was an Iraqi guy called Mo, a thin, stern-looking ex-army officer who ran the Iraqi nationals on the team. Stevie's relationship with Mo was similar to the one I'd had with Mohammed.

He clearly liked him a lot, had relied on him in very dodgy situations, but didn't ask too many questions about exactly who he was. I could see why. Mo was also the crew's chief armourer, and much of the weaponry he procured came from pals he had among the insurgents. Mo could get pretty much anything they wanted: Kalashnikovs for $200, Glock pistols for $1,000, belt-fed machine guns for $2,000. The only weapons off-limits were American M16s and M4s – not because Mo couldn't get hold of them, but because the chances were they'd belonged to some dead American serviceman, which could land someone in big trouble.

'You can order stuff at breakfast and by lunch it's on the table,' Stevie said. 'It used to be that you could only have pistols and Kalashnikovs, but things have got so rough round here now that nobody minds what you have.'

The crew were now equipped like a small army. As well as belt-fed machine guns in their pick-up trucks, they had several rocket-propelled grenade launchers, ready for emergencies. Stevie also carried five 'pineapples' – slang for grenades – and an entire daysack full of spare magazines for his Kalashnikov. When he'd started here back in 2003, he'd carried just two spares.

All the same, he agreed to take me out on a run to Al Asad, as long as I signed an indemnity form saying that I wouldn't sue if things went wrong. Things were all set to go, then disaster struck. Coming back into west Baghdad one day, Stevie's convoy was hit by an IED in the Abu Ghraib district, a known insurgent haunt. One of his Iraqi staff was killed outright, and another lost his arm. As they pulled over by the roadside, they saw two minibuses parked further up the road, which they figured were full of insurgents waiting for them. Some of the Basra Iraqis went into complete panic, crying, praying, convinced they were about to die. Stevie ended up having to fire his Kalashnikov over their heads to get them to their senses.

'It was total chaos,' he said. 'I'd temporarily lost my hearing from the blast, and I was running around with the medical kit trying to do first aid. The guy who'd lost his arm was just in a daze, wandering around going "Find my arm, find my arm". I ran around firing over people's heads, and then told them, "Right, form a defensive box. Anything that comes within a certain distance, you fucking blast it away. Man, woman, child, whatever. I will deal with the consequences".'

In the end, the feared follow-up attack never came. The convoy managed to turn around and take refuge in a nearby US army base. Even so though, Stevie's boss, cost-conscious as ever, wanted to know why they'd left the bomb-blasted vehicle by the side of the road. Not long after, Stevie quit Iraq.

'It was a cowboy operation, although it took the deaths and casualties of a severe contact to make me work it out,' he told me later. 'I have got to take responsibility for some part of that myself, I guess. But we were getting promises things would get better, and they never did.'

*****

I, too, was planning on leaving. In late March, a call came from the *Sunday Telegraph*'s foreign editor, Topaz Amoore, an answer to my prayers. 'Are you interested in coming back to London and working for us from here?' she asked. 'There'd be some work on the foreign desk, maybe a bit of travel abroad, but not Iraq all the time. I imagine you'd quite like to get out of there by now?'

I jumped at it. I had a feeling that, sooner or later, the law of averages was going to catch up with me. And there was so little you could safely do out here any more that it was no longer much fun, just a constant game of hide-and-seek with death.

My final tranche of reporting was a clutch of 'Iraq two years on' stories. They were similar to those I'd done the year before, but infinitely more downbeat. On the first anniversary of the war, the Coalition had defiantly pumped out press releases and statistics about how things had, despite what everybody said, got better. They reminded people that electricity was back to pre-war levels, that the police and the army were improving, and so on. This year, they weren't even bothering. I couldn't find a single Iraqi who wasn't pessimistic. Many were increasingly nostalgic for Saddam's time. A young woman I interviewed, Ruaa Jamal, told us how she carried a four-inch flick knife with her whenever she went to college, as protection against muggers and rapists. Not only was post-Saddam Iraq dangerous, she complained, it was crushingly boring. As a young, single woman in Saddam's time, she could walk around Baghdad at any time of night. Today, life was an endless, drudgy round of nights in, trips out chaperoned by male relatives, and the occasional sleepover at girlfriends' houses. I mentioned that now she at least had the freedom to complain. She replied that the novelty had worn somewhat thin after two years. Especially when nothing she complained about ever got better.

Even those who'd been truly happy when Saddam had been toppled were fed up. Down in Karrada was an artists' studio, one of the few places we could go to without risking getting kidnapped. It was home to a young painter called Bakr Mughtadh, who, just before the war, had got the call that every artist in Iraq dreaded. 'Come to the palace, Saddam's people want to see you', said the voice at the end of the line. Such invites usually meant one of two things, neither of them good. Either the artist had offended Saddam for some reason, and was due for a stint in the cells. Or, worse still, Saddam liked their work and wanted them to paint him. Which, if he didn't find the likeness flattering enough, carried the risk of much worse punishment. Bakr found himself being ordered to do a 10-foot-high presidential portrait. Yet as he set to work, he couldn't help wondering why Saddam had commissioned a relative unknown like himself to do it. Halfway through, he found out. Saddam's security goons turned up at his studios with the world's press in tow, and he was introduced as an ordinary, patriotic Iraqi, painting a picture of the beloved president who was about to lead his nation into war.

'I had to dance around like a clown before the world's TV – shame on me,' he said. 'When the invasion started I destroyed the picture, and for a long time after that I worked double time, producing many paintings. But now, after all this trouble? I've been unable to do anything for three months.'

He gestured round his small studio to his last, unfinished works. None were exactly masterpieces. In one, a horse fled an abstract chaos. In another, three elderly women sat together gloomily. One was his mother. She'd never had a chance to be happy in her entire life, he said.

'Painting is hard work, and requires a special kind of stable mood to do so,' he told me. 'You cannot do it with all this terror going on, when you have this impression of being at a continuous funeral.'

'Isn't hardship and strife supposed to be a kind of creative lifeblood?' I asked.

He shook his head. 'People who say that have never seen a carbomb.'

My last interview was with a guy called Alan Enwia, a gentle, agreeable Iraqi Christian who ran one of Baghdad's many copy-to-order record shops. I'd never met him before, but he was a well-known figure to anybody in town who liked pop music. While most Iraqis didn't know much beyond the Bee Gees and Dolly Parton, Alan was acquainted with everything from hardcore rave to Westlife. An Iraqi Andy Kershaw, his shop was a meeting place for many of Baghdad's funkier, Western-leaning teenagers, among them Iraq's only boy band, *Unknown to No-one*, for whom he was the manager. The lead singer was Nadim, who'd worked for me as a translator when Nasi had been arrested for a week. He performed along with two Shias, two Armenian Christians and a Kurd, a harmony in creed as well as song. They'd started up back in 1999, doing the obligatory pro-Saddam song to keep the authorities happy and starring in their own rather unconvincing MTV-style video, posing on a battered VW Passat. Then, just after the war, their big chance had come. With thousands of journalists still in Baghdad looking for stories, they'd had all the exposure any aspiring pop stars could dream of. Foreign A&R men spotted their potential as a novelty act, and within months they'd been picked by a British talent scout. It all looked like taking off. There was interest in their act from Fame Academy, invites from endless chatshows, even talk of a book. Barry Mason, who wrote the Tom Jones hit *Delilah*, penned a song for them, a thank-you number to the Coalition for toppling Saddam. Then, just as Alan and the boys were planning to go to Britain to cut their first record, it all went wrong. The Foreign Office, despite being desperately short of 'positive' Iraq stories to shout about, somehow had problems granting them visas. Time dragged on, and as the pressure of expectation got too much, the band members began falling out.

'We were all set to go to Britain,' Alan told me. 'The people behind it knew it could be a big hit. But the boys had difficulty with their visas, and no matter how much effort was made, they couldn't get in. They would have gone through the boy-band sausage machine, and they could have made millions, but it didn't happen.'

I was amazed at how philosophical he seemed. For Alan and his boys, it hadn't been one dream come true, but two – first to be freed from the pop-hating Saddam, then to become famous. I couldn't understand how he could even talk about it without ranting and raging about who'd messed up, who'd stopped it all going ahead, or whatever. The sense of lost opportunity must have been unbearable. Yet even if *Unknown to No-one* had finally lived up to their name, it could still have spelt disaster. The band's fame and wealth would have made their families targets for every kidnap gang in Baghdad. And if they'd been beamed around the world singing a thank-you song for getting rid of Saddam, they'd also have faced the wrath of insurgents.

In other words, no matter how bright the future had seemed, it was, at the end of the day, a lose-lose situation. And one that summed Iraq up, as far as Alan was concerned. 'It was a shame – we felt like we were on the very last step toward a dream,' he said. 'But in many ways, it felt like usual. In this country, you can never lead a normal life.' He paused for a moment. 'Not even in music.'

*****

A few days afterwards I returned to Britain to work at the *Sunday Telegraph*. Later that year they hired me as a full-time London-based foreign correspondent. It was perfect: a steady job, a chance to travel to countries other than Iraq, and the opportunity to re-connect with home again. Part of me felt that I should have stuck it out in Baghdad, seeing it through the grim times. But in a way, it was a bigger challenge to move on elsewhere. I didn't want to be known as someone whose only selling point was his willingness to work in a place that nobody else wanted to go. That, in its way, was no different to being a milkbottle on Cheryl Barrymore's doorstep.

Besides, there was the curse of the Al Dulaimi hotel to beware. Perhaps it was more a mundane statement of the law of averages. Stay in a dangerous place long enough, and eventually circumstances would conspire to undo you. My own little social circle in Baghdad was proof of that alone. I thought of all the people I knew whom the violence had touched. Ryan dead, his colleague Kirk vanished into thin air. James Brandon, Georges and several others kidnapped. Myself lucky to be alive after being shot perilously close to my vital regions. Yet none of them, myself included, could be described as gung ho, as courting or seeking trouble in any sense. Instead, trouble had come to us, despite all our efforts to avoid it.

Every time people said Iraq couldn't get any worse, it did. Summer 2003, when people's main complaint had been the lack of electricity, seemed like paradise compared to spring 2004, when the insurgency first really kicked off.

Spring 2004, in turn, look like the good old days by autumn 2004, when the kidnapping and beheadings started in earnest.

And 2005, meanwhile, saw the first signs of sectarian violence between Sunnis and Shias, brought on by growing Sunni anger at the Shias' dominance in government. Shias on pilgrimages to the holy city of Najaf were getting ambushed as they passed through the redneck Sunni farming towns *en route*. Sometimes their attackers would even ambush funeral cortèges, dragging bodies out of coffins strapped to the roofs of cars and ceremonially beheading them in front of the horrified mourners. It was hard to imagine any more provocative act and, despite Shia clerics calling for calm, revenge attacks soon began. This time, the Shias had the machinery of government on their side. Shia death squads – often operating within the police – began kidnapping, killing and torturing Sunnis. Ostensibly, they only targeted those they suspected of being insurgents but increasingly it was just anyone they didn't like. The Sunnis responded with ever more ferocity, carbombing crowded marketplaces in Shia neighbourhoods, sometimes killing hundreds at a time. Civil war began to look increasingly possible. Soon, pretty much everyone in Iraq was talking about it, except Coalition commanders.

In December 2005, I returned to Baghdad for a fortnight-long reporting trip. Beforehand, the prospect didn't unnerve me too much. With Sunnis and Shias increasingly at each other's throats, Westerners no longer seemed quite such a target. No journalists had been kidnapped since the spring. But in the weeks running up to the trip, that all changed. Norman Kember, an elderly British peace activist, was abducted along with three other colleagues in west Baghdad. And for the first time, the Al Hamra hotel was the direct target of a suicide bombing. It was a two-vehicle attack, a car followed by a truck. An annexe of the hotel was badly damaged, but the brunt of the blast was taken by a block of private flats next to the hotel, which was flattened: 15 Iraqis died and 40 more were injured. The foreign journalists staying in the Hamra were only saved because the truck got stuck in the crater made by the car. Had it got through, it would have destroyed the entire hotel.

So, once again, I turned up to Baghdad in a state of complete paranoia. Because I was now staff for the *Sunday Telegraph*, we had the benefit of being able to consult with a British security company based at the Hamra that advised most of the journalists there. It wasn't very reassuring. When I told their boss I wasn't planning on using a tail car to follow me around, he was decidedly unimpressed.

'It's extremely nasty out there at the moment, the risk of kidnapping is as high as ever,' he said. 'You really ought to think about it. If you find some drivers, we can train them up. I'm not trying to drum up business for the firm. I'm not a salesman. But this is your security we're talking about here.'

I asked him how much it would cost. The price he quoted ran into roughly what I was planning to spend for the entire fortnight. Plus I'd have to find two Iraqi drivers I could trust to turn up at the same time each day, something I knew would be all but impossible. And the training course would take two entire days, time we didn't have to spare. It wasn't that the *Sunday Telegraph* cut corners on safety. It just wasn't practical, financially or logistically, for just a fortnight of reporting. If we lashed that kind of money out every time we came here, we'd never be able to afford to go anywhere else. The next day, I told the security firm boss why I thought it was unmanageable. He remained unsympathetic. 'The fact is mate, you're talking about management. I'm talking about security. Your decision though.'

I stuck to my plan. Part of it was that my ego didn't really like having some ex-military type telling me how to do my security. Especially since I'd survived here nearly two years without any help. Yet knowing that someone else thought I was being reckless was not pleasant. I felt extremely uneasy for the entire fortnight.

The night before I went back to London I had a parting beer with Colonel Mohammed in the Summerland Hotel. He didn't know it was a parting beer, admittedly. These days, you always kept your exact date of departure from Baghdad a closely-guarded secret, lest the information fall into the wrong ears and someone planned a special farewell party for you *en route* to the airport. Even the staff at the hotel were kept in the dark until the very last minute, which meant there was seldom time to tip them all (a problem, given my theory that keeping them sweet might somehow buy their loyalty).

The Colonel looked good, wearing a smart new white jacket and a decent shirt. He had the air of a man prospering while Baghdad burned. As ever, he insisted on paying for the drinks, except for the two whisky miniatures that I'd brought him as a present from the duty free on the way over. They were tots of some extra-posh blend of Glenfiddich, which came in a special presentation pack. Mohammed examined one carefully, opened it, and poured it straight into his pint of lager.

'What are you doing?' I said, horrified. 'You can't mix whisky and lager together!'

'This is as per the way of the officers of the Iraqi military. It is to hide the bitter taste of the whisky.'

'But that's finest malt Scotch! It's 30 years old… you're supposed to enjoy the taste, not hide it!'

He shrugged and raised his glass. 'Hmm. It's very good.'

'Go on then, let me try one too.'

He opened the other one and poured it into my beer, decades of some Scots distiller's careful craftsmanship dissolving into an indifferent froth of Turkish lager. It tasted foul. No wonder it had never caught on beyond the officers' mess of the Iraqi Army.

I sipped away, trying not to gag. I asked Mohammed what he was up to. As ever, he was slightly evasive.

'Ah. Buying. Selling. You know.'

'No, not really. What?'

'Ah, some cars. Washing machines. Air conditioners. And some properties. Myself and some of my friends, we buy some old place, make it look clean and tidy, and then sell it.'

'Not selling guns, then, I hope?'

'Not guns.'

Whatever he was flogging, his new role as a Baghdad Del Boy seemed to be paying off. He claimed to be earning about $3,000 a month, far more than he'd ever done with me or Ultra Services. I suspected, though, that whatever success he was having owed as much to his ability to handle himself as his business acumen. Working in the property market in Baghdad would not be like being an estate agent in London. If a deal went sour, it wouldn't be settled in court. Still, it was better than going back into the Iraqi army. The Iraqi government was crying out for experienced officers to lead the country's new security forces. But such men also found themselves fast-tracked to the very top of the insurgents' hit list. Some of his old chums in the Ministry of Defence had been trying to persuade him to join them again, and had even promoted him to brigadier in his absence. But so far he'd refused. As a friend, I was glad his desire to earn a quick buck was greater than his desire to save his country.

More lager and whisky flowed. We reminisced on when we'd worked together, back in what we now saw as the good old days. The trip to Majar al Kabir, where he'd calmed and charmed the natives after they'd slaughtered the British Red Caps. The meeting the next day with his old enemy Kareem Mahood, the Lord of the Marshes, the man the Iraqi army had never been able to catch. An interview up in Tikrit with Saddam Hussein's tribal sheikh, an affable, whiskery old boy who looked a bit like the president's kindly elder brother. He'd talked fondly of hotel stays in London's Park Lane and had invited us onto his terrace for a glass of Johnnie Walker (Mohammed hadn't let us, he said the sheikh was just being polite). There'd been some good moments there, things we'd remember for the rest of our lives. And all because he'd happened to pull his car over when that strange Westerner, the first he'd ever met, had thumbed a lift on a street in Baghdad.

But that was a long time ago now. Iraq had changed, become terrifyingly vicious and nasty, the anger, poison and bitterness that had welled up under three decades of Saddam finally erupting like a long-festering boil. It was if the country was finally revealing itself in its true colours, having hidden behind an unbroken wall of politeness when I'd first got here. Frankly, it wasn't really a place where soft Western civilians like me could survive any more. Only the likes of Mohammed, the warrior breed, could survive. As he staggered drunkenly off to his car, I wondered whether we'd still be in touch when we were both old men, meeting up in Baghdad when it was finally peaceful and prosperous. If either of us lived that long, that was. I'd miss him for sure, in all his many roles: translator, fixer, bodyguard, colonel (staff) and friend. And, as my aching head screamed at me all the next day, purveyor of quite the most poisonous cocktail on the planet. There was only one name for it – the Chemical Ali.

*****

The curse of the Al Dulaimi hotel claimed its last victim a month later, in January 2006. It was a Saturday afternoon, and I was in the London office of the *Sunday Telegraph*, helping put the finishing touches to that week's paper. Suddenly the newswires flashed up a headline. 'Western journalist kidnapped in Baghdad.' A female. It was Jill. She'd gone to visit a Sunni politician in al Adel, a dangerous neighbourhood of Baghdad, and had been kidnapped on her way back. With her that day had been Alan Enwia, the former manager of *Unknown to No-one*, who did translation work in his spare time: the kidnappers had shot him dead and left his body in the street. Casual brutality like that was commonplace, and nobody gave Jill much hope of surviving either. Despite the huge hue and cry that went up over her disappearance, the word was she'd been passed on to Zarqawi's mob and was unlikely to stand much chance of being freed. It drove it home to me just how much risk we'd all been taking. It was no longer the sort of Boy's Own adventure stuff that I'd sought out there.

Jill was held for nearly three months, her face appearing in ghostly images on occasional videos released by her captors. Eventually she was freed, apparently without any ransom being paid. Nobody quite knew why, although it was certainly true that her case had aroused the pity of the Arab world in a way that other Western kidnap victims hadn't. Much was made of the fact that she was a woman, an Arabic speaker, and worked for the *Monitor*, a left-of-centre paper that had opposed the invasion. It was easy for the media to portray her as a caring, conscientious journalist who'd been trying to give a voice to the Iraqi people. Somehow, I doubted they'd have managed that with me. The *Sunday Telegraph* had been a staunch supporter of the war. And Mohammed, as my only close Iraqi friend, might not have been the most sympathetic of characters had he done a televised appeal on my behalf. I suspected it would have simply swiftened the executioner's blade.

During Jill's time in captivity, the *Sunday Telegraph* ran a feature piece she had written the year before for the *American Journalism Review*, describing the life of the small group of freelancers in Baghdad. Like me, she'd come to Iraq because mainstream journalism back home was boring her witless. While I'd had an epiphany outside

Cheryl Barrymore's, her piece began with a rant about covering dull municipal planning meetings in America. 'You'd rather jump off a cliff than cover one more zoning board meeting, and just when one of the biggest stories in years is developing in Iraq, those foreign correspondent aspirations seem ever further out of reach,' she wrote. 'There's only one way out. Pull up stakes, clean out that savings account and get on a plane to Baghdad.'

She went on to tell the tales of several of those who had, mentioning me and my bullet in the bum, and the Al Dulaimi and its curse. A few days later, a young shifter at the *Sunday Telegraph* – yet another poor bastard fighting tooth and nail for a contract – told me he'd read it over the weekend.

'I saw your name mentioned in that piece,' he said. 'Bloody hell.'

Fame at last! 'You should try it, mate' I said, trying not to look too smug at his mild admiration. 'Best thing I ever did in my life.'

Afterword

IT'S NOW JUST OVER five years since Saddam Hussein's fall. It's not been a pleasant five years in Iraq. The civil war between Sunni and Shia that was brewing in 2005 exploded full scale in 2006, and achieved what everyone hoped was impossible, by making things infinitely worse than they already were. Sectarian gangs were abducting, killing and beheading people in such numbers that Baghdad's morgues couldn't cope. A million horror stories bear this out, but one that sticks in my mind is about the city's tattoo parlours: they began offering to ink peoples' names and addresses onto their thighs so that their corpses could be identified if they turned up headless somewhere.

These days, I'm seldom in a position to report on such stories first hand. I now visit Baghdad only on brief trips of a couple of weeks at a time, and then usually in the company of US troops on 'embeds' or with professional Western security guards around me. Neither are ideal ways of reporting on the country, and in the old days I was a bit sniffy about reporters who used either. But ever since Jill Carroll's abduction in 2006, the prospect of chancing it alone is not tempting. As I write, another British reporter, Richard Butler, has just been released after being taken hostage, having spent two months in Basra with a sack on his head.

March 2007 saw the start of the 'troop surge', George W Bush's last-ditch attempt to damp down the civil war by flooding Baghdad with nearly 30,000 extra US soldiers. It has stabilised things a little, although these things are relative. In March 2008, for example, 1,269 Iraqis died violent deaths, according to an Associated Press count. That's an appalling figure by any normal standards, but it is less than half the peak figure of nearly 3,000 per month in December 2006. Respectable estimates put the number of Iraqis killed since the invasion at around 80,000, and up to two million have fled the country altogether. Many of the stack of business cards I have from my Iraq days fall into the 'dead or fled' categories. For those whom I still know about, fate has been both cruel and kind. Here's a brief round-up.

Colonel Mohammed remains alive and well, despite having spent much of the last two years on the run from the Mahdi Army, who found out about his military service under Saddam and sent him death threats. I last saw him in Baghdad a month ago, when he told me he was now working as a military adviser to the government, and had been promoted to the rank of general. He doesn't wear a uniform, nor does he have the chauffeur and bodyguards that he had in Saddam's time. But he does carry no less than four mobile phones.

Colonel Saba, my old driver, left Iraq for Australia after his teenage son was kidnapped in Baghdad. The boy was eventually released alive after a ransom was paid, but not before he was shot and injured by his captors. The Iraqi Ministry of Defence found a job for Saba as the Iraqi military attache to Australia, a post which then abruptly ended when there was a change of defence minister. Saba, facing the prospect of being returned to Iraq, successfully applied for asylum, but he has found it hard adapting to life Down Under. He wonders whether somewhere like Egypt – devoid of sex, booze, and free-and-easy Ozzie chicks – might be a better place for his kids to grow up.

John Dawkins, to the best of my knowledge, continues working as a contractor and businessman, while the murder of Ryan Manelick remains unsolved and under investigation. According to a blog written by Kirk von Ackerman's widow, US military investigators concluded that he was the victim of a kidnap attempt by Iraqi insurgents that went wrong. Omar Hadi, who travelled into Iraq with John and myself, went on to serve as an adviser to the Iraqi government for a while and now works for a developer in the United Arab Emirates.

Jill Carroll and Georges Malbrunot, my fellow denizens of the Al Dulaimi Hotel, now work full time for the *Christian Science Monitor* and *Le Figaro*, the papers for which they'd respectively been freelancing when they were kidnapped. It's incredible what you have to do to get a staff job these days.

I am now chief foreign correspondent on the *Sunday Telegraph*, travelling not just to Iraq but a wide range of other unloved countries around the world: Somalia, Chad, Iran, and Burma, to name but a few. After two years in Baghdad, though, nowhere seems quite that bad.

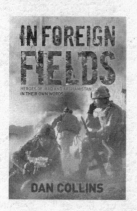

WASTING POLICE TIME...
THE CRAZY WORLD OF THE WAR ON CRIME
PC David Copperfield (£7.99)

PC DAVID COPPERFIELD is an ordinary bobby quietly waging war on crime...when he's not drowning in a sea of paperwork, government initiatives and bogus targets.

Wasting Police Time is his hilarious but shocking picture of life in a modern British town, where teenage yobs terrorise the elderly, drunken couples brawl in front of their children and drug-addicted burglars and muggers roam free.

He reveals how crime is spiralling while millions of pounds in tax is frittered away, and reveals a force which, crushed under mad bureaucracy, is left desperately fiddling the figures.

His book has attracted rave reviews for its dry wit and insight from The Sunday Times, The Guardian, The Observer, The Daily Mail, The Mail on Sunday and The Daily Telegraph;.

'Being a policeman in modern England is not like appearing in an episode of The Sweeney, Inspector Morse or even The Bill, sadly,' says Copperfield. 'No, it's like standing banging your head against a wall, carrying a couple of hundredweight of paperwork on your shoulders, while the house around you burns to the ground.'

"*A huge hit... will make you laugh out loud*" – **The Daily Mail**
"*Very revealing*" – **The Daily Telegraph**
"*Damning... gallows humour*" – **The Sunday Times**
"*Graphic, entertaining and sobering*" – **The Observer**
"*A sensation*" – **The Sun**
By PC David Copperfield – as seen on BBC1's *Panorama*
www.coppersblog.blogspot.com

**Available from all good bookshops
or from www.mondaybooks.com**

DIARY OF AN ON-CALL GIRL
True Stories From The Front Line
WPC EE Bloggs (£7.99)

If crime is the sickness, WPC Ellie Bloggs is the cure... Well, she is when she's not inside the nick, flirting with male officers, buying doughnuts for the sergeant and hacking her way through a jungle of emails, forms and government targets.

Of course, in amongst the tea-making, gossip and boyfriend trouble, real work sometimes intrudes. Luckily, as a woman, she can multi-task... switching effortlessly between gobby drunks, angry chavs and the merely bonkers. WPC Bloggs is a real-life policewoman, who occasionally arrests some very naughty people. *Diary of an On-Call Girl* is her hilarious, despairing dispatch from the front line of modern British lunacy.

WARNING: Contains satire, irony and traces of sarcasm.

> *"Think Belle de Jour meets The Bill... sarky sarges, missing panda cars and wayward MOPS (members of the public)."*
> **- The Guardian**

> *"Modern policing is part Orwell, part Kafka ... and part Trisha."* – **The Mail on Sunday**

£7.99 – and read her at **www.pcbloggs.blogspot.com**

**Available from all good bookshops
or from www.mondaybooks.com**

COMING SOON FROM MONDAY BOOKS:

PERVERTING THE COURSE OF JUSTICE
Inspector Gadget (Paperback £7.99)
PUBLISHED SEPTEMBER 2008

For the first time ever, a senior policeman – writing as 'Inspector Gadget' for fear of exposure – breaks ranks to tell the truth about the collapse of law and order in the UK.

With access to statistics about frontline police strength (much lower than you think), exclusive inside information on the political targets and interference which are bedevilling officers and detailed analysis of the lies politicians and senior police officers tell, his explosive book will reveal how bad things really are.

Controversial and gripping – and the long-awaited 'follow-up' to PC David Copperfield's *Wasting Police Time* – it will set the news agenda on crime and shock the nation.

**Available from all good bookshops
or from www.mondaybooks.com**

SO *THAT'S* WHY THEY CALL IT GREAT BRITAIN
How one tiny country gave so much to the world
Steve Pope (Paperback £7.99)
PUBLISHED APRIL 2009

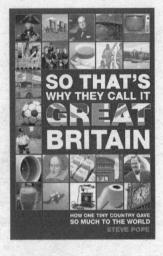

It covers less than half of one per cent of the earth's land mass, but is responsible for more 40% of the world's great inventions. The first car, first train, and first aeroplane *(sorry, Wright Bros)* came from Great Britain, as did the steam engine, the jet engine and the engine of the internet (the www protocols used online).

Britons created the first computer and the first computer game *(noughts and crosses)*, as well as the telegraph, the telephone and the television *(and the mousetrap, the lightbulb and the loo roll)*.

In almost every sphere – from agriculture and medicine to politics, science and the law – we have led the way for centuries.

Most of the world's major sports originated here – along with William Shakespeare and Jane Austen, The Beatles and The Stones, *Fawlty Towers* and *The Office*.

This book shows – without boasting, and with tons of humour, unknown facts and weird stories – just why our country is called GREAT Britain.

**Available from all good bookshops
or from www.mondaybooks.com**